The Bournias Family History, Heritage, and Personal Legacies

Page intentionally left blank for notes

The Bournias Family History, Heritage, and Personal Legacies

Genealogy of the Bournias family

By
PETER ANTHONY BOURNIAS
a.k.a.
PETROS-ANTONIOS BOURNIAS

Colophon:

Copyright © 2023 by Peter A. Bournias a.k.a. Petros-Antonios I. Bournias. All rights reserved.

No portion of this book may be reproduced, stored in a retrieval system or transmitted in any form including electronic, mechanical, photocopying, recording or otherwise without written permission of the publisher or the author in accordance with Copyright laws.

Limit of Liability / Disclaimer of Warranty:
The publisher and the author make no representations or warranties with respect to the accuracy or completeness of the contents of this work and specifically disclaim all warranties, including without limitation warranties of fitness for a particular purpose.
No warranty may be created or extended by sales or promotional materials.

Every effort has been made in the preparation of the content of this work to ensure the accuracy of the information presented. However, the information contained in the content of this work is sold without warranty, either express or implied. Neither the author, nor the publisher will be held liable for any damages caused or alleged to be caused directly or indirectly by the content of this work.

Any information, advice, or strategies contained herein may not be suitable for every situation.
This work is sold with the understanding that the author is not engaged in rendering legal or other professional services. If professional assistance is required, the services of a competent professional should be sought.

Readers should be aware that Internet websites listed in this work may have changed or may no longer exist between when this work was written and when read.

All physical and/or digital documentation containing personal information about the individuals included in this research are for historical purposes in accordance with the privacy laws of the EU and the USA.

The privacy laws of the EU and the USA protect the dissemination of data for living persons. Other physical and/or digital documentation from the Internet regarding individuals included in this research for historical purposes from other countries.

Typesetting:
This book was produced using TTF Arial, Calibri, and OFL Myriad Pro fonts for the titles, caption text, and tables in the English and Greek languages to properly preserve and present the information written in both languages.

This book is a work of non-fiction.
Book design: Peter A. Bournias
Cover design: Peter A. Bournias
Translations / Interpretations: Peter A. Bournias and Katerina Barbatsi

Edition notice:
First edition: March 2023
First published: March 2023
Published by: Lulu Press Inc.
Printed in the United States of America, and other global locations.

ISBN (International Standard Book Number): 979-8-218-16241-2 (PRINTED BOOK ONLY)

LCCN (Library of Congress Control Number):   2023903752

10 9 8 7 6 5 4 3 2 1

Author information and contact
　　　Peter A. Bournias also known as Petros-Antonios I. Bournias
　　　Visit my website at http://www.bournias.net/
　　　Email address bourniasfamily@bournias.net

Written requests to the author for permission should be sent to this address:
　　　Peter A. Bournias
　　　Ypolohagou Diakou Alexandrou 35
　　　Voula 16673
　　　Greece

INTRODUCTION

This is a non-fiction work about the Bournias Family History, Ancestry, Heritage, and Personal Legacies of family members.

The above photograph is the port of Chios Greece, the island where everyone with the family surname Bournias originates.

This photograph was taken from the hotel balcony of the hotel where my wife and I stayed in March of 2005 and I added the graphic text "Chios" to it.

While reading this, I believe you will realize that the island of Chios has an enormous history through the centuries and was historically a gateway to the east.

FORWARD

To understand the wealth and importance of the Greek island of Chios, the following were created:

The First School of Higher Education was founded in 1792, a library, a printing house, a hospital (with a nursing home, residence for the poor, an orphanage, Lovokomeio a refuge for Lepers in the area of Kofinas, a mental asylum), its own bank, and half of the commercial trade in the Mediterranean in 1822.[1]

This may or may not sound important to someone born more recently, or who has never visited Greece but consider the history and economics of the time two hundred years ago.

The University was founded in 1781 and had 700 students by 1818 offering a free education funded by the city of Chios.

The library was a contribution by a Chiotis named Adamantios Korais, and was built about 1772. It is a cultural heritage today, housing historical archives that were saved after the catastrophe of Chios in 1822. It housed one of the first printing presses of Chios.[2]

The most important product economically for Chios was Masticha[3]. From the year 1329 it resulted in 120,000 gold coins per year, otherwise known as Mastic, its production continues profitably into the 21st century, as is evident by the creation of the documentation included at the Chios Mastic Museum[4] that opened in 2016.

One of my discoveries is the history and controversy about one of our earliest relatives, a revolutionary of Chios in 1822.

I hope you find this work interesting and that you will have the opportunity to visit Chios someday, if you have not already, whether you are a member of the Bournias family or not.

The island of Chios is a museum of historical information with beautiful beaches, a fortress citadel, and locally produced products including Mastic, a plant resin exemplified historically by the tremendous value in both its monetary worth and the significance that it has in history and the museum.

Author's note:
First School of Higher Education, known as "**Η Μεγάλη Σχολή της Χίου**," (Megali Scholi tis Chiou), see more information at the Korais Library.

---

[1] Wikipedia, https://en.wikipedia.org/wiki/Chios
[2] Η Μεγάλη Σχολή της Χίου (Megali Scholi tis Chiou), https://www.koraeslibrary.gr/en/library/history
[3] Wikipedia, https://en.wikipedia.org/wiki/Mastic_(plant_resin)
[4] https://www.piop.gr/en/diktuo-mouseiwn/Mouseio-Mastixas/to-mouseio.asp

DEDICATION

To my grandparents Pantelis and Zabella who gave me and my brother their love even though we could never really know them or verbally learn more deeply about each other's characteristics and beliefs because of our language barrier.

To my loving spouse Katerina Barbatsi, who gives me all of her love; who patiently explaines some of the finer details about the idiosyncrasies, culture, traditions, and more detailed history of Greece. I further credit Katerina with starting my fever of tracing my ancestors while researching hers, and the arduous complexities of reading many of the handwritten Greek texts of the National Archives from the 19th and 18th centuries while using our combined knowledge of English and Greek to translate and interpret them.

My grandparents from Chios
Zabella and Pantelis playing the Bouzouki[5]
at their house in Vrontados about 1969

My father, aunt, and uncle
Ioannis, Maritsa, and Adiamantis
about 1945

---

[5] https://en.wikipedia.org/wiki/Bouzouki

TABLE OF CONTENTS

THE BOURNIAS FAMILY 3
HISTORY, HERITAGE, ... 3
AND PERSONAL LEGACIES 3
INTRODUCTION 6
FORWARD 7
DEDICATION 8
TABLE OF CONTENTS 9
PREFACE 13
    TIME TRAVELLING INTO THE HISTORY OF THE BOURNIAS FAMILY THROUGH GENEALOGY 13
    THE GREAT PHILOSOPHER HOMER 15
    HIPPOCRATES OF CHIOS 15
    CHIOS GREECE TRADITIONAL FOLKLORE AND ARTIFACTS 16
    SWEETS FROM CHIOS 17
    A MODERN DAY MAP OF CHIOS GREECE 18
    THE GREEK LANGUAGE AND THE DIALECT OF CHIOS 19
        A Smidgen of History about Chios and Greece and Asia Minor 20
THE BOURNIAS SURNAME 22
INCEPTION OF THE BOURNIAS SURNAME 23
GEOGRAPHICAL MAPPING OF THE SURNAME 24
GREEKS WITH THE SURNAME BOURNIAS IN GREECE 25
CHIAN SURNAMES 28
    OTHER CHIOT SURNAMES 31
    GREEK NAMING CONVENTIONS AND TRADITIONS 32
    ORIGINS OF GREEK SURNAMES 33
    DIASPORA AND FOREIGNERS TO GREEK LANGUAGE TRANSLATIONS 34
    FOREIGN FIRST NAMES FOR BIRTHS, BAPTISMS, AND THE GREEK ORTHODOX CHURCH 35
    FIRST NAMES OF GREEKS ABROAD 35
    NICKNAMES OR PARATSOUKLI (παρατσουκλι) 35
    HOW TO INTERPRET MIDDLE INITIALS OF GREEK NAMES 36
    GREEK NAME DAYS AND BIRTHDAYS 36
    MYTHS REGARDING THE MEANING OF THE SURNAME BOURNIAS 37
WORK AND PROFESSIONS 39
SOURCES OF NAMES AND VITAL RECORDS 41
RELIGION 43
    THE CATHOLIC CHURCH IN GREECE 44
THE GREEK MILITARY 45
    WARS IN GREECE AND CHIOS 46
THE EVZONS 47
BALKAN WARS 1912 - 1913 48
WORLD WAR I - 1914 TO 1919 49

THE GRECO-TURKISH WAR OF 1919 TO 1922	50
THE ASIA MINOR CAMPAIGN KNOWN AS THE GRECO-TURKISH WAR TO THE WESTERN WORLD.	50
WORLD WAR II - 1939 TO 1945	51
The Greek Army	*51*
The Greek Navy	*51*
The Greek Air Force	*51*
GREECE SURVIVED FORTY-EIGHT (48) YEARS OF WAR!	*52*
OBSTRUCTIONS IN GREEK GENEALOGY	53
POLITICS	54
FOREIGN INFLUENCE AND POLITICS	56
PIRATES	57
GENEALOGY OF THE BOURNIAS FAMILIES	58
A RARE MAP OF CHIOS	59
GENEALOGY SHORTHAND	61
INDIVIDUALS OF THE BOURNIAS FAMILY	62
LINEAGE OF THE BOURNIAS ANCESTRY MAIN CHART	63
APOSTOLOS BOURNIAS (ΑΠΟΣΤΟΛΟΣ ΜΠΟΥΡΝΙΑΣ)	*66*
Antonios A. Bournias (Αντώνιος Α. Μπουρνιάς), 1788 - 1865	*67*
THE REVOLUTION ON CHIOS ABRIDGED	*69*
The Massacre at Chios by Eugene Delacroix	*73*
A bust representing the figure of Antonios A. Bournias	*74*
What is OUR family relationship with Antonios A. Bournias?	*75*
Testimonial evidence of Antonios A. Bournias	*77*
Ioannis Bournias (Ιωάννης Μπουρνιάς), 1799 - death unknown	*80*
Petros D. Bournias (Πέτρος Δ. Μπουρνιάς), 1829 - death unknown	*81*
Emmanouil A. Bournias (Εμμανουήλ Α. Μπουρνιάς), 1832 - death unknown	*82*
Gregorios A. Bournias (Γρηγόριος Α. Μπουρνιάς), 1833 - 1904	*85*
Apostolis A. Bournias (Αποστολής Α. Μπουρνιάς), 1835 - death unknown	*86*
Othonos I. Bournias (Όθωνος Ι. Μπουρνιάς), 1844 - death unknown	*87*
Demetrios L. Bournias (Δημήτριος Λ. Μπουρνιάς), 1861 - death unknown	*88*
Historical photograph circa 1912 of the family	*88*
Michail A. Bournias (Μιχαήλ Α. Μπουρνιάς), 1866 - death unknown	*89*
Georgios A. Bournias (Γεώργιος Α. Μπουρνιάς), 1870 - 1950	*90*
Ioannis A. Bournias (Ιωάννης Α. Μπουρνιάς), 1877 - 1974	*92*
Pantelis P. Bournias (Παντελής Π. Μπουρνιάς), 1889 - 1976	*93*
Leonidas A. Bournias (Λεωνίδας Α. Μπουρνιάς), 1908 - 1997	*95*
Apostolis I. Bournias (Αποστολής Ι. Μπουρνιάς), 1915 - 1998	*96*
Loukas D. Bournias (Λουκας Δ. Μπουρνιας), 1922 - 1942	*97*
Ioannis P. Bournias (Ιωάννης Π. Μπουρνιάς), 1930 - 2021	*98*
Maritsa P. Bournia(s) (Μαρίτσα Π. Μπουρνιά) 1933 - 2022	*100*
Captain Adamantios P. Bournias (Αδαμάντιος Π. Μπουρνιάς), 1936 - 2001	*101*
BOURNIAS FROM SPARTOUNTA TO KORONI, KALAMATA, AND TEXAS	102
LINEAGE OF THE BOURNIAS ANCESTRY CHART OF TEXAS AND MESSINIA	107
Lineage of the Bournias Ancestry chart of Texas and Messinia	*112*
Panagiotis Bournias (Παναγιώτης Μπουρνιάς), 1842 - 1920	*114*
Georgios P. Bournias (Γεώργιος Π. Μπουρνιάς), 1880 –1944	*116*
William Pete Bournias, 1883 – 1951	*117*

BOURNIAS FAMILY MEMBERS NOT LINKED ON MY GENEALOGY CHARTS 131

Ioannis Bournias (Ιωάννης Μπουρνιάς), 1885 - 1970 KALAMATA 131
Ariadni Bournia, (Αριάδνη Μπουρνιά) 1953 - 1972 133
Apostolos Bournias 134

THE BOURNIAS SURNAME IN THE UNITED KINGDOM 136

SETTLEMENTS NAMED BOURNIAS 138

HOMES OF SOME BOURNIAS FAMILY MEMBERS 139

The home of Antonios A. Bournias in Parparia Chios 139
A PLAQUE ON THE HOME OF ANTONIOS A. BOURNIAS 140
The home of Gregorios A. Bournias 141

TRAVELING ON A STEAMSHIP 143

THE SS PATRIS 145

CONCLUSION OF RESEARCH 146

FAMILY RECORDS 147

A Birth Certificate of Ioannis P. Bournias of 1930 147
The Marriage Certificate of Pantelis Petros Bournias 1928 149
THE GAK OF CHIOS 151
Election List Chios Spartounta 1930 153
A list of Bournias from the Municipality of Kardamyla, Chios dated 1928 154
THE GAK OF ERMOUPOLI SYROS AND MYKONOS 155
Electoral List Municipality Syros 1871 159
GAK ERMOUPOLI SYROS AND MYKONOS 161
GAK ATHENS 163
GAK KALAMATA 164
GAK KALAMATA 165
MUNICIPALITY RECORDS OF KARYSTOS EVIA 166
GREEK ORTHODOX CHURCH BAPTISM AND MARRIAGE RECORDS 167
CEMETERIES 169

GREEK ARMY RECORDS 170

PESONTES OF THE GREEK ITALIAN WAR OF 1940 AND 1941 171
THE PARLIAMENT LIBRARY COLLECTION 172
CENSUS RECORDS OF GREECE 173
SHIP MANIFESTS 174
Ship Crew Lists 181
BNF GALLICA FRANCE ARCHIVE 182
Census Records of the United States 184
Voting Records of the United States 185

GENEALOGY CHARTS 186

PHOTOGRAPHY AND HISTORY 187

First photography on Chios 187
First Women Photographers in Greece 188
VRONTADOS CHIOS ABOUT 1930 189

- **BIBLIOGRAPHY AND ONLINE BOOKS** 190
  - *Bibliography* 190
  - *Some rare books found online* 190
  - *REFERENCES AND NOTES* 194
  - *Movies Regarding Greek History* 196
- **RESOLUTIONS OF GREEK HISTORY** 197
  - History is an inter-twined timeline of facts, consequences, circumstances, and delusions 197
- **INTERNET LINKS** 199
- **BOURNIAS FAMILY WEBSITES** 201
- **GLOSSARY / ABBREVIATIONS / ACRONYMS** 202
- **ANNOTATIONS** 202
- **ACKNOWLEDGEMENTS** 203
- **CLOSING REMARKS** 205
  - BIOGRAPHY OF THE AUTHOR 206

PREFACE
Time travelling into the History of the Bournias family through Genealogy

I am merely a speck in time in the genealogical journey through the Bournias family history and research to produce the family tree. Peter A. Bournias

I wrote this book to honor all of the Bournias family member's ancestry and heritage.

Some additional information has been noted by other family members and included, as well as the data used to update the family database and charts.

I was raised by my mother as my parents divorced when I was five. She was a Catholic, and so I was baptized twice, Catholic and Greek Orthodox.

My premier visit to the island of Chios was in August 1973 when I was nineteen years old. It was a culture shock coming from Manhattan, New York, considered by many as one of the most modern cities in the world. I stayed at the home of my grandparents in Vrontados with my grandfather Pantelis, my grandmother Zabella, my father Ioannis (John), and my stepmother.

I didn't know what to expect before I arrived. I found myself in a very old home that was minimalistic with antiquated furniture. It had electricity and a poor water supply. My father had just bought a television for his parents that offered only one channel, broadcasted for about three hours per day and was controlled by the military.

My visit to the market in the center of Chios was an interesting although a shocking experience. When we went to the meat market, I realized for the first time how different life was in Greece and that refrigeration was almost non-existent and a luxury, as I saw flies covering the meats.

I didn't know the Greek language; this made communication impossible as the Chiots lived in a world where English was uncommon then for the majority of the islanders.

After I returned to New York, I often thought about the trip and believe that these are situations where foreigners learn to appreciate the simplicity that life offers them after, and a new way of viewing their own life through such experiences.

Ten years later, I found myself wanting to leave New York, and decided to move to Greece. I learned the Greek language at the age of thirty when I moved to Greece from New York. Now almost forty years later, I have survived living in a country that many Greek born Diaspora cannot understand how I accomplished it when they tried but could not.

The most challenging part encountered in this research, apart from the Greek bureaucracy, is trying to link family members from Spartounta and Messinia that originated from Chios but travelled to Asia Minor, then immigrated as refugees back to Greece, and / or to Texas in the USA, and / or Australia, and elsewhere.

The subject of genealogy has taught me to appreciate not only Greece but also the history of Greece and about how and what the Greek people think. This is the very essence of understanding their continuous efforts to strive to maintain the great idea or "MEGALI IDEA" as a nation, to keep their language as pure as possible, and to maintain their network with the Diaspora. This has become even more burdensome today even though we now have so many ways of communication through technology.

While I will cite historical facts, I will not endeavor to write history in my writings, as I am not a historian. I will mention historical facts to provide proof about our ancestors.

As a foreigner, the research of the family allows me to connect the historical timeline of the past with my relatives, and this accentuates my thoughts on the introspection of their lives compared to the Diaspora, those who live or have lived abroad.[6]

The methodology involved in researching and analyzing the data of the family genealogy coincides with my studies of accounting, auditing, and information technology. Research requires objectivity to maintain the clarity of the information collected and then to organize it.

The information regarding our ancestors in this document is not written in a story format because I didn't see it as being a contiguous pieces of information from which I could do so. It is my first book, and I wrote it to be a historical record with biographical information, and an objective and factual analysis of the data discovered, with the exception of personal notes.

When I began the research around twenty (20) years ago, information was not available on any public computer. Later, only some of it was accessible via the Internet, and I extracted the most significant of all of it by visiting archives of various areas traveling around the main land and the islands, requesting vital records from municipalities (and being denied many times), reading Greek texts and then translating and interpreting the most relevant information into English.

Always question what you read and see!
Assuming that you have questions, some may be answered in this book.
It may be important if it is missing because this is OUR heritage.
If you have questions or additional information regarding a branch of the family, I would like to know about them or I will try to provide you with an answer if I have that information.
My genealogy research has not ended, once you begin, it becomes perpetual.

---

6 https://en.wikipedia.org/wiki/Diaspora

The Great Philosopher Homer

Chios is also known as a place where the great philosopher Homer taught, about 800 b. c.; his method of teaching is still in use today and is the foundation of western education.[7]

There is a rock known as Daskalopetra (teacher's rock) in the area known as Omiroupolis (Greek for Homer and Polis for city) that was supposedly used by Homer to sit and teach surrounded by students.
This rock is visited by many tourists that travel to Chios and is located in the area of Vrontados.

Image credit:
Internet / wikipedia.org

As technology progresses with the introduction of drones, many Greeks are now using them to film videos of the areas of Chios, and other areas. Some astonishing videos for different areas and topics regarding Chios on YouTube are available whether you know Greek or not.

Hippocrates of Chios

Hippocrates of Chios[8] was a Greek mathematician specializing in geometry and astronomer. He lived on the island of Chios, which is the fifth largest of the Greek islands and is much closer to Turkey than to mainland Greece, and later moved to Athens. He was influenced by Pythagorean[9] thinking, which was popular on the nearby island of Samos. He should not be confused with **Hippocrates of Kos**, the doctor and originator of the **Hippocratic Oath**[10], who lived about the same time.

---

7 https://en.wikipedia.org/wiki/Homer
8 Hippocrates of Chios – Wikipedia, https://en.wikipedia.org/wiki/Hippocrates_of_Chios
9 https://en.wikipedia.org/wiki/Pythagorean_theorem
10 https://en.wikipedia.org/wiki/Hippocratic_Oath

Chios Greece Traditional Folklore and Artifacts

I added two photographs about the clothing of the period from the 15th century to about the mid-1900 that help to explain the transition of Greece into a western country.

For those that will travel to Chios, there is a Folklore Museum.[11] Here is a video link about another folklore museum in Greece.[12]

Greece did not progress along the same timeline as the majority of Europe even through WWI and WWII, and therefore the Greeks remained in a vacuum as impoverished people. Their clothing began to change to more of a western dress style later in the 1900's when they started migrating to other countries. This allowed those who moved abroad to assimilate into western society and opened a new clothing industry that helped the Greeks in Greece to move forward by advancing the domestic economy after their 400 years of slavery by the Ottomans.

The photo on the left displays a freedom fighter of the period wearing a "fustanella," typical clothing for the period. The photo on the right is a similar transition by the freedom fighter who are known as a Tsolia or Evzon, a royal guard of the government that is comparable to a Marine.[13] [14]

Image credit: Internet / website author unknown

---

[11] A Folklore Museum in Chios http://gym-kallim.chi.sch.gr/index.php
[12] A YouTube, https://www.youtube.com/watch?v=BjvF2zKkoFA
[13] https://en.wikipedia.org/wiki/Evzones
[14] https://en.wikipedia.org/wiki/Marines

Sweets from Chios

The Bournias family were involved in the production of sweets too. There was a family owned and operated sweet shop on the corner of the port for many years where Chiots, and tourists alike, bought sweets as gifts for those on the island and to take back home.

Bournias and Michalakis in Chios produced this can of sweets. As you can see on the bottom of the can, produced by **ΜΠΟΥΡΝΙΑΣ & ΜΙΧΑΛΑΚΗΣ ΓΛΥΚΑ ΧΙΟΥ**. The partners were Georgios Bournias and Nicholas Michalakis from Kouronio Chios.

Other sweets such as Mastic, which is a hard rock like candy, produced from the sap of trees that only grows on Chios. During the old days, Mastic was so important that it was safeguarded because of its economic value and enormous benefits for health, and other byproducts.

Syrupy sweets called "sweets of the spoon".[15]

This image shows syrupy sweet baby eggplants.

The majority of families on the island of Chios made their own sweets from various fruits and vegetables. Some of the best tasting syrupy (γλυκό κουταλιού) sweets from Chios are produced with cherry, grapes, wild orange, lime, prunes, and even some vegetables.

Chios didn't have apples or pumpkin in those days, and one has to remember that they could only create something from the local produce available. Other sweets like Baklavas and "Kataifi" are made with pistachios and honey.

In other parts of Greece sweets were (and are today) made with walnuts, almonds, chestnuts, and other fruits like quince, strawberries, peaches, pears, and others locally available. A favorite sweet that is easy to carry around is dried figs. If milk (from a goat) was available then they could make cake-like deserts using flour and sugar. Sugar was an expensive commodity in the past as was coffee.

Image credit: Internet / website author unknown

---

15 https://en.wikipedia.org/wiki/Spoon_sweets

A modern day map of Chios Greece

Popular areas in noted in Greek and English on this map includes older area name that may have changed. Chios is populated by visiting Greek Diaspora speaking English in the months of July and August.

Not shown are the adjacent islands from the north clockwise are Kertis, Margariti, Glastria, Strovili, St. Stephanos, Prasonisia, Inousses, Pateroniso, Papapontikadiko, St. Panteleimon, Archontoniso, Pontikonisi, Gaidouronisos, Pasas, Vatos, Vataki, and Mastic villages or Venetiko Island, Pelagonisos, Nisaki, and other rocky islets.

Image credit: Internet / website author unknown

The Greek Language and the Dialect of Chios

The Greek language has undergone numerous changes over the centuries. This happens due to foreign influence, the use of slang, how the people use the language, determines how it affects our communication.[16]

In the bygone days, the Chiots developed a dialect or slang. This may have been to prevent the Ottomans from knowing what they discussed but I am not sure.[17]

The Greek Language I learned and taught today is called Demotic or Neo-Hellenic Greek. It uses three (3) accent marks. While most foreigners think that Greek today is extremely difficult, the previous versions were more demanding because of their use of many accent marks but was more precise according to many highly educated Greeks.[18]

What many foreign language users forget is that English, as well as other languages, are based on the Greek and Latin languages. These two languages comprise about seventy (70) percent of the English language. I will point out that "Greeklish" is considered improper to use because historically the Greeks used proper Greek even through the 400 years of occupation by the Ottomans that continues to be used today. Greeklish is considered rude and an apathetic method of writing Greek using Latin characters simply because you have to know Greek to write it that way.[19]

What is the importance of understanding how languages are constructed and how they affect us?
The Greeks will say their language is "rich" while the English language is "poor".
What does that mean? The short and simple explanation is that one word in Greek can have multiple connotations while one word in English is more narrowly defined.
Greek politicians love the Greek language because they can say something to a crowd of people and each person can interpret it in a different way.

Does this mean the Greek language is not explicit?
No, but to use Greek for example in the field of engineering requires an extremely good knowledge of the language by both the person who will write or speak about something and by those who will read or listen to it. Therefore, the English language is more adept for technical explanations. A proof of that is the technological progress of English language countries compared to Greece, the exception being ancient Greek for example the Antikythera Mechanism.[20]

---

16 The Greek Language - a history, Wikipedia, https://en.wikipedia.org/wiki/Greek_language
17 A list of words and phrases that have different words to express them in the dialect of the Chiots. http://kallimasia.blogspot.gr/2013/12/blog-post_8.html
18 http://www.chios24.gr/chios/language
19 https://en.wikipedia.org/wiki/Greeklish
20 Wikipedia, https://en.wikipedia.org/wiki/Antikythera_mechanism

A Smidgen of History about Chios and Greece and Asia Minor

Anatolia is likewise known as Asia Minor that became the country known today as Turkey but in the past, it was a part of the Byzantine Empire and populated by groups of people including Greeks, Armenians, Ottomans, and others. Greeks lived throughout Asia Minor for centuries and many spoke only Greek while others learned various languages of the people.[21] [22]

Chios was known as the gateway to the east and in 1304, the Genoese and the Giustiniani family ruled the island, and collected taxes for the Ottomans to maintain their rule.
In 1566, the Ottoman Empire took control of Chios.[23]

In 1453, the Byzantine Empire is lost to the Osman's known as the Ottomans as they capture Constantinople and rename it Istanbul. In essence, Asia Minor became the Ottoman Empire.[24]

From 1453, the Greeks endured, and then the Greek War of Independence in 1821 begins throughout Greece.[25]

The **First National Assembly** was established in Nafplio in January 1822 creating a constitution and standardized the Greek flag.[26]

The **Greek Revolution** began in March 1822. There are many discrepancies in the actual dates as recorded by Greek historians.

During the beginning of Easter, the **revolution on Chios** began in April 1822 led by Antonios Bournias, Lykourgos Logothetis, and a group of Samians from the island of Samos.[27]
The massacre followed and many Chiots fled to Syros, Mykonos, other areas, with many returning to Chios years after and others who did not. More details regarding this event and the family are presented in the research in this book.

In 1829, Russia defeats the Ottomans and helps Greece become independent thereby creating a bond of friendship between the two countries. This emboldened the establishment of the birth of the communist party in Greece subsequently.

Chios finally gained their independence from the Ottomans after the **First Balkan War** in 1912, 346 years after the occupation, although many will cite 400 years of occupation by the Ottomans. The Greeks including the Chiots endured and kept their language, religion, culture, and origin as Greeks intact throughout.

---

21 https://en.wikipedia.org/wiki/Anatolia
22 https://en.wikipedia.org/wiki/Byzantine_Empire
23 https://en.wikipedia.org/wiki/Giustiniani
24 https://en.wikipedia.org/wiki/Ottoman_Turks
25 https://en.wikipedia.org/wiki/Greek_War_of_Independence
26 https://en.wikipedia.org/wiki/Nafplio
27 https://en.wikipedia.org/wiki/Lykourgos_Logothetis

At the end of WWI in 1919, the Asia Minor Campaign started with the promise by the British Prime Minister to Eleftherios Venizelos that Greece could have additional land from Asia Minor.[28] This became **"The Asia Minor Catastrophe"** and historically known as **"The Greco-Turkish War (1919 – 1922)"**.[29]

At the same time, the rise of power had begun with Kemal Ataturk to achieve the national cleansing of the Ottoman Empire, "***Turkification***," starting the genocide of the Greeks, Armenians, Jews, and other Christians.[30]

The following two paragraphs depict what the Greeks of Asia Minor lost and experienced; the anger and hate that they had for the decision by Eleftherios Venizelos and his generals regarding the expansion of Greek territory immediately after WWI.

During the period of "**the exchange**" in 1923[31], the Greeks of Asia Minor, many rich and wealthy, lost everything and found themselves nowhere, exchanging homes and businesses for huts in an indifferent and hostile homeland of Greece, which faltered economically and politically.[32]

Here is a quote from the Greek High Commissioner of Smyrna, Aristides Stergiadis:
"It is better for them (the Greeks) to stay here, for Kemal to slaughter them, because if they go to Athens they will overthrow (revolt due to their losses) everything."[33] [34]

I included this information about Asia Minor because most people do not know why the Greeks affirm the genocide and loss of lives and property in the Asia Minor Campaign of 1919 to 1922. Many of our relatives lived, worked, prospered, and died fighting there.

The continued displacement of Christian groups living in Turkey happened again using a tax as justification, called "Varlık Vergisi," mostly levied on non-Muslim citizens in 1942 that forced Greeks and others in Istanbul to leave, and then again in 1964 - 1965 with the expulsion of Istanbul Greeks by the Turks to justify their actions.[35]

Author's comment
Turkey although a member of NATO continues to threaten Greece today claiming that the islands in the Aegean belong to them based upon history of the long dispersed Ottoman Empire. They continue to make false claims that the islands of Greece are theirs, and refuse to acknowledge the Treaty of Lausanne[36], and that Greeks lived throughout what is known today as Turkey for centuries before the Ottoman Empire even existed.

---

28 https://en.wikipedia.org/wiki/Eleftherios_Venizelos
29 https://en.wikipedia.org/wiki/Greco-Turkish_War_(1919%E2%80%931922)
30 https://en.wikipedia.org/wiki/Turkification
31 https://en.wikipedia.org/wiki/Population_exchange_between_Greece_and_Turkey
32 https://en.wikipedia.org/wiki/Anatolian_Greeks
33 https://en.wikipedia.org/wiki/Mustafa_Kemal_Atat%C3%BCrk
34 https://en.wikipedia.org/wiki/Aristeidis_Stergiadis
35 https://en.wikipedia.org/wiki/Varl%C4%B1k_Vergisi
36 https://en.wikipedia.org/wiki/Treaty_of_Lausanne

THE BOURNIAS SURNAME

The Bournias family has travelled throughout Greece and to other areas of the world from Chios and Evia[37] to these areas and other places around the world.

The Bournias family tree and history is a major work consolidating numerous generations of the family.

- Vrontados, Chios, Greece
- Mesta, Chios, Greece
- Arcadias, Peloponnese, Greece
- Harokopio, Messinia, Greece[38]
- Drama, Greece
- Arcadia, Peloponnese
- Crete, Greece
- Athens, Greece
- Mykonos, Greece
- Tsesme, Asia Minor, Turkey (today)
- Chicago, Illinois, USA
- Brooklyn, NY, USA
- Texas, USA
- France
- South East Asia
- Spartounda, Chios, Greece
- Karystos, Evia, Greece
- Lydoriki, Fokidos, Greece
- Koroni, Pilos, Messinia, Greece
- Vounaria & Kombi, Messinia, Greece
- Tripoli, Peloponnese
- Zakynthos, Greece
- Kalamata, Greece
- Naxos, Greece
- Smyrna, Asia Minor, Turkey (today)[39]
- New York, USA
- Florida, USA
- New Jersey, USA
- Australia
- and other areas and countries

---

[37] Evia or Euboea is an island, see https://en.wikipedia.org/wiki/Euboea
[38] Messinia or Messenia, see https://en.wikipedia.org/wiki/Messenia
[39] Smyrna is adjacent to Chios, see https://en.wikipedia.org/wiki/Smyrna

INCEPTION OF THE BOURNIAS SURNAME

I have followed the genealogy trail of the Bournias family throughout Greece beginning on the island of Chios dating back to the 1700's but the family surname may have started in France.[40]

While searching for records in France, I came across the surname **Bournihas** in the area of Puy-de-Dôme[41], Montpellier[42] and Thiers, an area of Clermont-Ferrand[43]. The surname that I found was Bournihas, which if pronounced using a French accent is similar to the Greek name of Bournias as the "h" is silent.

Travels by Bournias family members from Greece to other places in Europe, showed that some settled in Marseille.[44] I discovered some newspaper clippings in the Archives of France.[45]

I am fascinated about how and why Antonios A. Bournias was a friend of the Charles Nicolas Fabvier, French Ambassador[46] of the French Embassy or Consulate on Chios during that period in time, and why he fought in the Egyptian and Syrian campaigns with Napoleon's army against the Ottomans. I have to assume that he must have been able to communicate in French and that means that the family must have known the French language.

Researcher note:
Charles Nicolas Fabvier is mentioned as an ambassador.
https://en.wikipedia.org/wiki/Charles_Nicolas_Fabvier
https://en.wikipedia.org/wiki/List_of_ambassadors_of_France_to_the_Ottoman_Empire
https://en.wikipedia.org/wiki/French_campaign_in_Egypt_and_Syria
Charles Fabvier Napoleonic Soldier and Greek Hero[47]

Quote from another genealogist, unknown
>*Who we are is a product of multiple factors: genetics, environment, and opportunities (or lack thereof). So it was with our ancestors. Where they lived and how they lived framed their mortal existence; but it was their personalities which molded their lives.*

---

40 France, https://en.wikipedia.org/wiki/France
41 Puy-de-Dôme, https://en.wikipedia.org/wiki/Puy-de-D%C3%B4me
42 Montpellier, https://en.wikipedia.org/wiki/Montpellier
43 Clermont-Ferrand, https://en.wikipedia.org/wiki/Clermont-Ferrand
44 https://en.wikipedia.org/wiki/Marseille
45 https://en.wikipedia.org/wiki/Archives_Nationales_(France)
46 https://en.wikipedia.org/wiki/Charles_Nicolas_Fabvier
47 Charles Fabvier: Napoleonic Soldier & Greek Hero, from the website of Shannon Selin, https://shannonselin.com/2016/04/charles-fabvier/

GEOGRAPHICAL MAPPING OF THE SURNAME

In Greece today, the surname Bournias exists on Chios, and Evia next to Attiki although none are displayed, and in the Athens area of Attiki, as shown in this map from the website vrisko.gr. The same map displays populations of the surname by area using red dots.[48]

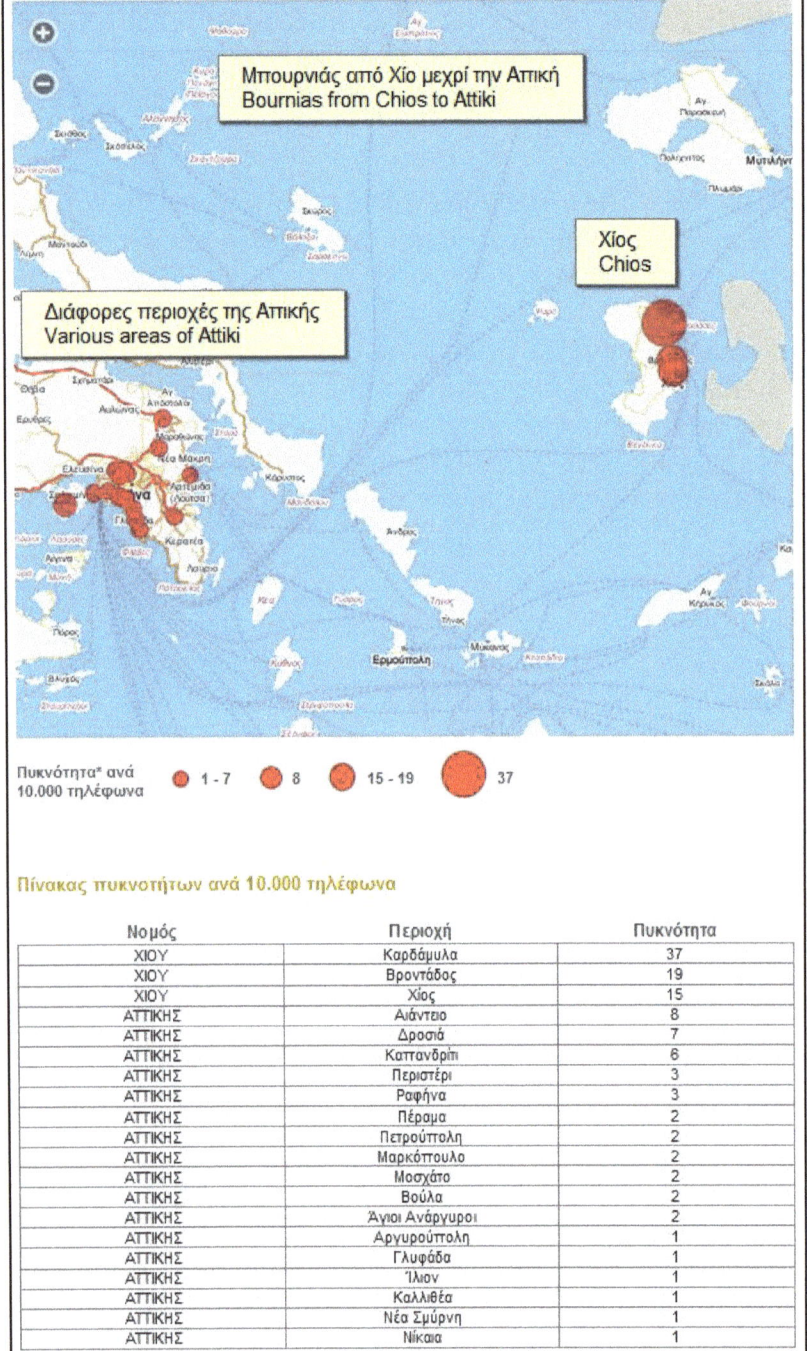

Researcher note:
The first telephone catalog of Greece was published by OTE, the national telephone company in 1909. It only listed 975 subscribers of the Athens area.

Image credit:
Internet / vrisko.gr

Νομός	Περιοχή	Πυκνότητα
ΧΙΟΥ	Καρδάμυλα	37
ΧΙΟΥ	Βροντάδος	19
ΧΙΟΥ	Χίος	15
ΑΤΤΙΚΗΣ	Αιάντειο	8
ΑΤΤΙΚΗΣ	Δροσιά	7
ΑΤΤΙΚΗΣ	Καπανδρίτι	6
ΑΤΤΙΚΗΣ	Περιστέρι	3
ΑΤΤΙΚΗΣ	Ραφήνα	3
ΑΤΤΙΚΗΣ	Πέραμα	2
ΑΤΤΙΚΗΣ	Πετρούπολη	2
ΑΤΤΙΚΗΣ	Μαρκόπουλο	2
ΑΤΤΙΚΗΣ	Μοσχάτο	2
ΑΤΤΙΚΗΣ	Βούλα	2
ΑΤΤΙΚΗΣ	Άγιοι Ανάργυροι	2
ΑΤΤΙΚΗΣ	Αργυρούπολη	1
ΑΤΤΙΚΗΣ	Γλυφάδα	1
ΑΤΤΙΚΗΣ	Ίλιον	1
ΑΤΤΙΚΗΣ	Καλλιθέα	1
ΑΤΤΙΚΗΣ	Νέα Σμύρνη	1
ΑΤΤΙΚΗΣ	Νίκαια	1

---

48 The above chart was extracted from the web site service of Vrisko.gr that provides an online Telephone Catalog for Greece. https://apps.vrisko.gr/apo-pou-krataei-i-skoufia-sou

GREEKS WITH THE SURNAME BOURNIAS IN GREECE

The following chart is a list of the surname from the website vrisko.gr, a Greek Telephone Catalog[49] covers people living in various areas of Greece such as Athens, Attiki, and the island of Chios, excluding areas such as Evia, and Messinia in the Peloponnese.[50] Translation to English is inclusive for Bournias and Bournia as both genders in Greek.

PREFECTURE	AREA	POPULATION	
Νομός	Περιοχή	Πυκνότητα	Area in English
ΑΤΤΙΚΗΣ	Άγιοι Ανάργυροι	2	Agios Anargyros
ΑΤΤΙΚΗΣ	Αιάντειο	8	Aianteio
ΑΤΤΙΚΗΣ	Αργυρούπολη	1	Argyroupolis
ΑΤΤΙΚΗΣ	Βούλα	2	Voula
ΑΤΤΙΚΗΣ	Γλυφάδα	1	Glyfada
ΑΤΤΙΚΗΣ	Δροσιά	7	Drosia
ΑΤΤΙΚΗΣ	Ίλιον	1	Hlion
ΑΤΤΙΚΗΣ	Καλλιθέα	1	Kallithea
ΑΤΤΙΚΗΣ	Καπανδρίτι	6	Kapandriti
ΑΤΤΙΚΗΣ	Μαρκόπουλο	2	Markopoulo
ΑΤΤΙΚΗΣ	Μοσχάτο	2	Moschato
ΑΤΤΙΚΗΣ	Νέα Σμύρνη	1	Nea Smyrni
ΑΤΤΙΚΗΣ	Νίκαια	1	Nikaia
ΑΤΤΙΚΗΣ	Πέραμα	2	Perama
ΑΤΤΙΚΗΣ	Περιστέρι	3	Peristeri
ΑΤΤΙΚΗΣ	Πετρούπολη	2	Petroupoli
ΑΤΤΙΚΗΣ	Ραφήνα	3	Rafina
ΧΙΟΥ	Βροντάδος	19	Vrontados
ΧΙΟΥ	Καρδάμυλα	37	Kardamyla
ΧΙΟΥ	Χίος	15	Chios

I didn't provide a total number for this chart because the real number of persons or families with a telephone listing may vary, and it may not include those with only mobile phone numbers.

Numerous family members are established in the United States with the largest group in Texas, others in Pennsylvania, New Jersey, and New York that originate from Spartounta. Similarly, many Chiot families in Australia originate from Spartounta.[51]

I have created numerous descendant charts according to locations of all the families from Greece, and abroad from information that I have discovered during my research or provided by other family members.

---

49 The above chart was extracted from the web site service of Vrisko.gr that provides an online Telephone Catalog for Greece. https://apps.vrisko.gr/apo-pou-krataei-i-skoufia-sou
50 https://en.wikipedia.org/wiki/Peloponnese
51 One of the regional units of Chios, https://en.wikipedia.org/wiki/List_of_settlements_in_the_Chios_regional_unit

Another geographical mapping of the surnames Bournias and Vournas[52] (un-researched) display their location in the Peloponnese in the area of Messinia[53] and Koroni[54].

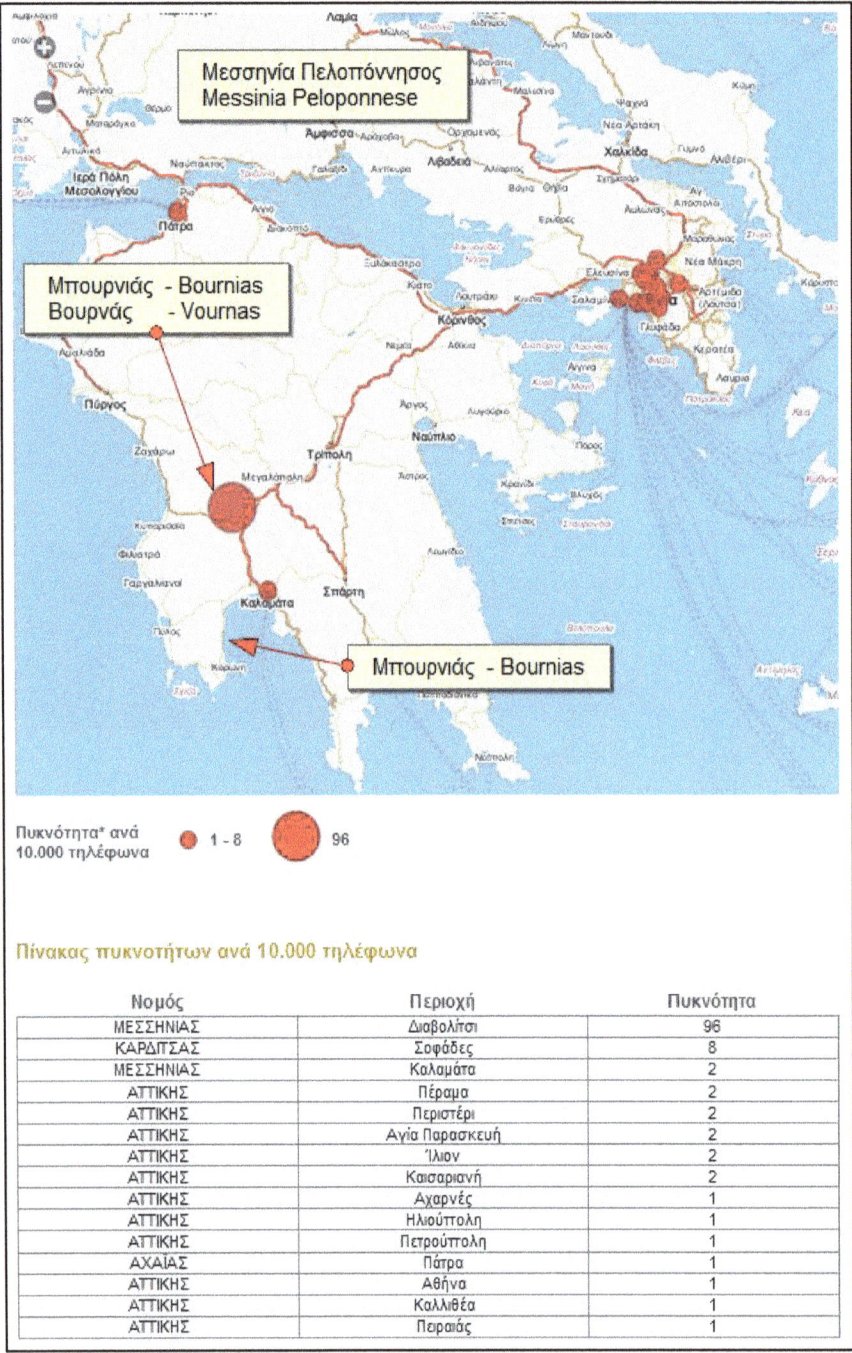

Image credit:
Internet / vrisko.gr

---

52 The Greek surname Vournas may be an incorrect recording of the surname Vournias or simply a misspelling.
53 https://en.wikipedia.org/wiki/Messenia
54 https://en.wikipedia.org/wiki/Koroni

This last mapping displays the surname **Vournias** that was originally Bournias and the movement of the family from **Chios** to **Cesme and Smyrna** to **Iraklion Crete**[55] and then to **Drama**[56] as I discovered in my research. In those days, imagine the difficulties of the journey as there were no means of mass transportation. The people carried their belongings walking over difficult terrain with little or no assistance from the Greek government. They were transported by ship first to Crete, then to Messinia, and then by decision of the government sent to Drama or other areas. More information about this is recorded in the following pages.

The following chart pertains to the surname Vournias in Greece.

Prefecture	Area	Population
Drama	Drama	2
Attiki	Nea Smyrni	1

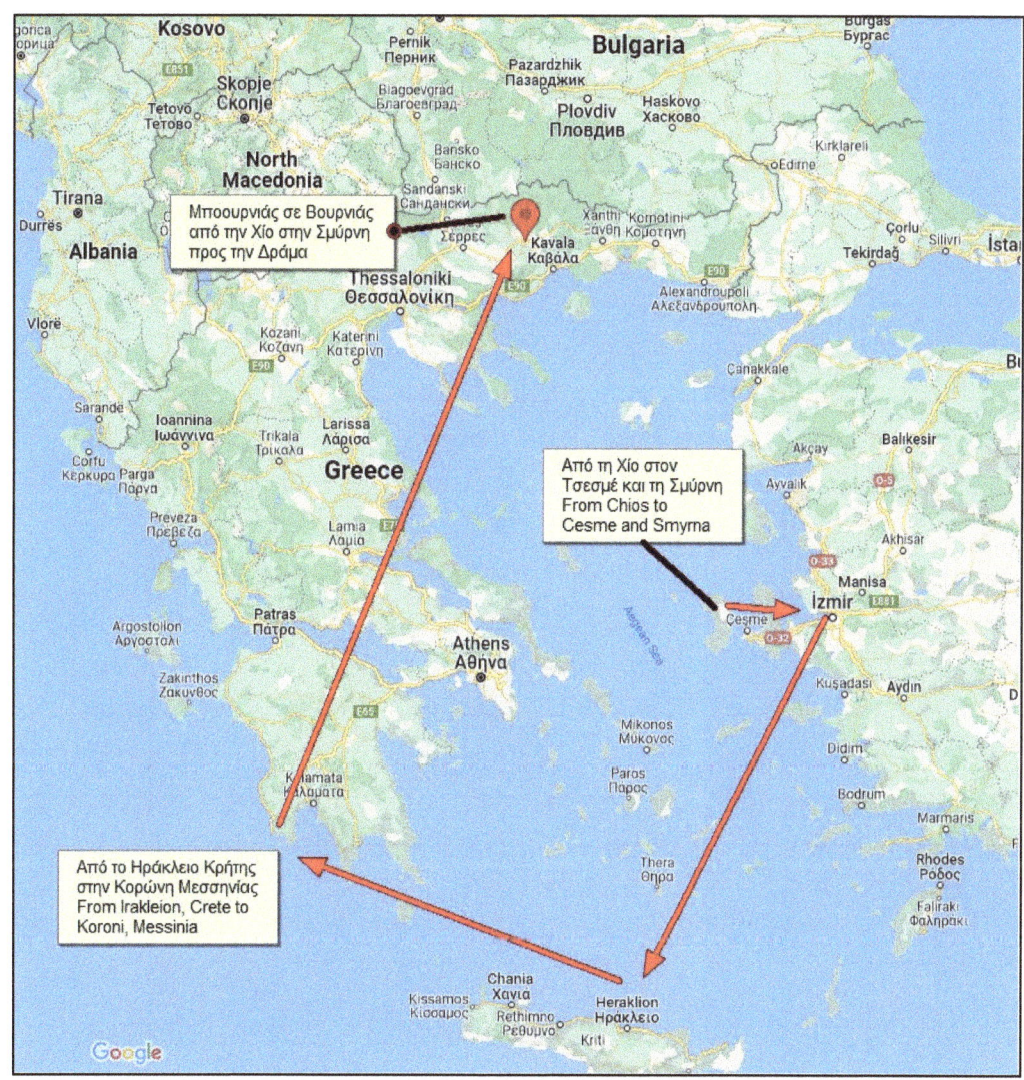

Image credit: Internet, table from vrisko.gr and map from Google Maps by google.com.

---

55 https://en.wikipedia.org/wiki/Heraklion
56 https://en.wikipedia.org/wiki/Drama

CHIAN SURNAMES

Some of my spelling may not agree with the assumed normality of the transliteration of Greek words into English. As an example, I do not agree with translations based on British English, substituting the letter "C" in English for a word or name written with a "K" in Greek.

Another difference in spelling is seen in the use of the letter "e" and "ι" Greek iota. English speakers will generally use "e" whereas Greek speakers will use the "ι" Greek iota. My explanation for this is that in Greek the "i" Greek iota has a higher pitch. Therefore as an example, when "Δημήτριος" is transliterated to English, I write it as Demetrios, whereas it may be seen as Dimitrios by Greek speakers. While I know that some may be upset by this kind of thinking, an explanation will follow.

Greek surnames starting with "ΜΠ" (are officially transliterated in English to "MP" by the government, and translate to "B" Latin alphabet) are considered to be of foreign origin.

You will not see the surname Bournias (Μπουρνιάς) in the following list, because the surnames on these two pages originate on Chios whereas the surname Bournias although appearing around 1700 is not evidenced to be an original Chiot surname.

The following is a list translated in English, and in Greek to preserve them correctly, the surnames found on Chios prior to 1820 and after.[57]

Latinized	Greek	Latinized	Greek
Angelakis	Αγγελάκης	Karavolas	Καράβολας
Angelikoussis	Αγγελικούσης	Kardoulis	Καρδούλης
Angelos	Άγγελος	Karmantis	Καρμαντής
Angeloudis	Αγγελούδης	Katradis	Κατράδης
Alatsis	Αλατσής	Katsounis	Κατσούνης
Alepos	Αλεπός	Kefalas	Κεφάλας
Aspiotis	Ασπιώτης	Kiminas	Κιμινάς
Vagianos	Βαγιάνος	Kontarnaris	Κονταρνάρης
Valantasis	Βαλαντάσης	Kontokostas	Κοντοκώστας
Vardalas	Βαρδαλάς	Kontris	Κόντρης
Kings	Βασιλές	Kopanos	Κόπανος
Vafias	Βαφιάς	Kopelos	Κόπελος
Ververis	Βέρβερης	Kordis	Κορδής
North	Βοριάς	Kotzembiris	Κοτζεμπίρης
Gemelos	Γέμελος	Kougiavlos	Κούγιαβλος

---

57 This list is from the following source:
Bulletin of the historical and ethnological company of Greece volume 3
Historical and Ethnological Society of Greece
Δελτίων της ιστορικής και εθνολογικής εταιρείας της Ελλάδος τόμος 3
Ιστορική και Εθνολογική Εταιρεία της Ελλάδος

Georgilis	Γεωργίλης	Koukounas	Κουκουνάς
Giannakis	Γιαννάκης	Kouloumoundra	Κουλουμούντρας
George	Γιώργος	Koutelas	Κουτέλας
Glyftis	Γλύφτης	Koutos	Κουτός
Goudes	Γουδές	Koutsoutos	Κούτσουτος
Gregos	Γρέγος	Koufolios	Κουφολιός
Gynaikotos	Γυναικωτός	Krikelis	Κρικέλης
Deligiannis	Δεληγιάννης	Ktistakis	Κτιστάκης
Dimitrakis	Δημητράκης	Kyriakas	Κυριακάς
Dimitros	Δημητρός	Laimos	Λαιμός
Diakogiorgos	Διακογιώργος	Liadis	Λιαδής
Dougias	Δούγιας	Libanos	Λιβανός
Embalomoutzounos	Εμβαλομούτζουνος	Lignos	Λιγνός
Zartaloudis	Ζαρταλούδης	Lyras	Λύρας
Zevros	Ζεβρός	Madias	Μαδιάς
Zoulotas	Ζουλότας	Makrinas	Μακρινάς
Thomas	Θωμάς	Makrinas	Μακρίνας
Kavouris	Καβούρης	Makrykostas	Μακρυκώστας
Kalmoukos	Καλμούκος	Maloupis	Μαλούπης
Kalogeros	Καλόγερος	Mantzavinos	Μαντζαβίνος
Kambylis	Καμπύλης	Mapas	Μάπας
Kapiniaris	Καπινιάρης	Martakas	Μάρτακας
Kapiris	Καπίρης	Martakis	Μαρτάκης
Karavadenios	Καραβαδένιος	Mavris	Μαυρής
Karavas	Καραβάς	Melis	Μέλης
Michalitsis	Μιχαλίτσης	Pyrovolos	Πυρόβολος
Monios	Μονιός	Rallis	Ράλλης
Monogios	Μονογιός	Rogas	Ρώγας
Moschos	Μόσχος	Samenas	Σαμενάς
Mouzalas	Μουζάλας	Svokos	Σβώκος
Mouselimis	Μουσελίμης	Silimas	Σιλημάς
Moustakas	Μουστάκας	Skarvelis	Σκαρβέλης
Balomoutzounos	Μπαλομούτζουνος	Skoinitis	Σκοινίτης
Barboutis	Μπαρμπούτης	Sousaris	Σουσάρης
Bilalis	Μπιλάλης	Spathogiannis	Σπαθογιάννης
Bolakis	Μπολάκης	Spanos	Σπανός
Mylonas	Μυλωνάς	Stavroulis	Σταυρούλης
Myxas	Μύξας	Stravelakis	Στραβελάκης

Myofas	Μυοφάς	Sykoutris	Συκουτρής
Mpsrakis	Μψράκης	Tzagaris	Τζαγκάρης
Neroklitis	Νεροκλίτης	Tzablakos	Τζαμπλάκος
Niamonitis	Νιαμονήτης	Tzapela	Τζαπέλας
Nikiforos	Νικηφόρος	Tzarouchas	Τζαρούχας
Nikolos	Νικολός	Tzigelis	Τζιγκέλης
Notias	Νοτιάς	Tzigros	Τζιγκρός
Xylas	Ξυλάς	Tziknas	Τζίκνας
Pagonis	Παγώνης	Tzirlis	Τζιρλής
Palios	Παλιός	Tzirokavlos	Τζιρόκαυλος
Pantelis	Παντελής	Tzolas	Τζόλας
Papagalakis	Παπαγαλάκης	Tornaris	Τορνάρης
Papazis	Παπαζής	Totonis	Τοτόνης
Papis	Παπής	Trifylios	Τριφύλιος
Papoulios	Παπουλιός	Tsatiris	Τσατήρης
Peratikos	Περατικός	Tsoumpos	Τσούμπος
Peristeris	Περιστέρης	Fatzis	Φατζής
Petikas	Πέτικας	Fatouros	Φατούρος
Pirounas	Πηρουνάς	Fatouteras	Φατουτέρας
Pistaras	Πιστάρας	Fikiaris	Φήκιαρης
Pistoliaris	Πιστολιάρης	Fissas	Φήσας
Poniros	Πονηρός	Foradis	Φοράδης
Pontikos	Ποντικός	Foros	Φόρος
Poradas	Ποραδάς	Fraggakis	Φραγκάκης
Poutis	Πουτής	Chandras	Χανδράς
Premenis	Πρεμενής	Harkia	Χαρκιάς
Proios	Πρώϊος	Hartoularis	Χαρτουλάρης
Fragkias	Φραγκιάς	Houmis	Χούμης
Frangos	Φράγκος	Psarelis	Ψαρέλης
Fokas	Φώκας	Psomataris	Ψωματάρης
Chalamantas	Χαλαμαντάς	Psomostithis	Ψωμοστήθης
Chalkias	Χαλκιάς	Psoras	Ψώρας

Other Chiot Surnames

Many of the families on Chios today may have migrated from Asia Minor through Northern Greece due to wars. Therefore, a question continues to exist as to whether the surname Bournias began in France. There is more to learn about this in the following pages.

The following list of surnames shown are found on Chios today although they appear in the **Pontus region,**[58] southern coast of the Black Sea of modern-day Turkey, which was inhabited by Greeks, Armenians, and other ethnic groups for centuries before it became the Ottoman Empire.

The Latin transliteration is based on the ELOT 743 standard for Modern Greek[59] **as used by the Greek government for Greek passports:**

Vorrias, Giomelos, Kakaris, Kaloutas, Karakatsanis, Karalis, Lavrentio Chrysovelonis, Tselepis, Karalis, Kleidas, Kolykas, Kosenas, Koutelos, Kozis, Livanos, Mathioudakis, Monios, Begakis, Bilmezis, Xylas, Rizos, Sarikas, Sarikides, Sarikakides, Sousouris, Stampoulos, Steliaras, Sfikas, Tsapalas, Fouroulis, Chatzimikes, Christofis, Psomataris, Flamos, and Firippis.

The original list is shown in Greek to preserve them correctly in the Greek language.[60]

Βορριάς, Γιόμελος, Κάκαρης, Καλουτάς, Καρακατσάνης, Καράλης, Λαυρέντιο Χρυσοβελώνης, Τσελεπής, Καράλης, Κλειδάς, Κωλυκάς, Κοσένας, Κούτελος, Κωζής, Λιβανός, Μαθιουδάκης, Μονιός, Μπεγάκης, Μπιλμέζης, Ξυλάς, Ρίζος, Σαρίκας, Σαρίκηδες, Σαρικάκηδες, Σουσουρής, Σταμπούλος, Στελιαράς, Σφήκας, Τσαπάλας, Φουρούλης, Χατζημικές, Χριστοφής, Ψωματάρης, Φλάμος, και Φιριππής.

---

58 https://en.wikipedia.org/wiki/Pontus_(region)
59 https://en.wikipedia.org/wiki/Romanization_of_Greek#Modern_Greek
60 The Association of Alatsatianon, "Surnames and origin" – "Alatsata, my lost homeland" by Fani Kleanthi, see the links below:
Σύλλογος Αλατσατιανών, απόσπασμα από το κεφάλαιο
"Επώνυμα και καταγωγή" - «Αλάτσατα, η Χαμένη Πατρίδα μου» του Φάνη Κλεάνθη
http://alatsata.net/index.php?option=com_content&view=article&id=70%3Ae-&catid=20%3A2009-08-18-09-20-23&Itemid=64&lang=el
https://en.wikipedia.org/wiki/Pontus_(region)#/media/File:Asia_Minor_in_the_Greco-Roman_period_-_general_map_-_regions_and_main_settlements.jpg

Greek Naming Conventions and Traditions

For most of the Greeks, tradition keeps the family names indexed or a sequence from generation to generation. The importance of this tradition is that it may have been the creation of the indexing system used by the Greek municipalities in their registries.

Greek first names

The Greek tradition in naming a child's first name is:
- first son is named after the (father's father) grandfather's first name
- first daughter is named after the (father's mother) grandmother's first name
- second son is the first name of the mother's father
- second daughter is the first name of the mother's mother
- Other children are often named after a Godparent, Saints, friends or relatives.

Normally, as the first child will have the name of the grandfather or grandmother of the father, it can be very helpful when creating a chart where you do not have true dates of birth for children when trying to establish the order of births.

The Greek custom of naming children after their grandparents quickly produces many individuals in the same lineage with almost the same name.

You may wonder how there is no confusion of similar family members but when you combine the names along with the middle initial of the father's first name and the year of birth, it develops into a patronymic[61] indexing system even if the names of the individuals are similar. In an analogy with information technology, the index is composed of multiple variables such as surname, first name, father, date of birth (*dd/mm/yyyy*).

This can be visually observed by looking at a genealogy chart and following the names. In some situations, the child may give the next name for a newborn child by an uncle or aunt, or godparent, or a foster parent, or someone who has wealth.

Normally, a son is never named after his father's first name unless the father has died before the child is named. Similarly, a daughter is never given her mother's first name unless the mother dies while giving birth.

What happens if a young child dies before baptism? Whatever name the child was going to receive is forfeited and the name of the next person in the family line is given, such as the first name of an uncle or aunt to the next newborn because superstition plays a role as it is considered a bad omen to give the same name again.

Lastly, on the subject of first names, many of first names in use today by foreigners are based on Greek first names, and many of them have both a male and corresponding female counterpart, example Alexander and Alexandra.

---

[61] An explanation of the Patronymic naming system, https://en.wikipedia.org/wiki/Patronymic

Origins of Greek Surnames

Many Greek surnames are based on patronyms, personal and / or physical descriptions, occupations and / or titles, foreign terms or localities, with patronyms being the most common. Greek surnames were created like surnames from most cultures, and they fall into the following categories:

From the father's name (patronymic)
Greek surname endings may indicate the area where a person possibly originated.
By adding, the equivalent of the English phrase "*son of*" to the end of the first name of the father, created new surnames. The suffix used varies according to the place of origin but this is debatable due to the movement of the Greeks due to numerous wars over the years.
Examples: "oglou" as in Skenderoglou (Asia Minor)
"poulos" as in Avromopoulos (mainly from the Peloponnese)

Personal or physical characteristics for a surname
Many surnames reflect some personal or physical characteristic of the original bearer, e.g. Kontos (short) forming Kontogiannis (short John), Xanthos (blonde / fair-haired) a combination that forms the surname Xanthogiannis (fair-haired John).

Titles seen as prefixes
Hatzi, from the Arabic Hajj (one who visited the holy land) at the beginning of a Greek surname, e.g. Hatzigiannis or Hatzi-Giannis, for someone or an ancestor who made a pilgrimage to the Holy Land and may have been baptized in the river Jordan. Another example is the title 'Mastro' indicates a master craftsman or worker, e.g. Mastrodemetrios as in Master Demetrios.

From foreign words or phrases
Some Greek surnames are derived from other languages such as in, the instance of 'Kara,' which is the Turkish word for the color black as in the surname Karageorgos (black George). The surname is Greek and does not signify foreign ancestry even though a part of it is from Turkey. It may signify the complexion of the individual or a characteristic or the personality.

Greek Cognomen
Many Greek surnames create a foreign surname such as a shortened version of the surname. An example is the surname Charalambopoulos or Haralambopoulos for which the surname Harris might be used.

Names from Work and Professions
I have noted the occupation for many of the relatives on the genealogy chart, and they range from farmer to factory worker to political ministers - (PM's) of local government and parliament. The majority of male Greeks worked as farmers and "fishermen" while women sewed clothing and rugs using a loom in the past, along with other occupation titles that no longer exist.[62]

---

62 https://en.wikipedia.org/wiki/Loom

Diaspora and foreigners to Greek language translations

Greek Naming Conventions to Latin by Various Methods of Translations:
- Greek Phonetic translation of names, e.g. Πέτρος to Petros
- Transcribing Greek names, e.g. Λεωνίδας to Leonidas
- Translating Greek names, e.g. Αντώνιος to Anthony
- Transliteration in accordance with the current standards of the Greek authorities

The correct translation of a foreigner's name to the Greek language from another is the phonetic translation or transliteration. Peter in Greek should be "Πήτερ or Πίτερ," and approved by the individual or parents, as the name translates into Greek with the equivalent being Petros, Pantelis, and Panagiotis.

The origins of most first names in Greek are from various periods in history such as ancient, Medieval, Modern or New Hellenic or Demotic Greek. Katharevousa was used from the 18th century until about 1980. It is considered "pure" Greek and its use is in many of the government documents that you will find even today.[63]

Your English name should be recorded as it sounds on legal documents unless the family wishes to choose a proper Greek name from their own relatives. Depending on the Greek official, they may tell you otherwise but you must insist and demand that it be recorded the way that you want. On a similar note, your signature should be recorded as used in your country of origin. You should not be expected to provide it written in the Greek language. The same holds true for Greeks or other Diaspora moving to other countries.

I have written this because I made the mistake of not knowing how the government functions, and not arguing with the Greek government employees who have very little understanding of logic and objectivity during the processing of my own paperwork.

I will mention that most families of Greek Diaspora living abroad do not know that they are responsible to declare births, marriages, children, divorces, and deaths at the Special Registry of Athens especially if they own property in Greece otherwise their relatives will face tremendous problems regarding inheritance and property transfers, as well as Greek citizenship for children. The Greek government expects you to know this even though they purposively procrastinate providing written information for the Diaspora.

If you should find yourself in need of a more persuasive excuse, demand to speak with a supervisor. If they have any intelligence then they will understand.

I am very proud to say that I have never paid any government employee a bribe or kickback known as "Baksheesh" to complete any paperwork in Greece.

---

63 https://en.wiktionary.org/wiki/Wiktionary:Greek_transliteration/Old

Foreign first names for births, baptisms, and the Greek Orthodox Church

For those who might be considering moving to Greece.
If you have a child and wish to use a foreign first name that is not associated with a Greek Orthodox Saint, then you may register the child in Greece. However, if you intend on baptizing the child in the Greek Orthodox Church you should be aware that you may have to choose a first name based upon a Greek Orthodox Saint.

First Names of Greeks Abroad

You may have some Greek friends and not even know it. The reason is that many Greeks who moved abroad may or may not have been accepted into their new societies.
There were both good and bad reasons including racial conflicts that made the Greeks change their Greek first and/or last names to help them blend into their new countries.

An example of this, the first name Adiamantis is also known as Diamond.
Others such as Hlias or Elias may change their name to Louis.

Others continue to use names that may be considered unusual by foreigners such as Pericles (Periklis) or Socrates based on the familiarity or popularity of the name, or based on royalty.

Another reason why it can be very laborious to trace foreign names back to Greek.
If you are researching your genealogy, it is better to work in the Greek language while researching for those of Greek origin.

Nicknames or Paratsoukli (παρατσούκλι)

In some cases surnames from nicknames refer to some event in the life of the individual that may be complicated to determine, e.g. Mavros (black) as in Mavrogiannis (black John).
Did his surname infer that he wore black clothing, or refer to his black beard, or dark complexion? Unknown.

Nicknames exist in English and in Greek, and sometimes they will be associated to a particular family member either male or female rather than a general population.

Examples:
Takis is also Panagiotis. Tasos *can be* Anastasios. Billy (Μπιλή) *can be* Vasilis.
Kiki or Koula *can be* Angeliki, Vasiliki, or Kyriaki. Rena *can be* Irene (Ειρήνη).
Effie *can be* Efstathia, Despina *can be* Debby, Dionysia *can be* Denise.
A common nickname for Konstantinos is Gus or Kostas, and for Konstantina as Dina.

Researcher note:
I use the phrase "can be" because many names are used to express from Greek to English and other names in any language.

How to interpret middle initials of Greek names

The middle initial is normally the father's first name under Greek Patronymic naming system, e.g. Ioannis P. Bournias, the "**son of**" Pantelis or Maritsa P. Bournia, the "**daughter of**" Pantelis.

Others may abbreviate the middle name, such as "Στ" may refer to Stephanos, or "Αδ" may refer to Adiamantis.

The middle initial is not applied for the mother.[64]

After marriage, women "inherit" the middle initial of their husband's first name.

Other ways of receiving a different middle name than that of the father is through baptism. In some cases, a child may receive the first name of a godparent or a person who baptizes or adopts the child as an honor or respect to them. This can be justified by the godparent or the adoptive parent provides for the well-being of the child.

In other cases, an adopted child may have living parents who could not provide care for the child due to economic uncertainties. In this case, the child would most likely been given to an uncle.

Greek Name Days and Birthdays

The majority of the Greeks celebrate name days.[65]

Name days are associated with a saint chosen at the time of baptism, which is when the first name of the child is declared.

Almost every Greek first name is associated with a calendar day corresponding to the saint assigned by the Greek Orthodox Church. Some Greeks celebrate Birthdays as well. The observance of the name day is based on the day, not the date.

What is the difference between a Greek Name day and a Birthday?

In western countries, many people celebrate a person's birthday with a party that usually consists of relatives and friends. The assumed normal situation is that the relatives and friends bring a gift to that person. In contrast, when a Greek celebrates a name day it is associated with a calendar date for the name of a Greek Orthodox Saint, and you can send felicitations to anyone who has the same first name whether you know them or not.

Furthermore, the person with the name day may offer food and drinks to their closest relatives, friends, or even those who may appear by chance at their door. Relatives and close friends usually bring a gift to the person with the name day, as giving a gift is recommended although not mandatory. Therefore, if you have a friend that has Greek heritage and want to surprise them, wish them a happy name day by saying "Chronia Polla".

---

64 https://en.wikipedia.org/wiki/Patronymic#Greek_and_Greek_Cypriot
65 Name Days in Greece, https://en.wikipedia.org/wiki/Name_days_in_Greece

Myths regarding the meaning of the surname Bournias

On more than one occasion, I have heard a variety of explanations trying to decipher the surname Bournias. Many last names have different meanings and origins, and they may apply across the borders of countries. Surnames like "Smith" are easily associated with work like, an ironworker or blacksmith, or "Carpenter" for someone who worked with wood.

A Bournias used as a bullhorn by sailors

Another such story is one where sailors on fishing boats heading into fog would use a type of megaphone or bullhorn to yell out into the fog and avoid collisions with other boats.

A vase called a bourinia in Greek
Image credit: Internet / website author unknown

Some believe that the surname has something to do with clay pottery such as a vase or jar as shown below.

Billie Bournias, another distant cousin by marriage from Texas sent me a copy of a letter that noted a story from the island of Andros, describing **clay pots known as "*bourinies,*"** but this has no connection to the meaning of the surname Bournias.

While researching the above word in Greek, it appears to be spelled incorrectly most likely due to it being from a Greek dialect.

I learned that there was a pharmaceutical jar (δοχείο φιάλες) used by pharmacies that were also similar to the word Bournias and this information also appears in the 14th to 16th century according to **Prof. Stephanos Kaklamanis**[66] who is a professor of Greek Philology.

A not so close variation is that of the Greek word (μπουνιά) pronounced "*bounia,*" which means punch. Another Greek word for a sudden gale, flurry, windstorm, or hurricane is bourini (μπουρίνι), which again has nothing to do with the name.
This can be found in the excellent dictionary that **Professor Georgios Babiniotis of the University of Athens** has defined in his dictionary of the Greek language.[67]

---

66 https://www.philology.uoc.gr/en/staff/stefanos-kaklamanis
67 https://en.wikipedia.org/wiki/Georgios_Babiniotis

Does the surname Bournias have a meaning?

I can't say because the surname may originate from another country and therefore it may have a completely different meaning, if it does.[68]

Does it matter though? Then again, must a surname really have a meaning?

No, surnames do not always have a meaning as they can originate in a variety of ways, some of which I have written in the following pages.

A surname can be created for almost any reason whether that is from a trade, a skill, a characteristic of a person, where a person lived, etc., or a new identity.

Greek surnames started in the Archaic Period of Greece to identify individuals based on their father's first name. This probably happened when multiple families began to name their children and to create a differentiation using the expression "son of".[69]

There are many books in Greece explain the creation of surnames, this is the most common.

«Τα Μυστικά των Ονομάτων: Τα Οικογενειακά Μας Ονόματα» (Τριανταφυλλίδης 2013), "*The Mystery of the Surnames*" by Manolis Triantafyllidis explains the roots of many Greek family surnames.

---

68 Surnames – Origins, https://en.wikipedia.org/wiki/Surname#Origins
69 https://en.wikipedia.org/wiki/Archaic_Greece

WORK AND PROFESSIONS
A LIST OF OLD & NEW PROFESSIONS IN GREECE

Occupations are an abundant source for surnames, e.g. Raftis (tailor), Papoutsis (shoemaker). Surnames beginning with Papa (priest) are numerous in Greece, like Papadopoulos (son of a priest), which is very common in the Peloponnese.

A partial list of professions that prosper while others became redundant in Greece.
I added words in English as an example of their pronunciation and/or explanation.

Some of these jobs may sound unusual but remember that in the near future there will be job titles of today that will be lost as the technology progresses.
Blank explanations that are evident. This is a partial list with my translations.

English	English pronunciation	Greek	Explanation of those that may no longer exist
Barber	koureas	κουρέας	
Barrel maker	varelopois	βαρελοποιός	someone who makes or repairs barrels or casks
Blacksmith	sideras	σιδεράς	
Bootblack	loustros	λούστρος	shoe shiner or in this case a boot shiner
Builder	oikodomos	οικοδόμος	construction worker
Butcher	kreopolis	κρεοπώλης	
carpenter	maragos xylourgos	μαραγκός ή ξυλουργός	
chandler	kyropoios	κηροποιός	person who makes candles, e.g. for lighting
carrier	vastazos	βαστάζος	person who carries stuff on his back for others
farmer	agrotis	αγρότης	
fisherman	psaras	ψαράς	
farrier	petalotis	πεταλωτής	person who makes and shoes horses
hunter	kinigos	κυνηγός	
merchant	pantopolis	παντοπώλης	similar to a grocery store that has a variety of goods
metal ware	kalaitzis	καλαϊτζής ή γανωτής	metal worker, adds improves objects, e.g. cookware
weaver	kalathas	καλαθάς	basket weaver
seamstress	kentistra	κεντήστρα	person who creates needlepoint
locksmith		κλειδαράς	
Fish net maker	koskinas	κοσκινάς	person who makes nets

jeweler	kosmimatopoios	κοσμηματοπώλης	person who makes jewelry
Olive oil producer	loutrouviaris elaiotrivis	λουτρουβιάρης ελαιοτρίβης	person who presses (squeezes) oil from olives
mastic farmer	mastichoparagogos	μαστιχοπαραγωγός	harvest Mastic trees, raw material chewing gum
bee keeper	melissourgos	μελισσουργός	
midwife or doula	mamy or mayia	μαμή ή μαία	woman who assists at child birth, a doula
miller	mylonas	μυλωνάς	person who grinds or mills, e.g. wheat
blanket or quilt maker	paplomatas	παπλωματάς	
shoemaker	papoutsis	τσαγκάρης ή παπουτσής	
producer of souma	Paragogos soumas	παραγωγός σούμας	person who makes Raki, an alcoholic drink from figs
confectioner	pastelas	παστελάς - ξηροί καρποί	person who makes and sells sweets and nuts
photographer	fotografos	φωτογράφος	
potter	angeioplastis	αγγειοπλάστης	person who makes ceramic pottery and decorations
puppeteer	karagkiozopaichtis	καραγκιοζοπαίχτης	
saddler	samaras	σαμαράς	person who makes saddles
sailor	naftis	ναύτης	
tailor	raftis	ράφτης	
Tanner	Virsodepsis	βυρσοδέψης	person who makes animal hides into leather
tinker	ganomatis	γανωματής	person who makes things by request
tobacco producers	kapnoparagogos	καπνοπαραγωγός	
weaver	yfantra	υφάντρα	person who makes clothes or rugs
wine producer	Paragogos krasiou	παραγωγός κρασιού	
woodcutter	xylokopos	ξυλοκόπος	

SOURCES OF NAMES AND VITAL RECORDS

Genealogy research uses vital records as documentation to prove what has been discovered.[70] Alternative methods such as verbal confirmations, as well as sources from abroad including government or legal documentation, and documentation from relatives can be acceptable proof.

Genealogical proof is a problem in Greece as many records have been destroyed during many of the conflicts and other natural disasters over the years. As such, there are problems with attaining them assuming that they are available in different areas of Greece and for different time-periods; therefore, there is no simple answer as to whether or not you may find them.[71]

Greek vital records are not centralized or available via the Internet, except if you are a direct lineage family member, father or mother or son or daughter.
A direct lineage family member must know where the individual was from, the municipality, to make the request from the local municipality.

Most records of birth are in the locality of where the individual was born.
If you do not know that, then you will have a dubious time trying to find family records, and may not find them because of changes of jurisdiction of areas by the Greek government. Similarly, records of death can be unattainable for various reasons besides bureaucracy. Generally, obituaries are not published.

Many vital records from 1925 generally include records of birth, marriage, and death and are available from the municipality and sometimes from the Greek Orthodox Church or the national archives. Marriages performed by the Church from 1925 were supposed to be recorded by the municipality. Records from the municipalities prior to 1925 may or may not be digitized. Digitization of vital records using computers began around 1960 beginning with the 1925 records.

The Greek Orthodox Church, gravesites (assuming the grave exists), municipal electoral lists, and the Greek Military are other sources and noted elsewhere in this document.

Records from abroad such as, Ellis Island are known to be incomplete; have various errors, and misspellings. If possible, municipal and even church records from abroad are preferred as a starting point for genealogical research.

Another factor or variable regarding genealogy research in Greece regards the Julian and Gregorian calendar. Greece was the last Eastern Orthodox country in Europe to adopt the Gregorian calendar for civil purposes. Under military administration following the 11 September 1922 Revolution, effective on 1 March 1923. The Greek calendar, Wednesday 15 February 1923 was followed by Thursday 1 March 1923.[72]

---

70 https://en.wikipedia.org/wiki/Vital_record
71 https://en.wikipedia.org/wiki/Genealogical_Proof_Standard
72 https://en.wikipedia.org/wiki/Adoption_of_the_Gregorian_calendar#Adoption_in_Eastern_Europe

Historical records may be available from the General Archives of Chios in the Korais Library, founded by Adamantios Korais[73], and at the central office of the General Archives of Athens.[74]

Records from the archives include but may be limited by year and location:
- Newspapers
- School Records
- Electoral Catalogs or Voter lists
- Land Registries, legal documents
- Migration Records (e.g. from Asia Minor), and other sources
- Most records are in the Greek language.

Municiple and church records are uncommon but some may exist at the GAK.

Area or location refer to local area of a particular location, e.g. records for those from Harokopio, Messinia may be found either at the General Archives in Messinia or at the municipality in Koroni, Messinia.

A photograph of the **First Gymnasio (Secondary) School built in 1792** on the left and the **Korais Library** (down the street on the right) where the **General Archives of Chios** is located in the center of Chios.[75]

Image Reference: P. Bournias, Sept. 2018

---

73 https://en.wikipedia.org/wiki/Adamantios_Korais
74 http://www.koraeslibrary.gr
75 Also known as the First School of Higher Education

RELIGION

The majority of Greeks belong to the Greek Orthodox religion.

Exceptions to this are the result of mixed marriages with spouses of other religions. In Greece, there are other religions but the Greek Orthodox Church is the official state church. Most European countries have an official church and religion.

The first name of the child was officially recognized upon baptism.
Births were recorded when the child was baptized and may combine the date of birth. Marriages were recorded by the church prior to 1925; afterwards by both the church and the local municipalities. Marriages were usually performed at the church in the nearest village or city where the bride resided.

The Greek Orthodox Church Records and Archives
The Greek Orthodox Churches began to create registries of baptism and marriage roughly around 1825 and continue today. I have photographed some pages pertaining to individuals with the surname Bournias from 1866 and the 1900's.

There were many reasons for this; some were to prevent polygamy, to prevent marriages between close relatives, and the creation of organized family records.

Information recorded by the "*Mitropoli*" is a copy of the information from other local churches. The church too was affected by the depredations of wars and due to the destruction or loss of local church records. It began centralizing the local church records at the "*Mitropoli*" for each area. The organization of the "**Μητρόπολη**" (Diocese) serves as a central church with jurisdiction of the local area churches.

Most Chiots belong to local parishes and I have noted the names of the parishes for various families based on the information from electoral lists on my charts.
The dates that they recorded births or baptisms may have been delayed for very long periods as the local churches had to supply their information to be recorded into separate books held by the "*Mitropoli*". In one case, I found the delay was four (4) years.

The Greek Orthodox Church generally continues to retain their own archive for records of baptism and Marriage but some records from other locations may be found at the General Archives. You must be able to identify the closest location to obtain this from either the "*Mitropoli*" or the local church of the area where the family lived.

Researcher note:
If you are wondering why I write "***Mitropoli***" in quotation marks, it is because many individuals loosely transliterate the Greek word "**Μητρόπολη**," which is a Greek Orthodox Cathedral to the word Metropolis that translates to a large city in English.

THE CATHOLIC CHURCH IN GREECE

The Catholic Church has operated on Chios since 1592 with Jesuit priests.

A Catholic Church exists today on Chios and the Diocese of Chios is responsible for many of the nearby islands.[76]

In Greece, the Catholic Church along with other religions such as the Anglican, Methodists, Baptists, Hellenistic Judaism, and others do exist although the majority are not visible by the average visitor.[77] They are what the Greeks refer to as Latin religions.

The island of Syros is about fifty percent Greek Orthodox and fifty percent Catholic, and both churches are visible when traveling to the island as they are at the peaks of the hills as you enter the port area.

Syros is a central location for government municipal offices for many of the Aegean islands. It became a refuge by the people of Chios to escape to during the revolutionary war of 1821 and an area on one of the hillsides are where the Chiots lived.

Ermoupoli and upper Syros
The Catholic Church in the photograph on the top right with the blue dome.

Image credit: Internet / website https://en.wikipedia.org/wiki/Syros

---

76 https://en.wikipedia.org/wiki/Syros#Religion
77 https://en.wikipedia.org/wiki/Hellenistic_religion#Hellenistic_Judaism

THE GREEK MILITARY

In Greece, all male citizens are registered at birth for the purpose of conscription and required to enter into military service, thus creating the registry of boys (males).

Women have served in the past and may now officially join the military but are not drafted.

For Diaspora considering moving to Greece and younger than the age of 50, ask your local Greek embassy or consulate about the requirement of you or your male children being required to serve in the Greek military, it may be mandatory.

In the past, Greek officers could only marry if their wife to be had a dowry.

Researching individuals using the Greek military has proven to be the most difficult to attain records of ancestors. They have stringent requirements due to security of their information and will only provide records for a direct family ancestor assuming that the record is available. You can make a request whether or not you know if your ancestor was an officer.

I sent a written request to them and asked as of what years are records available.
Written requests are always necessary as proof that you made a request.
Never rely on verbal requests with any government employee or official.

The Greek military finally answered my request writing that they do not have records prior to 1880 and that they have begun to put some records of the deceased online.

I made a written request for my grandfather's military record and received it. Unfortunately, I cannot publish it because they required that I sign a non-disclosure specifically stating that I would not.

While I understand that *"loose lips sink ships,"* I would think that many changes have taken place in the Greek Theatre of War but I guess not.[78]

I have retrieved and extracted a list of the **BOURNIAS FALLEN IN ACTION** from the Greek Army, which they made available through an online database, with the English translation of the records toward the end of this document.

The wars in the following pages display the courage and endurance of the Greeks, the justification of the number of bankruptcies, and the personal losses of wealth and family, and their unwanted transformation into immigrants from Asia Minor and on the mainland to other countries.

---

78 https://en.wikipedia.org/wiki/Loose_lips_sink_ships

WARS IN GREECE AND CHIOS

There were many wars that involved Greece both directly and indirectly and many conquerors through the 19th and 20th centuries. Besides the Ottomans (Turkish) rulers, Chios was under the rule of the Venetians, and the Genovese.

There was a tremendous interest in the island of Chios by the Venetians. Even today, the surviving surnames of Venetian families exist and claim their origin as Chiots.

Britain and France both had consulates on Chios. According to a book, *"Covel - Early Voyages and Travels in the Levant from the Diary of Master Thomas Dallam, 1599 – 1600"* with extracts from the *"Diaries of Dr. John Covel, 1670 – 1679,"* Britain had a consulate established on Chios around 1513.[79]

When we look at a map of Greece, we must bear in mind that prior to the modernization of military transportation, many invaders marched through northern Greece or sailed to islands and ports of the mainland killing and decimating entire areas. This and the economy of Greece that forced Greeks to migrate to other areas of Greece or abroad either temporarily or permanently.

The Greek Wars since the revolution in Greece[80]

WARS	BEGAN	ENDED
The Greek Revolution	1821	1829 [1]
Cretan Revolution	1866	1869
Greek-Turkish War [2]	1897	1897
The Macedonian Conflict [3]	1904	1908
First Balkan War	September 1912	May 1913
Second Balkan War	June 1913	July 1913
World War I	June 1914	November 1918
Asia Minor	May 1918	October 1922
World War II	September 1939	September 1945
Greek Civil War [4]	March 1946	August 1949

Researcher note:
1. The Independence of Chios along with other islands occurred in 1912 not 1821.
2. The Cretan Revolution involved Greece and United Kingdom, France, Italy, Austria-Hungary, Germany and Russia against the Ottomans.
3. The Macedonian Conflict is likewise known as the Macedonian Struggle.
4. It should be noted that the Greek Civil War continues to be a very sensitive issue today and should not be discussed.

---

[79] https://www.gutenberg.org/ebooks/61660
[80] https://en.wikipedia.org/wiki/List_of_wars_involving_Greece

THE EVZONS

As many show an interest in the military uniforms of the Greeks. I decided to begin this with the Evzons as they are highly respected miltiary combatants.[81] Prior to the Balkan war of 1912 many soldiers used either clothing of the Evzon or modified versions as uniforms.

The Evzon known colloquially as Tsolias are considered to be an elite regiment that began in 1867 and were typically in the service of the king, the military, and the government. Today, they are commonly seen at the Tomb of the Unknown Soldier and at the Presidential Mansion in Athens.

The Evzones (plural) wear a fustanella, a white pleated skirt like kilt that was commonly worn by Greek men since the 12th century until about the early 1900's.[82] It is a heavy piece of cloth with around four hundred (400) pleats. During the winter months, thermal underwear is worn under the fustanella to provide warmth. Their shoes known as tsarouchia are made of multiple pieces of leather. They carry loaded rifles with ammunition.

The prospective Evzon is chosen based on the following physical characteristics criteria: 1.88 to 2.05 meters in height, excellent physical and mental condition, good character and moral, trustworthy and loyal to the mission of the King's Guard.

Image credit: Internet / website levantineheritage.com, Greek occupation of Asia Minor 1919

---

81 Wikipedia, https://en.wikipedia.org/wiki/Evzones
82 Wikipedia, https://en.wikipedia.org/wiki/Fustanella

BALKAN WARS 1912 - 1913

Greece fought in two Balkan wars. In the first Greece fought against the Ottomans.
In the second Greece fought against Bulgaria.

With the Balkan wars, Greece did not have the economic resources to maintain many uniforms for museums from the wars and photographs of the soldiers are generally not available except for those that photographed themselves for their families.

The following uniforms were typical for the soldiers from Chios who fought in the multiple wars that took place during various years between Greece and the northern areas known as Albania, Northern Macedonia (changed from FYROM previously Yugoslavia), and Bulgaria.
They carried swords as well as pistols, and rifles. Their means of travel were by foot across hundreds of kilometers and some regiments used horses.

A group of soldiers from Chios, no family relation that I know of.
They are seated on whatever is available as this was a primitive studio photograph.
No known family relations in this photograph.

Image credit: Bottom right translation, as posted on FB from the archive of K. D. Chalkias

WORLD WAR I - 1914 to 1919
Soldiers of the Greek Army preparing for the First World War.

There are many outposts throughout Greece and visitors may see them but it is considered illegal to photograph them without the permission of the camp commander.

Bottom legend translation:
Presentation of the flag at the Fourth Regiment of Serres (northern Greece).
No known family relations in this photograph.

Image credit: The Greek Army Historical Archive, https://dis.army.gr/

The Greco-Turkish War of 1919 to 1922

The **Asia Minor Campaign** known as the Greco-Turkish War to the western world.[83] Greece under Venizelos began the war because the British Prime Minister David Lloyd George promised Greece territorial gains at the expense of the Ottoman Empire.[84] The justification by Greece was that the Ottoman Empire was **Anatolia**[85] and it was a part of Ancient Greece and the Byzantine Empire before the Ottomans conquered the area in the 12th to 15th centuries. The fall of the Byzantine Empire[86] occurred with the Fall of Constantinople in 1453.[87]

The war started when Greece proceeded with the expansion from Smyrna.
The Greek military failed by its generals in August 1922, effectively ended the war with the recapture of Smyrna by Turkish forces and the destruction by the great fire of Smyrna. Another noted battle is that of Bergama.[88]

Greek soldiers near the Ermou River during the Asia Minor Campaign 1919 - 1922
No known family relations in this photograph.

Image credit: Wikipedia

---

83 https://en.wikipedia.org/wiki/Greco-Turkish_War_(1919%E2%80%931922)
84 Wikipedia, Η Μικρασιατική Εκστρατεία - The Asia Minor Campaign
https://el.wikipedia.org/wiki/%CE%9C%CE%B9%CE%BA%CF%81%CE%B1%CF%83%CE%B9%CE%B1%CF%84%CE%B9%CE%BA%CE%AE_%CE%B5%CE%BA%CF%83%CF%84%CF%81%CE%B1%CF%84%CE%B5%CE%AF%CE%B1#cite_note-30
85 https://en.wikipedia.org/wiki/Anatolia
86 https://en.wikipedia.org/wiki/Byzantine_Empire
87 https://en.wikipedia.org/wiki/Fall_of_Constantinople
88 https://en.wikipedia.org/wiki/Battle_of_Bergama

WORLD WAR II - 1939 to 1945

Greek territories to protect encompass the main land, 31 islands, and numerous islets.

The Greek Army

The war theater for Greece during the second world warl took place in northern Greece and on both the eastern and western sides, and southern areas of the country at sea. Despite the size of the military, Greece was a curse to Hitler's plans forcing him to order more Italian and German resources to stop the Greeks. The battle in Crete is hailed as the most successful.

The Greek Navy

The pre-Dreadnought battleship Kilkis (previously the USS Mississippi) was sold together with her sister ship the Lemnos (previously the USS Idaho) by the US government in 1914 to Greece. Both were sunk by German JU87 dive-bombers in the port of Piraeus on 23 April 1941.

The executive commander of the Navy was the Chief of the Admiralty, Admiral A. Sakellariou. Under his command were 6,300 regular naval officers, men, 11,000 reservists, and the following vessels:
- 2 old battleships (armored cruisers) built in 1905 and 1906
- 2 old light cruisers, 4 old destroyers, 4 Hydra Class (Italian) destroyers,
- 13 old torpedo boats, 2 motor torpedo boats (MTBs), and 6 submarines.[89]

As the Greek mainland is essentially surrounded by the sea and having numerous islands, it is famous for having many sea captains; therefore, the Navy was and is the strongest military force in Greece covering the majority of its borders.

The Greek Air Force

The Air Force was a small air service unit of the Army before 1950 and had only 250 officers and 3,000 men. The Minister of the Military was responsible for the air services maintained by the Greek Army and Navy.

Many of the Greek pilots underwent training in England, and although outnumbered first by the Italians and then by the Germans, the air service put up a stubborn resistance in the campaigns of 1940-41. The Polish made PLZ P24-F fighter of the Greek Air Force was a formidable opponent to the Italians and the German in 1940 to 1941.[90]

Today, the Greek government has instilled the importance of the Greek military and has proposed the importance of military protection as a country of the EU to the European Defence Union[91] and NATO.[92]

---

[89] Wikipedia, https://en.wikipedia.org/wiki/List_of_battleships_of_Greece
[90] Wikipedia, https://en.wikipedia.org/wiki/PZL_P.24
[91] https://en.wikipedia.org/wiki/Common_Security_and_Defence_Policy
[92] https://en.wikipedia.org/wiki/NATO

GREECE SURVIVED FORTY-EIGHT (48) YEARS OF WAR!

If you have not realized the power of the Greeks and their military, then look at the period from 1897 to 1945. The continuous years of war devastated the country with an incomprehensible loss of lives, not to mention the loss of property. That is a tremendous number of waring years and is one of the main reasons that Greece has been economically destroyed. War destroyed Greece economically as the first two loans were received in 1824 and 1825 for the War of Independence.

The first bankruptcy occurred in 1827. Europe used this as foreign influence politically to appoint the first king of Greece, Otto as a justification to recgnize the independence of Greece in 1832. Another loan was issued and another bankruptcy occurred in 1843. More loans was issued and insolvency occurred again in 1893. The economics of Greece has been affected by many factors, war is the first, and corrupt politicians are the second major reason. Other reasons for Greece's loans include the modernization of infrastructure.[93]

Greece is now attempting to share its burden of protecting its borders as a European Union member. This of course means the creation and participation of a European military.

Our great grandfathers, grandfathers, and fathers have been fighting even before 1821. Many of them survived!
This is why you and I are here, but sadly, other Bournias family members are not.

Image credit:
The above image was found on Facebook (creator unknown) and it displays the tenacity and determination of the Greeks to fight for their country resisting the occupation of the Italian and German military for two hundred and nineteen (219) days.

---

[93] Greece Has a Long History of Debt and Bankruptcy, Antonis Diniakos and Giannis Androulidakis, https://www.vice.com/

OBSTRUCTIONS IN GREEK GENEALOGY
Nature and the Destruction of Greek Vital Records

During the research of the Greek ancestry, I learned that nature and war also inhibit the search for vital records because of their destruction. War, earthquakes, and fire destroyed numerous records depending upon the damages inflicted upon the buildings that housed the records.

The following information is to help you understand the events that had a devastating impact upon the lives of those who you may be searching for and explains the lack of vital records.

The catastrophic earthquakes of 1881, 1886, and 1949 affected the areas of Chios and Messinia and especially that of Komboi where many of the Bournias family from Asia Minor lived.[94, 95]

"On the island of Chios, 3550 people were killed and 7000 injured during the earthquake on 3rd of April 1881. In 1883, old buildings collapsed in Chios during the October 15 earthquake with the epicenter in Turkey between Urla and Cesme (120 people were killed - 3600 houses collapsed in the central area). Strong aftershocks followed on October 22 and November 1 (Milne 1912; Karnik 1971). The settlement of Komboi in the area of Koroni suffered extensive damage during the great catastrophic earthquake of 7.5 on the Richter scale, on August 27, 1886, focusing on Filiatra, which struck Messinia and Ilia. The earthquake almost completely destroyed the cities of Filatra, Gargaliana, Hora (then known as Ligoudista), Methoni, Koroni, and another 123 villages of mainly western Messinia. Pyrgos, Marathopoli, Pylos, Kalamata, the islands of Strofades, and 37 villages were damaged, which suffered significant damage, while 65 more villages in the Peloponnese were also affected. In all, about 6,000 homes collapsed or were destroyed or left uninhabited, and there were 326 dead and 796 injured. The aftershocks that followed, most notably that of September 6, 1886, completed the destruction. Hundreds of aftershocks occurred, many of them as devastating as the main earthquake, until 1894."

The following Time-periods of earthquakes and tsunamis that affected Greece, Turkey, and other areas that were above the magnitude of 6.5 and can destroy areas and older buildings:

DATE	LOCATION
February 1810	Crete, Heraklion
October 1840	Halki, west of Rhodes
October 1856	Rhodes, Crete
February 1867	Cephalonia a.k.a. Kefalonia
March 1867	Lesbos a.k.a. Mytilini
April 1881	Chios, Greece and Cesme, Alacatı Turkey[96]
August 1886	Filiatra, south west Messinia[97]
April 1894	Atalanti, Phthiotis, Greece
July 1949	Chios Cesme Strait[98]

---

94 Chios 1881, https://www.oasp.gr/node/585
95 Chios 1883, https://www.oasp.gr/node/586
96 Major destruction of buildings, homes, and the loss of records on Chios.
97 Filiatra 1886, https://www.oasp.gr/node/666
98 Chios-Cesme Strait, https://hal.archives-ouvertes.fr/hal-00299270/document

POLITICS
Greeks love politics, they live for it.

In general, the conservative party correlates to New Democracy, while the socialist party is known as PASOK. A few belong to the liberal wing party, known as the communist party or KKE, along with the party known today as Syriza, a coalition of the radical left that is a mixture of various political parties.

Some political parties have changed their names to avoid being associated with past transgressions of mismanagement and corruption while others complacently deny any illicit, illegal wrongdoings, and responsibility.

Other parties such as the "Independant (USA) / Independent (UK) party," a term that has nothing to do with liberal as distorted by some countries such as England and the USA as left wing.[99] This word was based on the Greek word for politics: autonomous (ανεξάρτητος).[100]

Astonishingly, a small percentage of the people consider themselves devoted to the idea that a king should reign in Greece.

Various areas of Greece identify to particular political parties. This can be seen in the election results from the statistics produced. The Greek political parties have nothing in common as being similar to that of other western nations.

If you think that the voting system of Greece is unusual, you may not realize that the development process over centuries has made it into one of the most valid.

After all, the ancient Greeks developed the first democratic system of voting that used black and white pebbles.[101] This contributed the advancement of the modern day voting system.

The Greek voting system is not corrupt. Corruption in voting starts with politicians affecting the votes of citizens.

---

[99] https://en.wikipedia.org/wiki/Independent_voter

[100] An English Greek online dictionary, https://www.wordreference.com/engr/Independent

[101] http://blogs.getty.edu/iris/voting-with-the-ancient-greeks/

Some clippings from various sources regarding the Bournias surname participation in parliamentary and local elections for Chios.

"Forty-eight of our fellow citizens were the ones who had the honor of becoming the chosen ones of Chios, gaining the anointing of MP, with previous in the relevant list is Leonidas Bournia, who was elected 9 times. Andreas Polemidis and Nikos Zorbas follow with 7 electoral victories and then Elias Aspiotis, Alex. Pachnos, Georgios Misailidis and Antonis Kotsakas who were elected 5 times."

Leonidas Bournias, (Λεων. Μπουρνιάς), page 2.[102]

"In Chios, two combinations were made. Both declared to be Venizelists.
In the first to receive the anointing of the Independent Party
Christoforos Rodokanakis, Augustis Kouvelas, Leonis Kalvokoresis, Alex participated. Choremis and Mich. Tselepidis.
Andreas participated in the second Venizelist combination, which formed the basis of the later anti-Venizelist faction.
Polemidis, Elias Aspiotis, Stef. Rallis, **Georg. Bournias** and Ioannis Casanovas. Candidates were independents, the Venezuelan Theod. Petrokokkinos and Adam. Bahas, the only one who declared himself anti-Venezelist."

"The Electoral Court annulled the election of Vict. Koukouridis. In the by-elections held on April 25, 1921, the elected member of the Anti-Venezuelan government ANAST was elected. ANDREADIS with 3377 votes out of 4729 votes cast. **Georg. Bournias *received 2573*, while Andr. Polemidis 2491.**"[103]

Georg. Bournias, page 3, 4, 5, 7.[104]

"In those first national elections (31/3/1915) the political climate was revealed in Chios as it had been formed at that time in the rest of Greece. Territory. In the electoral battle, two combinations of Venizelists were presented ("independent " and "People's Venizelos Combination"), a combination of Anti-Venizelists and an anti-Venizelos candidate (D. Bahas)."

"There were a total of 12 candidates, all active members of the Chian Society. Most of them were already involved in the public life of the island and some of them continued to contribute to the public and dominated for several years in the local political life, leaving behind a "good and good" name!"

"The names of those first candidates were: Christoforos Rodokanakis, Al. Choremis, Leon. Kalvokoresls, Ellas Asplotls, Mich. Tselepidis, Th. Petrokokkinos, Aug. Kouvelas, Andreas Polemidis, Stef. Rallis, **G. Bournias**, D. Bachas, I. Casanovas."[105]
"The result of the ballot showed the first five deputies of Chios, according to the then valid voting system, the "majority ballots," which were the first 5 mentioned above..."

---

[102] ΠΑΡΑΔΕΙΣΗΣ, ΣΩΤΗΡΗΣ. "1915 - 2015 Ένας αιώνας βουλευτικές εκλογές στη Χίο," ekloges_sti_chio_1915-2015. self published, 2019
[103] Georg. Bournias is Γεωργ. Μπουρνιάς shortened for Georgios Bournias.
[104] ΠΑΡΑΔΕΙΣΗΣ, ΣΩΤΗΡΗΣ. "1915 - 2015 Ένας αιώνας βουλευτικές εκλογές στη Χίο," ekloges_sti_chio_1915-2015. self published, 2019
[105] Καββάδας, Κώστας Στεφ.. "Ξεφυλλίζοντας τα πεπραγμένα περασμένων Βουλευτικών εκλογών στην Χίο 1915-1964." alithia.gr, Λονδίνο, Αύγουστος 2019, https://www.alithia.gr/politiki/xefyllizontas-ta-pepragmena-perasmenon-voyleytikon-eklogon-stin-hio-1915-1964

FOREIGN INFLUENCE AND POLITICS

Foreign politicians have provided both positive and negative influence in the progress of Greece over its history.

The majority of times, foreign politicians have endeavored in enriching their own countries at the expense of the lives of Greeks. The British are the most notorious for giving the advantage towards Ottomans during its occupation of Greece.

Even today, Britain while no longer a member of the European Union after the Brexit[106] is allied with Turkey primarily for commercial reasons. A reason for this may be that the previous Prime Minister Boris Johnson's paternal grandfather Wilfred Johnson was of Turkish decent.[107]

The largest political influence was brought upon the Greeks by its own politicians who abused their powers by using jobs for votes and graft. By doing so, they brought economic instability to Greece requiring foreign loans and the consequence of foreign control of the country by the International Monetary Fund[108] and the European Union.[109]

---

106 https://en.wikipedia.org/wiki/Brexit
107 Wikipedia, Family and ancestors , https://en.wikipedia.org/wiki/Boris_Johnson
108 https://en.wikipedia.org/wiki/International_Monetary_Fund
109 https://en.wikipedia.org/wiki/European_Union

PIRATES
The island of Chios is said to have a pirate base.

According to information that I have seen, the area where Antonios A. Bournias lived may have been a pirate stronghold, a small village built with a wall surrounding it like a castle for defense. It may be that the Bournias family may have established themselves originally in Parparia and Pirama as pirates, and this may be how the name Bournias is linked to the name Bournihas from France.

On another website that I found on the Internet, it mentions the existence of pirates that attacked the village of Kourounia located on the higher slopes, North West of Spartounta. During those times, Chios had watchtowers to warn the locals of imminent danger from the sea and fires. The watchtowers are shown on many maps of Chios.

Researcher note:

See the bibliography for these references:

Mixalakis, Giannis Kourounia. History, Athens, 2013.

Extracts from the diaries of John Covel (1870-1879.
In the above text, the following are mentioned:
Early Voyages and Travels in the Levant
The Diary of Master Thomas Dallam, 1599-1600.
Extracts from the Diaries of Dr. John Covel, 1670-1679.
With Some Account of the Levant Company of Turkey Merchants.

According to some of the following books, the Ottoman Empire used pirates, including those in Greece, to attack and loot ships from other countries.

CHIUS VINCTA
CHIUS LIBERATA
Catholic Pirates and Greek Merchants

GENEALOGY OF THE BOURNIAS FAMILIES

Sometime in the 1700's, it all started on an island in the Aegean Sea.

Here begins the heritage of the family surname introducing our great, great, great grandfather Apostolos Bournias who lived in the area known as Parparia on the island of Chios in Greece.[110]

During my research of the Bournias ancestry, I stumbled across a relative, Antonios Bournias who fascinated me and captured my curiosity in learning more about him and his relationship to the family history, and explored more about him.

I read numerous articles and books in Greek and in English, and learned about those who condemned his actions for his attempt to free Chios from the Ottomans.

I hope that the rest of this book provides you with an interesting look into the Bournias family and the relatives that have made a mark whether good or bad in history.

The Sphinx of Chios is the symbol used by the ancient Greeks for the island of Chios.
It depicts grapes, an amphora of wine, and the Sphinx, with the word Chios written in Greek.
The word sphinx originates from the ancient Greeks.[111]

The location of Chios in the Mediterranean made it a "commercial hub" during this time-period where shipping was the most important method of transportation to move goods from one country to another.

Another reason is the existence of Mastic, a substance from tree sap that was important for health reasons giving the island great economic wealth during this time-period.

Image Reference: Wikipedia, https://en.wikipedia.org/wiki/Sphinx

---

110 Wikipedia, https://en.wikipedia.org/wiki/Chios
111 Wikipedia, https://en.wikipedia.org/wiki/Sphinx

A RARE MAP OF CHIOS

A visual history of the areas on the island of Chios

This book shows detailed names of the older villages that are scattered around the island that are important when researching both the history of the island and the movement of the people. The map is rare because it shows the factual names of areas.

The red arrows indicate the major population of Bournias families inhabit such as Chios (Hora, the capital of Chios and port), Vrontados, Parparia, Pirama, Spartounda, and Mesta.
When looking at the next map, imagine yourself on the island in the year 1700.

If you follow the mountain path from Parparia or Pirama to Kastron (now called HORA), you can see the largest road that leads from that side of the island to the area of Vrontados. Of course back then, there were no 4x4's with the exception of horses and donkeys. This would be the immediate path to cross the island to reach the main port and Hora the principal city. The fortress citadel in Hora was where the battle for independence would be fought to free the island of the Ottomans rulers.

Chios has a rugged mountainous terrain and if you were living in the area of Pirama then you would probably be a farmer and have to transport your fruits and vegetables to anywhere that you could sell them including the Kastron (the central area known then as the castle more appropriately a fortress citadel). Now think of walking and working around mountains. If you were lucky, you might have a donkey to help carry what needed to be carried.

You might be poor since the Bournias family were not wealthy wearing a typical dress style that the Chiots did which means that for a man it would be a type of round cloth hat or no hat, loose shirt, short jockey styled pants, and either shoes or no shoes.
The women would wear a loose blouse, a wrap type of skirt, a cloth type of bra and underwear if you could afford it, and either shoes or no shoes.

There was no running water from pipes, no electricity, and the only other means of transport to get to the Kastron from other areas was by small boats from area to area or to the old central market.

Image credit: (next page)
The map on the following page is from the book, "*A History of the island of Chios a.d. 70 – 1822*," that was translated into English from the work of Dr. Alexander M. Vlasto noted as "*XIAKA*" or "*The History of the island of Chios from the earliest times down to its destruction by the Turks in 1822*".
I have added red arrows indicating approximately, where Bournias family members lived.

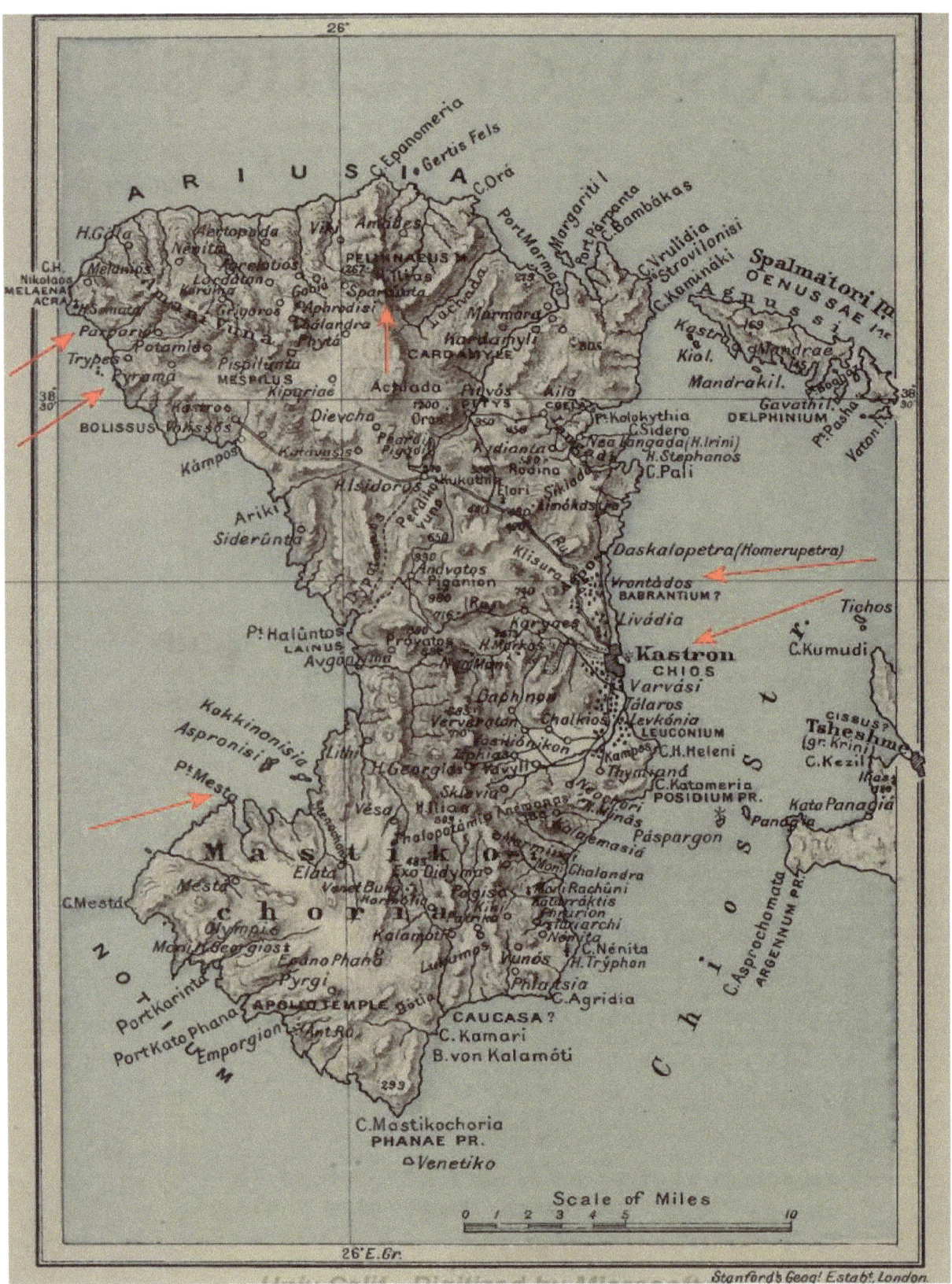

GENEALOGY SHORTHAND

Notes on how to read and understand the genealogy information on my charts.
I use the following abbreviations on my charts. The descriptions shown here.[112]

Abt. is sometimes shown as **circa,** which means <u>about or around</u> as in the time-period or year. In some cases, abt. will mean during the time-period when an exact date is not shown.

In cases where a year is shown without an exact date, it does not mean that it is not an exact year but that there no document has been obtained to substantiate the exact date.

EXPLANATION OF THE GENEALOGICAL SYMBOLS
ΕΞΗΓΗΣΗ ΤΩΝ ΓΕΝΕΑΛΟΓΙΚΑ ΣΥΜΒΟΛΑ

A basic genealogical tree including divorce

Ένα βασικό γενεαλογικό δέντρο συμπεριλαμβανομένου και του διαζυγίου

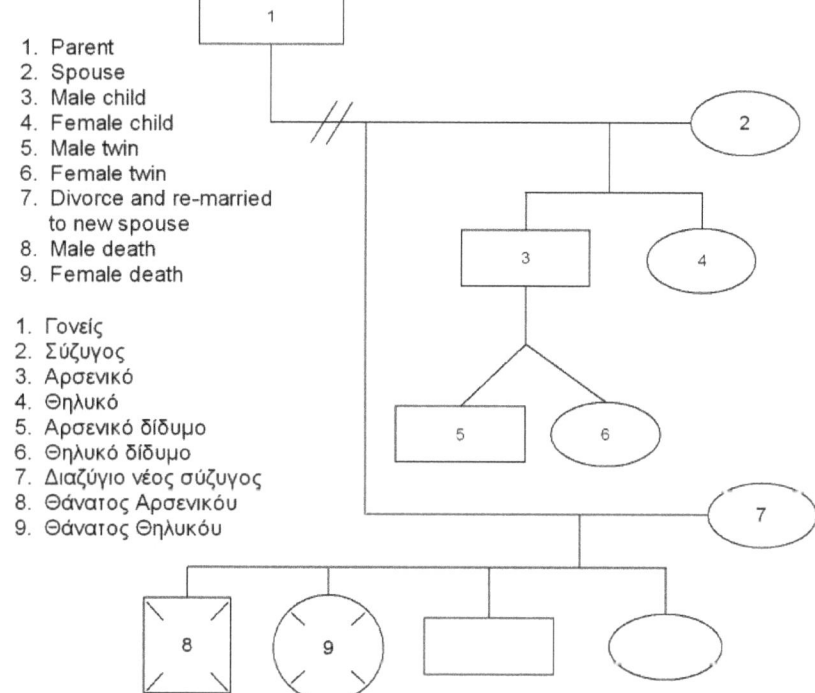

1. Parent
2. Spouse
3. Male child
4. Female child
5. Male twin
6. Female twin
7. Divorce and re-married to new spouse
8. Male death
9. Female death

1. Γονείς
2. Σύζυγος
3. Αρσενικό
4. Θηλυκό
5. Αρσενικό δίδυμο
6. Θηλυκό δίδυμο
7. Διαζύγιο νέος σύζυγος
8. Θάνατος Αρσενικού
9. Θάνατος Θηλυκού

- b. for birth and is sometimes shown as DOB, which is the date of birth.

- d. for death and is sometimes shown as DOD, which is the date of death.

- m. for marriage and is sometimes shown as DOM, which is the date of marriage.

- Nee is used to designate the maiden surname.

Image credit:
Created by P. Bournias

---

112 Abbreviations & Acronyms for Genealogy - The Accepted genealogy project. (n.d.). eni_Family_Tree. https://www.geni.com/projects/Abbreviations-Acronyms-for-Genealogy-The-Accepted/3096

Individuals of the Bournias family

For those of you who do not know, the **Land Registry**[113] (Υποθηκοφυλακεία) has records of property transactions, indexed by surname of the individuals buying and selling property. To obtain copies of records from them requires either a **Lawyer (Δικηγόρος)** or a **Notary Public**[114] **(συμβολαιογράφος)**.

Land registry records are not digitized or computerized and copies of the documents are charged based upon an appointed clerk of the registry office. Photograph is not allowed for land registry records unless you are willing to pay an exorbitant price for them, as photographs are considered copies and the price is set by the individual appointed to the land registry.

As such, I did not explore the Land Registries, although I do know that some records hold information about dowries, adoptions, inheritances, and foster parenting of children. The reason for this is due to the amount of time that one has to dedicate reading and copying by hand various information that might be contained in them, in an awkward and cramped environment of the Greek civil services.

An awkward environment by my definition is not having a table or chair to be able to examine documents, photograph records, and/or write notes. The facilities of the Greek Orthodox Church except for the "*Mitropoli*" of Kalamata are similarly awkward environments for researchers.

From my own family, I know that many relatives had small farms to grow fruits and vegetables, and some had chickens and goats, necessary for the sustenance of the family. They prepared the land that they had, sewed the crops, and harvested them when ready. At the same time, many of them worked as various labor.
I have provided a listing of work and professions depending on their education.

In the family lineage, it is obvious that the better educated the person was, the more likely they could advance in status. This is generally true even today and will become more obvious as you read about the individuals below and see the progress of family branches on the charts.

I am sorry to say that the majority of listed individuals are male members of the Bournias family because of the challenge in researching the female members of the family. Women were recorded only on birth / baptism certificates or marriage records. They were recorded later in the 20th century after they received the right to vote in the electoral lists.

While I would like to have discovered some texts written by primogenitors of the various branches of the Bournias family, I did not find any at any of the archives, except for a journal by Antonios A. Bournias that may have provided more insight into their daily lives.

---

[113] https://en.wikipedia.org/wiki/Land_registration
[114] https://en.wikipedia.org/wiki/Notary_public

Lineage of the Bournias Ancestry Main Chart

Many of the children's names repeat as they honor their grand parents as is customary.

First Tier

Apostolos Bournias (Απόστολος Μπουρνιάς), about 1760, Parparia, Chios, Greece
    Spouse first name unknown, surname Kolovos (ΚΟΛΟΒΟΣ)
    Mother's maiden name Chaniotis (ΧΑΝΙΩΤΗ), Parparia, Chios, Greece

Second Tier - Bournias_family_GR_main_left

Demetrios A. Bournias (Δημήτριος Α. Μπουρνιάς), birth: about 1785
    Spouse unknown
        Georgios D. Bournias (Γεώργιος Δ. Μπουρνιάς), birth: late 1700's to about 1825
        Leonidas D. Bournias (Λεωνιδας Δ. Μπουρνιάς), birth: about 1810
        Petros D. Bournias (Πετρος Δ. Μπουρνιάς), birth: about 1829

Second Tier - Bournias_family_GR_main_right

Antonios A. Bournias (Αντώνιος Μπουρνιάς), born 1788
    1st Spouse of Antonios A. Bournias, unknown, killed during the revolution
        1st child of Antonios, name unknown, birth: unknown, killed during the revolution
        2nd child of Antonios, name unknown, birth: unknown, killed during the revolution

    2nd Spouse of Antonios A. Bournias
    Argentou Maggina (Αργεντού Μάγγινα), Aegina, and Karystos, Evia
        a) Emmanuil A. Bournias (Εμμανουέλ Α. Μπουρνιάς), birth: 1832
        b) Gregoris A. Bournias (Γρηγόρης Α. Μπουρνιάς), birth: 1833
        c) Apostolos A. Bournias (Απόστολος Α. Μπουρνιάς), birth: 1835
        d) Smaragda A. Bournia (Σμαράγδα Α. Μπουρνιά), birth: about 1837
        e) Eleftherios A. Bournias (Ελευθερίος Α. Μπουρνιάς), birth: about 1839

Ioannis A. Bournias (Ιώαννης Μπουρνιάς), born about 1799
    Spouse **Elisavet** (Ελισάβετ), surname unknown
    Their children were:
        a) Othonos I. Bournias (Όθωνα Ι. Μπουρνιάς), birth 1844 Syros or Athens
        b) Demetrios I. Bournias or Vournias* (Δημήτριος Ι. Μπουρνιάς ή Βουρνιάς*)[115]

---

[115] * Researcher note: The surname change was discovered in the Asia Minor records. There is more information regarding this in this document.

Third Tier - Bournias_family_GR_main_left

Demetrios A. Bournias (Δημήτριος Α. Μπουρνιάς), about 1785

Georgios D. Bournias (Γεώργιος Δ. Μπουρνιάς), late 1700's to early 1800's
Spouse Ploumi, first name unknown
Ploumi, nicknames Ploumitsa, Ploumia (Πλουμί, nicknames Πλουμίτσα, Πλουμία)
Their children were:
    a) Antonios G. Bournias (Αντώνιος Γ. Μπουρνιάς), about 1853
    b) Agapia G. Bournia (Αγαπία Γ. Μπουρνιάς), 1854
No additional information discovered for these individuals.

Leonidas D. Bournias (Λεωνίδας Δ. Μπουρνιάς), about 1810
Spouse unknown
No additional information discovered for these individuals.
Their children were:
    a) Demetrios L. Bournias (Δημήτριος Λ. Μπουρνιάς), about 1861
    b) Kyriakos L. Bournias (Κυριάκος Λ. Μπουρνιάς), 1866
    c) Antonios L. Bournias (Αντώνιος Λ. Μπουρνιάς), 1870

Petros D. Bournias (Πέτρος Δ. Μπουρνιάς), about 1829
Spouse **Kalliopi** (Καλλιόπη), surname unknown, 1854
Their children were:
    a) Demetrios P. Bournias (Δημήτριος Π. Μπουρνιάς), about 1871
    b) Nikolaos P. Bournias (Νικόλαος Π. Μπουρνιάς), about 1874
    c) Antonios P. Bournias (Αντώνιος Π. Μπουρνιάς), about 1879
    d) Georgios P. Bournias (Γεώργιος Π. Μπουρνιάς), about 1882
    e) Stamatia P. Bournia (Σταμάτια Π. Μπουρνιά), about 1887
    f) Pantelis P. Bournias (Παντελής Δ. Μπουρνιάς), about 1889

Third Tier - Bournias_family_GR_main_right

Antonios A. Bournias (Αντώνιος Μπουρνιάς), born 1788

Emmanuil "Manouil" A. Bournias (Εμμανουήλ Α. Μπουρνιάς), 1832
Spouse unknown
Their children were:
    a) Georgios E. Bournias (Γεώργιος Ε. Μπουρνιάς), about 1850
    b) Demetrios E. Bournias (Δημήτριος Ε. Μπουρνιάς), 1853
    c) Antonios E. Bournias (Αντώνιος Ε. Μπουρνιάς), 1855

Third Tier - Bournias_family_GR_main_right – continued

Apostolos A. Bournias (Απόστολος Α. Μπουρνιάς), about 1835
    Spouse Vasiliki (Βασιλική), surname unknown, 1841
    Their children were:
        a) Antonios A. Bournias (Αντώνιος Α. Μπουρνιάς), 1861
        b) Konstantinos A. Bournias (Κωνσταντίνος Α. Μπουρνιάς), 1864
        c) Mihail A. Bournias (Μιχαήλ Α. Μπουρνιάς), 1866
        d) Leonidas A. Bournias (Λεωνίδας Α. Μπουρνιάς), 1868
        e) Georgios A. Bournias (Γεώργιος Α. Μπουρνιάς), about 1870
        f) Panagiotis (Panagis) A. Bournias (Παναγιώτης (Παναγής) Α. Μπουρνιάς), 1872
        g) Ioannis (Yiangos) A. Bournias (Ιωάννης (Γιάγκος) Α. Μπουρνιάς), about 1877
        h) Ariadni A. Bournia (Αριάδνη Α. Μπουρνιά), birth: unknown
        i) Eleni A. Bournia (Ελένη Α. Μπουρνιά), birth: unknown
        j) Klementini A. Bournia (Κλημεντίνη Α. Μπουρνιά), birth: unknown

Gregoris A. Bournias (Γρηγόρης Α. Μπουρνιάς), 1833
    Spouse unknown
    Their children were:
        a) Georgios G. Bournias (Γεώργιος Γ. Μπουρνιάς), about 1850
        b) Antonios G. Bournias (Αντώνιος Γ. Μπουρνιάς), 1865
        c) Sophia G. Bournia (Σοφία Γ. Μπουρνιά), 1875
        d) Periklis G. Bournias (Περικλής Γ. Μπουρνιάς), birth: unknown

Smaragda A. Bournia (Σμαράγδα Α. Μπουρνιά), about 1837
    No information discovered regarding this individual, spouse and/or children

Eleftherios A. Bournias (Ελευθερίος Α. Μπουρνιάς), about 1839
    No information discovered regarding individual, spouse and/or children

Researcher note:
Please refer to the genealogical ancestry chart provided separately.
The chart provides additional information and more tiers of ancestors that are allowed in accordance with the privacy laws for historical purposes.
The fourth tier is not provided in writing as it becomes too complicated to separate the family branches in writing.

APOSTOLOS BOURNIAS (ΑΠΟΣΤΟΛΟΣ ΜΠΟΥΡΝΙΑΣ)

Born about 1760 in Parparia, Chios.

Top of the main chart

Apostolos Bournias is a pivotal individual for both the left and right sides of the main chart of the Bournias families.

I begin this section with Apostolos Bournias who is essentially the first member of the Bournias family of Chios, as I was not able to uncover any further information prior to or about him.

He married a woman with the first name unknown and surname Kolovou (Kolovos).
I believe her mother's surname was Chanioti(s) (Χανιώτου), and were from the villages of Parparia, Chios based on a testimony in the book by Viou. (Viou 1987)

Apostolos Bournias had the following children born in Pirama:

Demetrios A. Bournias, born about 1785
Antonios A. Bournias, born 1788

I believe that Apostolos had more children based upon the number of siblings birthed during those times, but as the time-period of their lives was entwined with the Massacre of Chios in 1822 no additional records were discovered.

According to the testimony #24 on page 62 of Petros D. Bournias, who was born in Pirama about 1829, a resident of Livadia, and the children above were all born in Pirama.[116] (Bournias 2013)

I learned that there was a Priest named, Papa-Demetrios Chaniotis the archimandrite[117], a superior abbot at the church in Pirama. He may have been a relative of the spouse of Apostolos Bournias. He provided a testimony #25 on page 65 regarding the preparations for the revolution in the area of Psallida near a cave in the area of Spartounda.

---

[116] Bournias, Peter A. HISTORICAL TESTIMONIALS FOR ANTONIOS BOURNIAS, 2013.
[117] https://en.wikipedia.org/wiki/Archimandrite

Antonios A. Bournias (Αντώνιος Α. Μπουρνιάς), 1788 - 1865
Antonios A. Bournias, a.k.a. Hatzi-Antonios Bournias

From the main chart – right side by year of birth.

The families of Antonios A. Bournias.
The name of his first spouse and their two children remain unknown.
The name of his second spouse was Argento Maggina, birth unknown, location unknown.

Researching the surname of his second spouse as transliterated from Greek to Maggena, and/or Maggina, and/or Magkaina, I verified that the surname Maggina exists on the islands of Aegina and Evia.

According to the "*Historical testimonials for Antonios Bournias*," page 16 noted that, Argento Maggina was from Chios but Antonios met her and married her in Aegina.

The following information regards the children of his second spouse.
Here I had to use what I call "genealogical interpretation" to estimate the years of birth and to deduce the approximate years of previous ancestors, as minimal information was discovered.

Genealogical interpretation of year of birth:
Antonios A. Bournias, born 1788, died 1865, age 77, moved to Aegina about 1827.[118]
Antonios has finished his military career after 1825 based on the date of his personal journal, and married his second spouse around 1830 or 1831 at the age of about 42 or 43, Emmanuil was born about 1832 or 1833 according to an electoral list from Aegina that showed Antonios was about 44 years old.
This provides a fair estimation that the years of birth are accurate.

Estimated (~) years of birth of his children from his second marriage:
Emmanuil	1832 [119]
Gregoris	1833
Apostolos	1835 [120]
Smaragda	~1837
Eleftherios	~1839

---

118 Χιακόν αρχείον Ιωάννου Βλαχογιάννη - Archives of Chios Ioannis Vlachogiannis, 1924, v.1, pp. 451 - 453
119 Researcher notes: The year of birth for Emmanuil was verified based on his age in an electoral catalog of 1867 for Aegina.
120 The year of birth for Apostolos is 1835 from a gravestone at the First Cemetery of Athens, although the Municipality of Karystos in Evia note it as 1888 that correlates to the son of Antonios of 1861. See the documentation of the Municipality of Karystos Evia, Bournias-Dimos-Karystos-Evia.jpg

Emmanuil A. Bournias profession was noted as being a fisherman. He ventured into the Kelebesion Anneon region of Asia Minor and returned through Koroni Messinia. Along with his family, they were sent to Drama in Northern Greece with the surname changed to Vournias. More details about him are in his biography that follows.

Gregoris A. Bournias, more details about him are in his biography that follows.

Apostolos A. Bournias became a poet, archeologist, and notary public; more details about him are in his biography that follows.

Smaragda A. Bournia(s), no further information was discovered.

Eleftherios A. Bournias, no further information was discovered.

At this point, I must digress to provide a historical synopsis about the revolution on Chios as the details provide insight as to what happened on the island, its people, and how it affected the lives of the Bournias families.

Researcher note:
According to a sentence from the book "*Περίπατος με την Αγγελική*" (Walking with Angeliki), the author "*Έρση - Αλεξία Χατζημιχάλη*" (Ersi-Alexia Hatzimihali), Angeliki writes that Antonios Bournias had land in the area of Athens known today as Patission. In that time-period, the area of Patission in Athens was a prominent place to live.

As I have not found any written documentation that Antonios Bournias built a home there, he may have bought the land as an investment or for his children. The land was donated to the Greek Orthodox Church by the grandmother known as Areti, the spouse of Gregoris Bournias, who was from Syros.[121] (Έρση 1999)

---

121 Περίπατος με την Αγγελική, Χατζημιχάλη Έρση, 1999

THE REVOLUTION ON CHIOS ABRIDGED

On Easter Sunday, April 23, 1822, Antonios Bournias with other Chiotans and freedom fighters (the number varies from 300 to 2000 depending on the book) from the island of Samos began their attempt at a revolution.

During the hostilities between the Ottomans and the people on the island of Chios, Greece, a Chiotis named Antonios Bournias lived in the village of Pirama in 1788.
Antonios Bournias was also known as Hatzi-Antonios Bournias, the "Hatz" being someone who made a pilgrimage to the Holy Land.[122]
Parparia and Pirama are located in the North-West mountainous area of Chios.

Antonios Bournias served under Napoleon in his campaigns before attempting to overthrow the reign of the Pasha in Chios. He attained the position of an officer for his services in the African, Sardinia, and the Egyptian wars. Being a friend of the well-known Lycurgus Logothetis[123], he tried to persuade Alexandros Ypsilantis[124] and later Demtrios Ypsilantis[125] to provide support for his plan.[126]

In an attempt to find additional support for his plan, he went to the island of Samos where he met with four other men from Chios. After attaining the help of these men, they planned to storm the fortress citadel of the Pasha, which is the fortress citadel of Chios at the port.

The Pasha already knowing that the revolt would take place requested help from *Ottoman Empire*.[127] Pasha Kara Ali rushed to Chios from Asia Minor to stop the revolt with 7,000 men.
They burned the homes and killed 40,000 residents of the island.[128]

The attempt failed due to the traitorous upper class of Chios who preferred not to lose their business with the Ottomans. They informed the Ottomans prior to the revolt and the revolutionists along with a majority, thousands of the population of the island were slaughtered.

A large number of residents fled from the island of Chios to the island of Psara, the Cyclades, and the Peloponnese.

---

[122] https://en.wikipedia.org/wiki/Hatzi
[123] https://en.wikipedia.org/wiki/Lykourgos_Logothetis
[124] https://en.wikipedia.org/wiki/Alexander_Ypsilantis
[125] https://en.wikipedia.org/wiki/Demetrios_Ypsilantis
[126] https://en.wikisource.org/wiki/1911_Encyclop%C3%A6dia_Britannica/Ypsilanti_(family)
[127] There were many Pasha's in the Ottoman Empire, and Turkey did not exist at the time.
[128] https://en.wikipedia.org/wiki/Nasuhzade_Ali_Pasha

There are numerous reasons that the efforts of Antonios Bournias to free Chios failed:

- A prior attempt by freedom fighters from Spetses one year before failed
- Ypsilantis did not coordinate with the freedom fighters from the main land
- The promised support that he was to receive did not arrive
- The "gerontes" or elders of Chios betrayed the revolution

His attempts against the Pasha ultimately cost the life of his first wife, his two children, and his personal wealth. This forced him to flee, wounded, using a sailboat to the island of Psara, a small island to the north of Chios. From Psara, he traveled to Evia, Syros, or Aegina to recouperate from his wounds.

The Greek women that did not wish to become sexual slaves to the Ottomans committed suicide or threw themselves off higher grounds to avoid being taken alive.
Women and children that were captured either became slaves or were lost forever as they were taken to Turkey never to be seen again.
The Chiotan women taken for sale in the Ottoman Empire were killed to satisfy a sacrificial Muslim ritual.

From 1822 until about 1861, residents from the island of Chios were under the watchful eye of the Ottomans who controlled their lifestyle to prevent any further uprisings.

Antonios fought the Ottomans again in the area of Moria in the Peloponnese after his wounds healed, and he returned to Chios in 1827 to continue his fight.

A large number of residents fled from the island of Chios to the island of Psara, and to the islands of Syros, Mykonos, and the Peloponnese.

Later on the island of Aegina, he married his second wife. It is possible that this woman's surname was (Μάγκαινα), which transliterates to Maggena or Maggaina depending on the pronunciation.

Antonios had five children with her by the names of Emmanuil, Apostolos, Gregoris, Smaragda, and Eleftherios. His first child Emmanuil was born in 1832.

In reality, the island of Chios was finally and officially free from the Ottoman rule in 1912 even though Greece as a nation celebrates the 25 of March as their day of independence.

An excerpt from the book "**The Massacre at Chios**," depicts the horror by the Ottomans due to the selfishness of the elite of Chios who informed the Pasha about the revolution and who paid with their own lives, as described by the words of the British Ambassador.

"Taken as a hostage and hanged by the Turks at Chios in the Massacre of Chios 6 May 1822." The dungeon in which <u>47 of the island's leaders (demogerontes) were hanged</u> exists today at the castle of Chios.

Above the door a plaque reads:

"In this dark dungeon in the year 1822, 74 members of noble Chian families were kept prisoner as hostages of the Turks, and from here on 23rd April 1822 after untold suffering, the Bishop of Chios, Mitropolitan Plato, and 46 others were hanged: they died for their faith and for their country."

"An obelisk in marble from Skyros now marks the spot, close to the walls of the kastro by the fountain, where the long line of swinging corpses ended stretched from that point to the Porta Maggiore [Main Port of Chios]. Standing in a recess on the side of Vounaki Square, now known as The Way of The Martys, the obelisk names Loukas Vlasto was among the 47 who were murdered there. To engender greater terror, the Turks hung the bodies from trees around the city centre for three days, having already ridiculed Mitropolitan [Bishop] Plato by placing a Turkish cap, a 'tiara', on his head.
The heads of Mitropolitan [Bishop] Plato and the leader, Makarios were placed on pikes on the ramparts and pelted with stones by Turkish fanatics. The others too were decapitated and their heads shipped to Constantinople where the Sultan displayed them in victory 'pyramids' to demonstrate his great victory over the 'infidels' of Chios. (See 'Greek Fire' Ch. 5).
The headless bodies were given to the Jews who dragged them to the harbor's edge and threw them into the Aegean. Breasts, genitals, ears, noses and fingers were shipped to Constantinople and strewn about the streets. Only the nobility were hanged. Villagers were kept imprisoned until they died of malnutrition or disease."

The British, Austrian and French vice-consuls were then induced to convince about 1,000 in hiding in the countryside that they were being offered an amnesty. They were horrified to find that the Vahid pasha then ordered them all to be killed.

"The Turkish admiral hanged a further 70 from the yardarm of his flagship. Around 5,000 Chiots (mostly prosperous merchants and diplomats) were abroad at the time of the massacre. Another 15,000 managed to escape before the arrival of the captain pasha's Turkish troops invaded the island. Of those on the island who remained alive, records show that 41,000 Chians were deported to slavery in Turkey. In Constantinople, some were offered for sale at 100 piastres each. Mass circumcisions of young Christian Chians took place in Constantinople while women were sent to the brothels."

In May 1822, the British Ambassador in Constantinople, Viscount Strangford, wrote:

"My Lord, The Transactions at Scio [Chios] appear to have been of a most horrible description, and the ferocity of the Turks to have been carried to a pitch which makes humanity shudder. The whole of the Island, with the exception of the Twenty-four Mastic Villages [uniquely valuable to the Turks], presents one mass of ruin. The unfortunate inhabitants have paid with their lives, the price of their ill-advised rebellion [against being absorbed into the Ottoman Empire]. The only persons who have been spared are the women and children, who have been sold as slaves".

See Public Records Office: F.O. (Turkey) 78, vol. 108, no. 73, 'The Massacres of Chios described in Contemporary Diplomatic Reports', Ed. Philip Argenti (London, 1932)

"The terror even extended to Chian merchants living in Constantinople. Viscount Strangford wrote on 25 May 1822: "The most tragical occurrence took place on the Eighteenth (Instant), when, in spite of the assurances so often given to me by the Porte, that she considered those unhappy men as perfectly innocent, and that no offence could be alleged against them, the Ten Sciot [Chiot] Hostages residing here, were publicly beheaded. They were all persons of good repute, great connections in Trade, particularly with the English merchants, and of large and honourably acquired fortunes. Their fate is deeply regretted even by the Turks; the better class of whom do not scruple to inveigh against this transaction, as an unnecessary cruelty, and to attribute it entirely to the barbarous system of terrorism which Halet Effendi pursues for the sake of diverting public attention from his own misdeeds"

(See Public Records Office: F.O. (Turkey) 78, vol. 108. no. 74. 'The Massacres of Chios Described in Contemporary Diplomatic Reports', Ed. Philip Argenti (London, 1932)".

The Ottomans (Turks and/or Turkish rulers) a historical clarification
I mention this because many people incorrectly refer to them as the Turks but historically they were the Ottomans because Turkey was not officially founded then as a country. The Ottoman Empire existed since the 14th century until the 1922 when they officially became Turkey in 1923.[129]

---

[129] https://en.wikipedia.org/wiki/Ottoman_Turks

The Massacre at Chios by Eugene Delacroix

The artist Ferdinand Victor Eugène Delacroix was inspired by this event created this portrait, which hangs in the Louvre of Paris.[130]

Image Reference: Wikipedia, https://en.wikipedia.org/wiki/The_Massacre_at_Chios

Author's comment:
There may be a family member that attempts to accomplish something good but due to circumstances (including timing and luck) may be categorized as bad by others, and then again, they simply may have had a bad moral character. Peter A. Bournias

---

[130] https://en.wikipedia.org/wiki/Eug%C3%A8ne_Delacroix

A bust representing the figure of Antonios A. Bournias

Today, the Bournias family has spread throughout Greece, has traveled and populated many other countries around the world. The family name is known in various villages as well as in Hora, the city center of Chios, the village of Spartounda, and the area known as Livadia. Many of the family members are well known for their contributions in the areas of politics, law, commerce, accounting, health, musicians, actors, medicine, and engineering.

A picture of the author with the bronze sculpture[131] bust of Antonios (ANTONIS) Bournias found in his village near the church of Agios Ioannis Prodromos in Pirama (Pyrama) on Chios.

Descriptive characteristics of Antonios A. Bournias:

In some of the Greek texts that I have read, he was depicted as a strong, bold person, fearless of the Ottomans, and he would threaten them if he saw them bullying other Chiots and even taunt them into fighting with him.

Another description writes about him returning from his battles as a soldier in the army of Napoleon dressed in a manner that depicts the fanciness of a gallant officer with a feather in his hat, walking with a strut of superiority.

The fact that Antonios Bournias came back to Chios later in life must have caused him great pain regarding the loss of his first wife and children, as well as that of the pain and suffering of the people on the island.

---

[131] Researcher note: Please see the acknowledgement toward the end regarding Mr. Leonis Stylianos and this bronze sculpture bust.

What is OUR family relationship with Antonios A. Bournias?

His father was Apostolos Bournias, the first person on the descendant's chart of the Bournias family from Chios.

Antonios A. Bournias was the brother of Demetrios A. Bournias (The "A" for Apostolos) and therefore our great-great grandfathers.

Have you ever seen or read the story about "*Braveheart?*"[132] If yes, then you should recognize a scene where William Wallace realizes that he has been betrayed by a nobleman. It is a very moving scene that must have been realized by Antonios Bournias, who was betrayed by the noblemen of Chios at the time. Unlike William Wallace who lost the love of his life before he became a revolutionist, Antonios Bournias lost his first wife and two children during the war.

I know that some Chiots will disagree with my view about Antonios Bournias.

I have to consider myself lucky when working with my Greek family genealogy.

The fact that one of our relatives was a revolutionist provides historically written documentation about his life and legacy. On the other hand, due to the Massacre at Chios a tremendous amount of documentation and records prior to 1821, including the Korais Library, and then again in 1881 due to a major earthquake was destroyed.

This information has helped in the development of understanding why all of the members of the Bournias family are originally from Chios, and whom the descendants are that I have recorded in the creation of the ancestor charts that I have accumulated.

My own lineage is from the area of Vrontados Chios where my father Ioannis (John) Bournias and Grandfather Pantelis Bournias were born and my Great-grandfather Petros Bournias lived.

Additional information was extracted from the notes of Stylianos Leonis, a Chiot from the village of Pirama, who along with others from the villages of Pirama and Parparia hold Antonios Bournias in high esteem.

I have translated excerpts from the original Greek text of the book "**Massacre at Chios from the mouth of the Chiot People,**" into English with notes, as a separate PDF file is available for download from my website. In this text, my great grandfather Petros Bournias narrates part of the story of what happened during the time of the revolution. From this text, Petros states that he was born in a house in Pirama.

It reveals the viciousness and cruelty of the slaughter by the Ottoman soldiers and their use of Moors (African mercenaries) that slaughtered the Chiots during the uprising and have accounts by witnesses supporting Antonios Bournias at his trial by the Greek government.[133]

---

[132] Braveheart, https://en.wikipedia.org/wiki/Braveheart
[133] Moors, https://en.wikipedia.org/wiki/Moors

Antonios Bournias <u>was found not guilty by the military tribunal</u> but many Chiots continue to blame him for what happened without placing any blame on the upper class elders who betrayed him and his men.

The military tribunal found Demetrios Ypsilantis guilty and attributed him with the failure.[134] Nothing was noted about the elders.

While resentment exists among some Chiots today regarding Antonios Bournias, I hope that my writing about him maintains the objectivity necessary to allow the reader to make their own decision about the blame of the Catastrophe of Chios.

During the years, 2020 and 2021 Greece celebrated their 200 Anniversary of Independence.
A television historical documentary was released named, "*Περί Ελευθερίας*" that translates to "About Freedom". The documentary was presented by the Greek SKAI Channel[135] by Aris Portosalte [136], with professors of history on the **national holiday of March 25, anniversary of the War of Independence**.[137]

Apart from being very descriptive in the presentation of historical facts, a segment of this documentary was the first time that any inference was made about the fact that the revolution on Chios was lost due to betrayal.

I want to believe that Antonios wanted to liberate Chios but not through the vanity of leadership or at the loss of his wife and children to do so. To do otherwise would be the akin to the worse character in a person.

I have not discovered any information about him during his service with the French Army.

These are two street signs near the center of Chios.

The top one refers to the Platia or Town Square of Georgios Choremis.

The second refers to Antonios Bournias Street.
The English "AD." is wrongly transliterated using the Greek "ANT" because D is the sound for NT.

---

134 Demetrios Ypsilantis, https://en.wikipedia.org/wiki/Demetrios_Ypsilantis
135 https://en.wikipedia.org/wiki/Skai_TV
136 https://en.wikipedia.org/wiki/Aris_Portosalte
137 Περί Ελευθερίας, https://www.skai.gr/news/politismos/peri-eleytherias-premiera-ntokimanter-skai-200-xronia-elliniki-epanastasi

Testimonial evidence of Antonios A. Bournias

The translation of historical testimonials for Antonios Bournias is based on testimony of various individuals at the Parliament in Greece.

The historical testimonials are important because of the accusations that the slaughter of Chios was caused by Antonios Bournias and the testimonies proved that he was not guilty, which otherwise would have marked him a traitor for life.

Antonios Bournias was brought before the parliament to stand trial and was found not guilty by the Greek government. Based on the verdict, he was provided with a retirement for his efforts.
Obviously, if he was found guilty, he would never have received the retirement.

He wrote fifty pages of memoirs on parchments of paper that I have photographed but not translated and interpreted yet because they are hand written in very old Greek that is very intricate to read.

The image on the previous page is one of the hand written pages of the personal journal of Antonios Bournias, on pieces of paper parchment that are folded and are kept at the central Athens office of the General Archives of Greece.

Researcher note:
The memoirs were donated to the General Archives of Greece as reference K84 as a manuscript under the heading "From the Journal of Antonios Bournias about the Military Campaign of Chios in 1822".

ON A PERSONAL NOTE
After reading the above texts and translating parts of it that refer to Antonios into English, it is my opinion that the writer Mr. Vlastos appears to be biased in his writings and slant the work toward the benefit of those who betrayed Antonios.

I came back from a trip to Chios (March 22 2005) and after researching again and found that the Vlasto family were one of the privileged and elite families at the time of the Greek revolution.

It appears that while others were fighting for their independence, the wealthier families were using their financial strengths to accommodate their life-style, more so by not encouraging the fight for independence and to promote a do not instigate attitude since their life-styles were less affected by the Ottomans. Many of those families still exist today.

Further, it appears that this is common of many situations and that it is more apportioned for true patriots to be the ones who will sacrifice themselves for their beliefs. The position by the "elders" brought about the traitorous act upon Antonios Bournias by those who were financially comfortable doing business with the Ottomans.

The wealthy merchants of Chios persuaded the leaders of the fighters from Samos to turn their back Antonios leaving him with an ill-equipped bunch of farmer freedom fighters causing the loss of his family, his wealth and possessions, and giving the Ottomans an advantage in numbers and therefore losing the battle.

As a result, the fighters from Samos in their greed, decided to raid the homes of the Chiots and take whatever wealth they could since they knew that the Ottomans would probably kill most of them anyway. This increased the chaos among the Chiots that turned into a blood bath.
Therefore, the inception of the revolution turned into a nightmare negatively marking the name of Antonios Bournias historically.

During the same time, Catholics began burning Mosques, and the Ottomans began killing and looting, including around 200 monks, in the monastery of Nea Moni, and other villages. (ΚΑΡΑΒΟΛΟΥ 2019)

John Cartwright, British Consul-General in Constantinople, filed a report on May 25, 1822 stating:[138]

> "Chios, with the exception of 25 of the Mastic Villages was a complete scene of desolation- the air corrupted by the stench of dead bodies had produced an infectious disorder on board the Turkish Fleet which was daily carrying off its' victims. The fate of the unhappy survivors in the tragedy of Chios is miserable indeed - the females and children doomed to slavery from which there will be little chance of redemption, as all possible means are taken to prevent the sale of them to Christians. The hostages who were confined in the Castle of Chios as well of those who were here have been put to death."

The Sultan sent approximately 30,000 soldiers and resistance by the Chiots was impossible. Nearly the entire male population was massacred and their wives and children sold as slaves. Not only were the inhabitants decimated, but churches, homes, and villages were burned to the ground.

I have recorded various facts including many from the Library of the Parliament regarding Antonios Bournias as some Chiots continue to blame the Bournias family name for the massacre after 200 years.

---

[138] M., F. H. (n.d.). The Massacres of Chios, described in Contemporary Diplomatic Reports. Edited, with an Introduction, by Philip P. Argenti. Pp. xxxiv + 242 ; 3 plates. London: John Lane, 1932. 12s. 6d. | The Journal of Hellenic Studies. Cambridge Core. https://www.cambridge.org/core/journals/journal-of-hellenic-studies/article/abs/massacres-of-chios-described-in-contemporary-diplomatic-reports-edited-with-an-introduction-by-philip-p-argenti-pp-xxxiv-242-3-plates-london-john-lane-1932-12s-6d/7D3180D77526CBD6B03F19EC2EA96B6B

From the Library of the Parliament regarding Antonios Bournias

Testimonial references for Antonios Bournias by Hatzi-Giannakis of Pyrgos and Georgios Sklavos of Chios, dated 1822, March 22, Chios to the Parliament, number 94.[139]

The testimony by Hatzi-Giannakis and Georgios Sklavos declare that Antonios Bournias should have been declared a hero for his efforts and criticize the elders for their love of money and cooperation with the Ottoman enemy.

---

139 Image referernce: GAK Athens, P. Bournias, ΜΠΟΥΡΝΙΑΣ ΧΑΤΖΗ - ΑΝΤΩΝΙΟΣ - 0 - 0641766.gif

Ioannis Bournias (Ιωάννης Μπουρνιάς), 1799 - death unknown

Ioannis Bournias, born about 1799, father unknown, birth location Chios.

From the main chart – right side by year of birth.

A handwritten record from the Registry of Citizens of the Municipality of Ermoupoli, shows that that he moved from Chios to Ermoupoli Syros escaping from the results of the revolution in 1822. In the same document is his request for Greek citizenship again.[140] This may sound unusual but if the area where you lived was under the Ottoman rule, then you would have to request to renew your Greek citizenship even though the area may have originally been a part of Greece.

The name on the record is Ioannis Bournias and does not indicate a middle name or the name of his father. From the dates in this information, I estimated that he was born about 1799, and as I have not discovered any other branch of the family in this time period, I believe that he could be a brother of Demetrios born about 1785 and Antonios born 1788. There were many others from Chios listed on this record.[141]

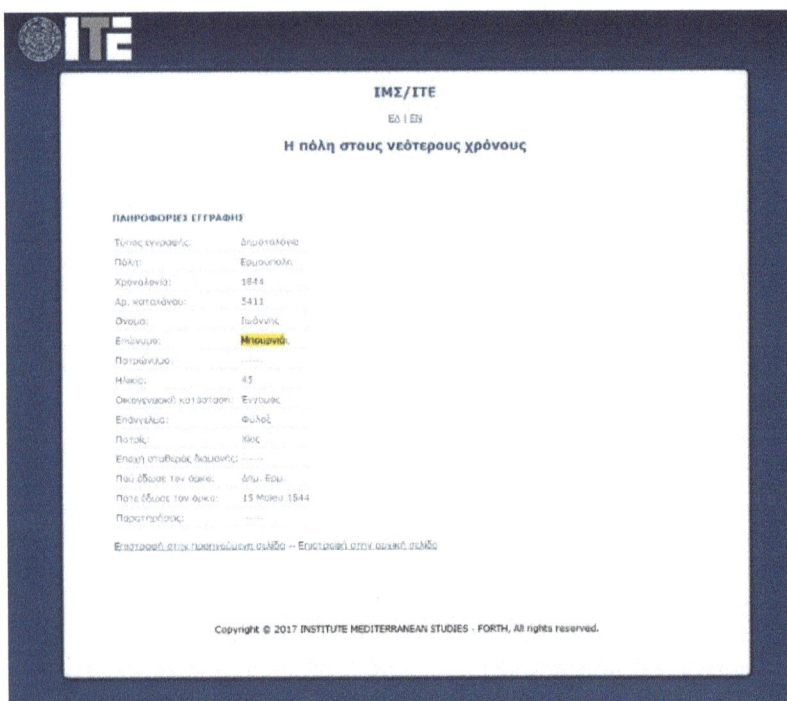

Translation of document from the GAK Syros - Ioannis Bournias 1844

Ioannis Bournias, middle initial or father unknown, born about 1799, location unknown, profession Port / Coast Guard.
He was married, age 45, and he was uneducated according to the document.[142]
This record was discovered online at the IMS website dated 1844. After more research, I discovered that the name of his spouse was Elizavet and they had two sons, Othonos born 1844, and Demetrios.

A reference to Demetrios in the Refugee List from Asia Minor indicates that he was also known as Vournias, and that he returned from the area of Tzifout-Bourgaz Derkon near Constantinople Turkey, and that he may have been born about 1840 to 1850.

Image Credit: IMS, 1844 Ioannis Bournias age 45 Guard Chios.jpg

---

140 Translation of document from the GAK Syros - GAK-Syros-Ioannis-Bournias-1844.pdf
141 Moved-Bournias-Ioannis-moved-from-Chios-to-Ermoupolis-1822.jpg
142 GAK-Syros-Ioannis-Bournias-1844.pdf

Petros D. Bournias (Πετρος Δ. Μπουρνιάς), 1829 - death unknown

Petros D. Bournias, son of Demetrios, was born about 1829 in Pirama Chios.

From the main chart – left side by year of birth.

His spouse was Kalliopi (Calliopi), surname unknown born 1854, died prior to 1928. They had six children that I have documented and based on the waring years, they had them late in life.

I first read about Petros D. Bournias, my great grandfather, while reading the Historical Testimonials for Antonios Bournias. In that document, I learned that he was a resident of Livadia in Vrontados Chios at the time that he knew Antonios A. Bournias.

My father never mentioned him but that was because he never knew him. I deduced this one day and asked my father about Petros receiving a blank look from him. Then I told him who Petros was and that he never met him because he died before my father was born in 1930.

I concluded that Petros and his spouse Kalliopi (Calliopi) were deceased prior to the wedding of my grandfather Pantelis in 1928, and therefore the birth of my father in 1930, as this was the only logical conclusion as to why my father never knew them.
As a basis of proof that Petros D. Bournias probably died before 1930, he is not listed as a voter in the Electoral Catalog of 1930.

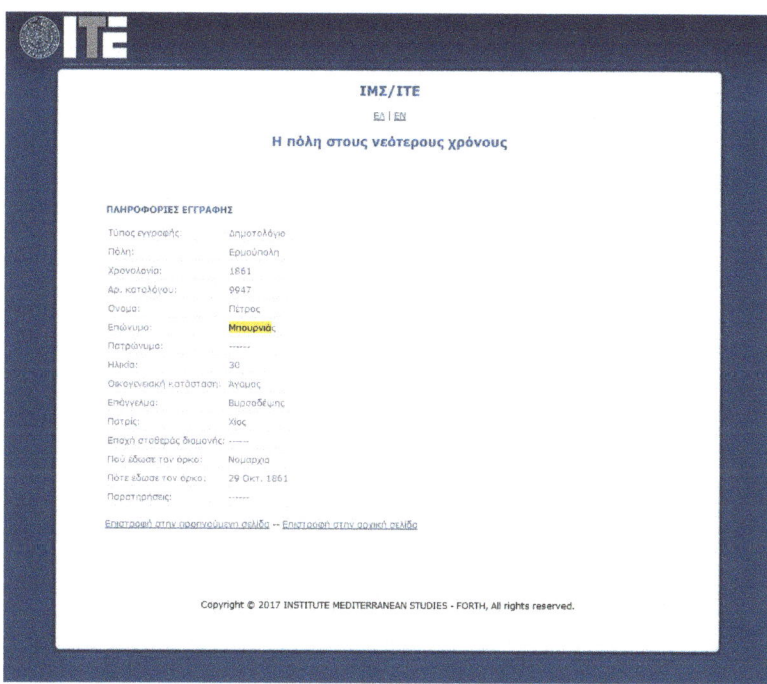

Reference from Syros:
Registry of Citizens of the Municipality of Ermoupoli Syros
Year   1861
Name   Petros
Surname   Bournias
Age   30
Family Status   Single
Profession   Tanner
Homeland   Chios

Where was the constitutional
oath given?   Prefecture[143]
Date?   29 Oct. 1861
Comments   None

Image Credit: IMS, 1861 Petros D Bournias age 30 Tanner Chios.jpg

---

[143] The Constitutional oath was a request to become a Greek citizenship again. This may sound unusual but if the area where you lived was under the Ottoman rule, then you had to renew your Greek citizenship even though the area was originally a part of Greece.

Emmanouil A. Bournias (Εμμανουήλ Α. Μπουρνιάς), 1832 - death unknown

Emmanouil A. (Manolis) Bournias (Εμμανουήλ (Μανώλης) Α. Μπουρνιάς), He was the first son from the second marriage of Antonios A. Bournias born in 1832 on Aegina as noted in the electoral catalog of 1867.

From the main chart – right side by year of birth.

Georgios E. Bournias, born about 1850 on the island of Aegina and was the first child of Emmanouil A. Bournias. He became the foster child of his uncle Apostolos A. Bournias of 1835. Generally, this happened in families that were either very poor or to introduce them to a profession of the foster parent as an apprenticeship.

Georgios E. Bournias ventured into **Kelebesion Anneon region of Asia Minor** around 1922. Georgios is the decedent of the Vournias Family that lives in the Kyrgia Drama. I found his name in the "*15 ΟΝΟΜΑΣΤΙΚΟΣ ΚΑΤΑΛΟΓΟΣ ΑΓΡΟΤΩΝ ΠΡΟΣΦΥΓΩΝ*," (*15th catalog of immigrant farmers*)[144] that fled Asia Minor between 1919 and 1922.

His surname of Bournias may have changed to Vournias during the flood of immigrants from Asia Minor by the Greek government possibly misconstruing the Greek "ΜΠ" (Μπουρνιάς) for the Latin "B" (as in V for Vournias - Βουρνιάς). See the third line in image that shows **Βουρνιάς ή Μπουρνιάς Δημ. του Ιωάννου** (Vournias or Bournias).

Βουρνέλης Κωνσταντίνος του Δημ.	ᵓ	59000-20
Βουρνέλης Κυριάκος του Λεωνίδα	ᵓ	61485
Βουρνιάς ή Μπουρνιάς Δημ. του Ιωάννου	Κελεμπέσιον-'Αννέων	63271
Βουρνοβαλή ή Γκεριγκιώντη Μαγδαληνή του Ιωάν.	Μαινεμένη-'Εφέσου	186117 Μ.
Βουρνοβαλής Γεώργιος του Κων)τίνου	Βαϊνδήριον-'Ηλιουπόλ.	5671
Βουρνουζούρης ή Καλπουρτζής Εμμ. του Ιωάννου	Βρύουλλα-Βρυούλλων	155732

Image text translation: Demetrios son of Ioannis, Kelebesion Anneon, file # 63271.

Image Credit: Υπουργείο Γεωργίας Επιτροπή Αποκατάστασης Προσφύγων B.pdf, pp. 199.

During a trip from Kalamata to Koroni in October 2017, I found a record in the Registry of Boys (Males) referring to an Emmanouil Bourniadakis, son of Georgios, born in 1881, but I did not know or believe at the time that he had any connection with the Vournias family.

Emmanuil (Manolis) Bourniadakis - Εμμανουήλ (Μανώλης) Μπουρνιάδακης, born 1881 Koroni, Pilos, Messinia. Manolis was his nickname.

---

[144] The catalog of immigrant farmers are record volumes from the Ministry of Agriculture Refugee Rehabilitation Committee of Asia Minor that was a list of the Greek immigrants.

I discovered numerous Bournias family members in the Registry of Boys of Koroni, Pilos in Messinia. I have not discovered any other person with the surname Bourniadakis (a combination of Bournia and a common Cretan surname ending - akis).

The family may have changed their surname to Bourniadakis to hide their real identity from the Ottomans in case they were fugitives, as this was a known practice.

Due to the Catastrophe of Asia Minor, the family returned from Asia Minor to Crete and then to Koroni, Pilos in Messinia where Emmanuil G. Bournias was born, and then to Kyrgia Drama, as many refugees from Asia Minor were sent to northern Greece by the government in that time.

Μπουρνιᾶ Σταυρίτσα χήρα τοῦ Γεωργίου τὸ γένος Βασιλ. Κυραβασιλείου	Κε'εμπέσιον - 'Αννέων	87629
Μπουρνιᾶς ἢ Βουρνιᾶς Δημ. τοῦ Ἰωάν.	,	63271

Image text translation:
Bournia Stavritsa, widow of Georgios, nee Vasil, (Vasilis) Karavasileiou, Kelebesion Anneon, file # 87629.

Image text translation:
Bournias or Vournias Dem. (Demetrios), son of Ioan. (Ioannis), Kelebesion Anneon, file # 63271.

The next image contains the same name recorded under "B" most likely as a cross-reference to the same application number.

Βουρνέλης Κυριᾶκος τοῦ Λεωνίδα	,	61485
Βουρνιᾶς ἢ Μπουρνιᾶς Δημ. τοῦ Ἰωάννου	Κε'εμπέσιον-'Αννέων	63271
Βουρνοβαλῆ ἢ Γκεριγκιώντη Μαγδαληνὴ τοῦ Ἰωάν.	Μαινεμένη-'Εφέσου	186117 Μ.

Image text translation:
Vournias or Bournias Dem. (Demetrios), son of Ioan. (Ioannis), Kelebesion Anneon, 63271.

I have linked these individuals to their ancestors on the main genealogical chart from the Vournias family chart.

Image Credit:
Υπουργείο Γεωργίας Επιτροπή Αποκατάστασης Προσφύγων Β.pdf, pp. 200.
Refugee List of Relatives from Asia Minor - Vournias.jpg
Υπουργείο Γεωργίας Επιτροπή Αποκατάστασης Προσφύγων Β.pdf, pp. 184 as 746.
Refugee List of Relatives from Asia Minor 1922.jpg

A copy of the Registry of Boys from the Municipality of Koroni, Pilos, Messinia.

Line #	Last name	first name	father	YOB	Location
16	Bourniadakis	Emmanouil	Georgios	1881	Koroni

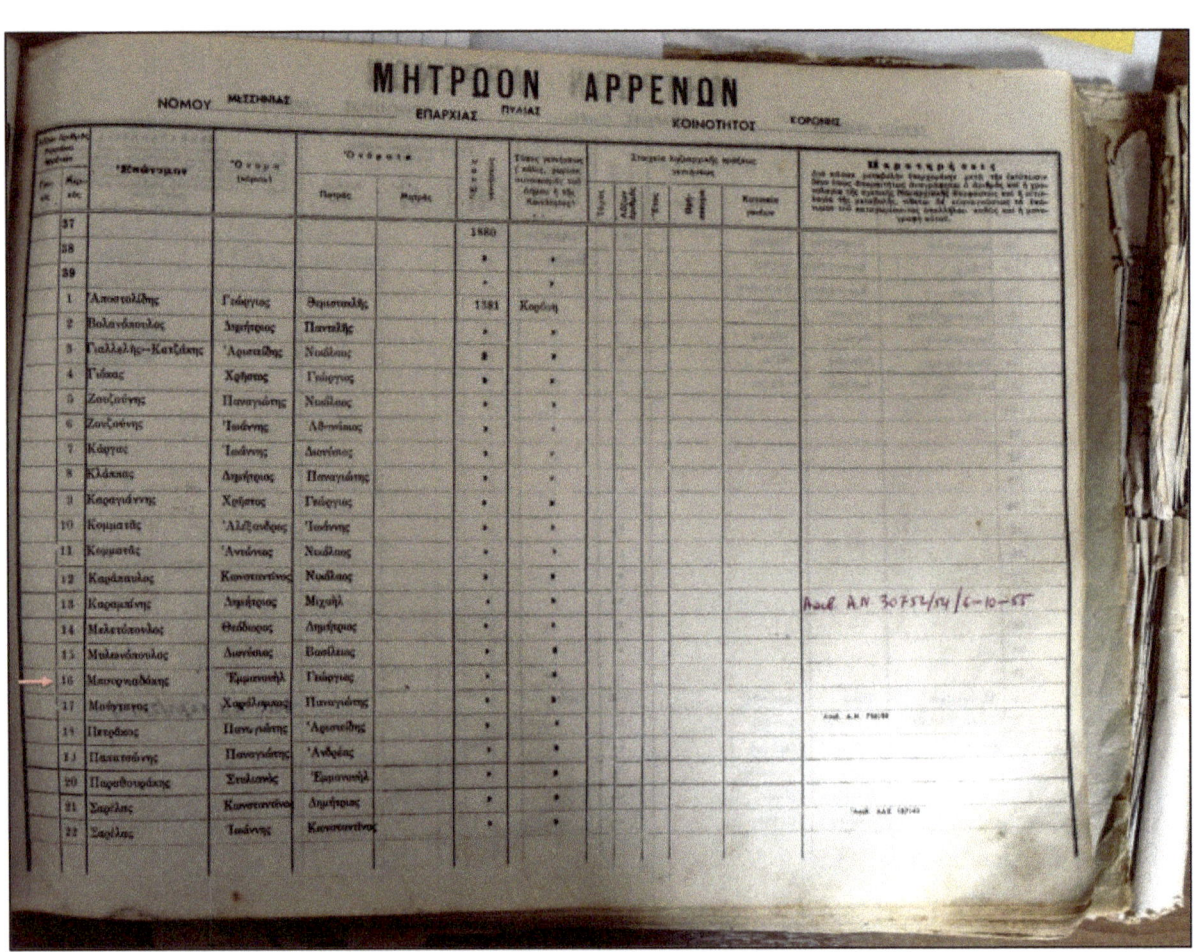

Image credit: Municipality of Koroni, Pilos, Messinia, P. Bournias

Gregorios A. Bournias (Γρηγόριος Α. Μπουρνιάς), 1833 - 1904

Gregorios A. Bournias, a son of Antonios A. Bournias born on Aegina in 1833.

From the main chart – right side by year of birth.

Gregorios A. Bournias lived on Hadrian Street in Athens, and was a Notary Public, a poet, and an archeologist. The building where he lived is a classical Greek building that exists today in the area of Plaka in Athens. His spouse was Areti, surname unknown and she was from Syros or Skyros. They had four children: Georgios 1856, Antonios 1851, Sophia 1875, and Pericles year unknown.

The following was extracted from the: Government Gazette official journal (ΦΕΚ), issue #75, dated March 15 1888, and **The Akropolis Newspaper**, issue #2079, dated Feb. 24, 1888.[145]

"In 1872 was appointed notary. In 1882, Mr. *Gregorios* Bournias *was supposedly involved in illegal* dealing regarding ancient coin collections after which he was barred as a notary public and provided his knowledge and personal services *to the* Verger library of ancient writings."

The court document alleges that he bought ancient coins that were ancient artifacts. Then he attempted to sell them to the museum at a higher price to make a profit. The museum claimed that he was illegally in possession of ancient coins that are considered artifacts based upon Greek government law and that he should not have attempted to make a profit from them.

After reading the information, I could not determine the exact facts of the case based on the way they were recorded and I remain uncertain as to what actually happened.
If I were to say that there was a possibility that the museum curator did not receive a kickback of the transaction based upon my knowledge and experience of how corrupt some people can be, then I would have to agree with the charges.

In the photograph, he is wearing two crosses, which were only given to people of notoriety. Unfortunately, due to the quality of the image, I am not able to see the crosses clearly and identify them in a reference book that I have about such medals.[146]
His home still exists today, and I have included photos of it later in this document.

---

[145] Bournias-Gregorios-Akropolis Newspaper issue 2079 dated Feb 24 1888 a36039.pdf
[146] ΓΡΗΓΟΡΙΟΣ_Α_ΜΠΟΥΡΝΙΑΣ-Gregorios-A-Bournias-1833-Aegina-72660-72660-1-PB.pdf

Apostolis A. Bournias (Αποστολής Α. Μπουρνιάς), 1835 - death unknown
Apostolis A. Bournias is also noted as Apostolos was born in Athens in 1835.

From the main chart – right side by year of birth.

Apostolis A. Bournias was a son of Antonios A. Bournias of 1788.

He was married to Vasiliki, surname unknown, born in 1841 on Evia and died in 1914 as is written at her grave.

They had ten children many of which became lawyers, members of parliament, and a Mayor.

Apostolos was a Greek lawyer, and became the foster father to Georgios E. Bournias of 1850, the son of Emmanuil of 1832 his brother.

Researcher note:
I have not included a photograph of the grave that is located at the 1st Cemetery of Athens out of respect for the family. This is where Vasiliki was buried but Apostolis may have been buried in the area of Karystos, Evia.

Othonos I. Bournias (Ὄθωνος Ι. Μπουρνιάς), 1844 - death unknown

During March 2018, while searching the archives of GAK Athens, I discovered an image of an election poster.

It shows an Othonos "Otto" I. Bournias born about 1844, and he was the son of Ioannis Bournias of 1799 and his mother was Elisavet (Ελισάβετ), surname and location unknown. Otto is the nickname for Othonos.

From the main chart – right side by year of birth.

Othonos Bournias, son of Ioannis, was a candidate for the position of Deputy Mayor of Athens as depicted and written in the image.

As many children were given the first names of royalty those days, his first name most likely coincides with that of King Otto of Greece.

I later found a record that Ioannis moved from Chios to Ermoupoli, Syros in 1822 it is most likely that Otto was born in Athens.

Although he campaigned for Mayor of Athens, peculiarly have not discovered any further information about him.

Image credit:
Internet / http://www.elia.org.gr

Image text translation:
Othonos Bournias
Candidate
Deputy Mayor of Athens

Demetrios L. Bournias (Δημήτριος Λ. Μπουρνιάς), 1861 - death unknown

Demetrios L. Bournias was born around 1861, and lived in the area of the Parish Agia Marina Kaloplytou, as noted in the Electoral list of the Municipality of Chios of 1930.

From the main chart – left side by year of birth.

He was married to Fotini, surname unknown, and they had nine children: Evangelia, Georgios, Angeliki Marika, Nikolaos, Ioannis, Chrostoforos, and Despina.

Demetrios was the son of Leonidas of 1810, the brother of Georgios, and my great grandfather Petros of 1829. The details of the clothing in this photograph are fantastic. Their clothing may have been the best that they had when they were photographed but the material and sewing stand out and exemplify the design of the period. This photograph provides a wonderful glimpse of the past from Chios, excluding the background from the photographic studio.

Historical photograph circa 1912 of the family

Image credit: Personal photograph of Leonidas G. Bournias

Michail A. Bournias (Μιχαήλ Α. Μπουρνιάς), 1866 - death unknown

Michail A. Bournias, born about 1866, death unknown, location unknown, a businessperson in commerce.

From the main chart – right side by year of birth.

I discovered this newspaper clipping that he owned a store in the area of Monastiraki.

The newspaper clipping translates as follows:

The first paragraph, three lines, is unrelated about someone looking for a job.

New Goods Store
Flannel & Stockings
Michail A. Bournias
137 Ermou Street
Athens

The new store is stocked with a variety of commercially sewn goods.

All types of undergarments, socks, stockings, underwear, laces, handkerchiefs, scarves, baptism garments including sizes for young children.

Although the address still exists in the area of Monastiraki, the store does not.

Image credit:
Internet / Facebook author unknown, newspaper unknown.

Georgios A. Bournias (Γεώργιος Α. Μπουρνιάς), 1870 - 1950
Georgios A. Bournias born 1870, the son of Apostolos of 1835.
From the main chart – right side by year of birth.

Georgios was a student of law became a lawyer, a reporter (his own newspaper under his wife's name as management, and a political minister.

George Bournias was the grandchild of Antonios Bournias of 1822, one of the two leaders of the revolutionary army during the revolution of Chios in 1822. He was inspired by the spirit of his grandfather.

He was originally introduced in 1886 to the Military Preparatory School of Corfu from where he graduated in 1888 as a sergeant.

His goal was to serve two years in the Army to acquire the right of entrance into the Military School from which after three years of studies he would acquire the rank of Lieutenant.

After the military, he became a lawyer, a journalist and published the newspaper Eleftheria (Freedom) with his spouse Maria A. Papaontelidi on Chios, and a member of parliament.

Maria A. Papaontelidi is noted as the owner, manager, and publisher of the newspaper. They had two daughters.

Image text translation:
"Georgios Bournias, Hero of the 20th of Dec. at Karfotou" (in the area of Kardamyla Chios)

Image Reference: Internet / Wikipedia / Βικιπαίδεια

The Military School postponed its operation of classes indefinitely, and so he departed from the ranks of the army and resumed his legal studies at the National University.

In the war of 1897, he served as a reserve sergeant in the second Battalion of new recruits. After six months of service, he was promoted by the commander Major Anastasios Stymfaliadis to the rank of an officer.

In 1912, he abandoned his commercial business in Smyrna Turkey, and came to Athens, where he asked to enlist at the age of 42.

At the military base of Katechaki in Athens, he became a volunteer sergeant of the Athens guild. He requested and received approval from the Ministry of Defense and gained permission to form and lead 75 voluntary army recruits that arrived on the island of Chios on the steamer [ship] "Elda" on December 13, 1912.

The above extract is well written and documented, composed by a distinguishable in social status and fiery enthusiasm: The young corporal Agamemnon Zachos a lawyer, John Grammenos from Izmir (the first stationmaster of Vrontados), the Chian captains Koufopantelis Constantine (who later became Mayor of Vrontados) and Leonidas Margaronis, Constantine Tsouros or Chademenoso, Miltiadis C. Lemos, Miltiadis Panag. Lemos, Evangelos Saliaris engineer Ioannis Chalkias sailor, Constantine Foros, student literature, Zannis Chrysovelonis a banker from Romania, Michael convenient merchant, Constantine Theotokas Chiotis a lawyer in Cairo, Giannaropoulos Michael a trader from Karystos, Ioannidis Themistocles, a lawyer the Limassol of Cyprus, Saralee Nikolaos, a merchant Karystos Tampakopoulos John of Smyrna, G. Vassilopoulos from Kefalonia, Panopoulos from Kefalonia, Kitrilakis from Kefalonia and Podimatas from Kefalonia.

By the persistent request of George Bournias, he was sent to Kardamyla in Chios and acted decisively in the Battle of Karfotou of December 20, 1912.[147]

During his call of duty, Georgios Bournias served in the Greek Army of 1912; he led a special group of Chiotan volunteers as freedom fighters and distinguished himself in the **Battle of Karfotou**.

From the book, Chios and Chiotans through the ages by Philippou L. Chrysovelonis, Athens 1938 (in Greek).

---

[147] Website reference in Greek with a synopsis of "The Battle of Karfotou," http://www.arxeion-politismou.gr/2020/02/maxi-tou-Karfotou-Xiou.html?spref=fb

Ioannis A. Bournias (Ιωάννης Α. Μπουρνιάς), 1877 - 1974
A Greek lawyer and a Member of Parliament (MP) in Evia.
From the main chart – right side by year of birth.

Ioannis A. Bournias was the son of Apostolos of 1835 born in Karystos, Evia.
He was married to Eleni Bournias 1894 - 1988.
He was buried in the First Cemetery of Athens on January 21, 1974.
They had a son Apostolos I. Bournias 1915 – 1988 and a daughter Maria birth unknown.

On February 27, 1895, he was served at the Faculty of Law of the University of Athens.

He created the legacy of the Kybelis G. Bournias* Foundation of Ioannis A. Bournias and Helen Bournia in memory of Apostolos I. Bournias 1915 - 1998 and Vasiliki Bournia and their offspring in Karystos Evia.

In the elections of 1910, he was elected deputy for the Independent Party in Evia for the first time and re-elected in the years 1912, 1915, 1917, 1928, 1932, 1936 and 1946.

Ioannis A. Bournias worked as a lawyer and served as Deputy Minister of Justice in 1932 in the government of Eleftherios Venizelos, as Minister of Justice and interim Minister of Agriculture, in the Greek government of Dimitrios Maximos, and was appointed Minister of Transportation, serving in that position from 27 January 1947 to February 1947.

Ioannis Bournias of Apostolis was born in Karystos in 1877. He studied law and practiced law. He joined the Independent Party (KF) in 1910, with which he became a politician and was elected member of parliament for Evia in the electoral contests of 1910, 1912 and May 1915, while he abstained from the elections of December 1915, agreeing with the decision of the party. He became a politician again in the elections of 1928 and was elected deputy of Karystia with the KF. He was re-elected Member of Parliament for Evia with the same party in 1932 and took over as Deputy Minister of Justice (5.6.1932-6.9.1932) and then Minister of Justice (6.9.1932-4.11.1932) in the government of Eleftherios Venizelos. In the elections of 1933 he governed in the province of Karystia with the KF without being elected, while in the elections of 1935 he abstained, joining the decision of the Venizelos faction. He became a politician in the elections of 1936 and was re-elected deputy of Evia with the KF.
After the war, Io. Bournias joined Stylianos Gonatas in the political crisis that broke out in the KF in the spring of 1945 and participated in the formation of the National Independent Party, with which he was elected MP for Evia in the 1946 elections and took over as Minister of Transport (27.1.1947 17.2.1947) in the seven-party government of Dimitrios Maximos. In the elections of 1950 he ran in the region of the former Municipality of Athens as an independent and in 1951 he ran, for the last time, in the region of Evia with the KF again without being elected. Ioannis Bournias passed away in January 1974.[148]

Researcher note: * I found no record of a Kybelis G. Bournias.

---

148 Curriculum Vitae of Greek MPs, 1946-1956 - Βιογραφικό Λεξικό Ελλήνων Βουλευτών, 1946-1956, https://greek-parliament-members.anavathmis.eu/%CE%BC%CF%80%CE%BF%CF%85%CF%81%CE%BD%CE%B9%CE%AC%CF%82-%CE%B9%CF%89%CE%AC%CE%BD%CE%BD%CE%B7%CF%82/

Pantelis P. Bournias (Παντελής Π. Μπουρνιάς), 1889 - 1976

Pantelis P. Bournias was born 1899 in Vrontados Chios, and died on February 2, 1976.

From the main chart – left side by year of birth.

The Electoral list of the Municipality of Chios for 1930 has the wrong year of birth for him but I have attained some of his records including the family status, marriage, death and military.

Pantelis P. Bournias was a quiet but stern individual, and he was my grandfather.
He liked cats, and played the Bouzouki. I included another photo of my grandparents in my dedication. Although he was a farmer, he served in three wars and later worked at the tannery factory nearby their home in Vrontados.

I believe that this photograph of my uncle Diamantis, my grandfather Pantelis P. Bournias, and my grandmother Zabella A. Varia working in the field behind their home in 1953 was taken by my father Ioannis P. Bournias.

Image credit:
P. Bournias

Unfortunately, I could never communicate with my grandparents during my trip to Greece in 1973, as I never learned the Greek language before moving to Greece.
I sometimes wonder what they would say if we could speak to each other now.

I felt lucky to be given the military record as the military archive informed me that records were available mainly regarding officers. Upon receiving the scanned copy of the document, they never informed me as to the rank my grandfather had or any other information.

The military record is written on very thin paper, so thin that you can see the writing on the next page, something like "Pergamenata Parchment Vellum or Interleaving tissue paper".

I did not include an image of the document, as the military archive required that I sign a non-disclosure. I believe that the handwriting by various military personnel on the document is enough to protect any secrets, as it is unintelligible to read.

Apart from the years of wars, I was able to decipher that he was wounded but could not the pertinent information or circumstances.

I believe that my grandfather was a quiet man because of what he may have experienced while in the military. I was fortunate to locate his military record. I did not know that he served in the Greek Army during three wars until I saw his military record.
The Second Balkan War of 1913, World War I of 1914, and the Greco-Turkish War (Asia Minor) of 1918. My father never mentioned it, and I was too young to think about the history of my family during the short time of my first visit to Chios.

His spouse was Zabella A. Varia (Ζαμπέλλα Α. Βαρία), born on Chios 1904 in Vrontados Chios, and died on November 9, 1981. They were married on July 5, 1928 at the church of Agios Panagias Erithianis. She was the daughter of Adamantios Varias (Αδαμάντιος Βαρίας) born 1874, profession fisherman, and his spouse Efterpi (Ευτέρπη), surname unknown, birth and location unknown. They had three children: Ioannis, Maritsa, and Diamantis.

I have partially researched my grandmother's side of the family but discovered that they may have originated from northern Greece.

I think that anyone who reads this, and especially those who have children, should consider telling them about their earlier life and that of their parents.

Researcher note:
Translation of vital records by P. Bournias
Translation of the Certificate of Family Status - Bournias Pantelis 1889.pdf
Translation of Certificate of Death for Pantelis P Bournias 1976 .pdf
Translation of Certificate of Marriage for Pantelis P Bournias 1928.pdf

Leonidas A. Bournias (Λεωνίδας Α. Μπουρνιάς), 1908 - 1997

Leonidas A. Bournias was born in Athens in May 9, 1908*, and died in June 1997.[149]

From the main chart – left side by year of birth.

Born on Chios, he studied at the Law School of the University of Athens and initially worked as a lawyer.[150]

In 1930 he obtained a law degree and married a distant cousin **Vasiliki (Vasoula) K. Bournia** born 1912 and died 2006, the daughter of the lawyer **Konstantinos A. Bournias born 1864**.

He was a lawyer and a Greek politician and was a political minister and a Member of Parliament (MP) nine times on Chios.
He served in the Greek government as a political minister of Chios on different parties during:
(Democratic Socialist Party: 1950-1951,
Greek Rally [Ελληνικός Συναγερμός]: 1951-1952, MP 1956-1958, 1958-1961, 1961-1963, 1963-1964, 1964 -1967, and New Democracy: 1974-1981).
In 1932, he was appointed special secretary of the Minister of Justice, Ioannis Bournias.

Image credit: Internet / Wikipedia / Βικιπαίδεια

In 1935, he joined the newly formed Democratic Party of George Papandreou.
In 1946, he became director of the political bureau of the Democratic Socialist Party.
Secretary General of the Ministry of Interior (1947) and Merchant Marine (1952 - 1956).
He continued in 1961 with the EPE in 1974, in 1978, and with New Democracy.
In 1981, he announced his retirement from active political life, but remained a Member of the European Parliament.

Leonidas Bournias wrote the book **"The Greek Merchant Marine" (1950)**. This work is considered an international standard as it relates to shipping on a worldwide basis.

I met Leonidas Λ. Bournias during one of my trips to Chios with my father around 1985, and at his law office in Omonia Square in Athens.

---

149 * His date of birth has two different dates, reason unknown.
150 Wikipedia Λεωνίδας Α. Μπουρνιάς,
https://el.wikipedia.org/wiki/%CE%9B%CE%B5%CF%89%CE%BD%CE%AF%CE%B4%CE%B1%CF%82_%CE%9C%CF%80%CE%BF%CF%85%CF%81%CE%BD%CE%B9%CE%AC%CF%82

Apostolis I. Bournias (Αποστολής Ι. Μπουρνιάς), 1915 - 1998

He was born in Athens in 1815 and died Feb. 14, 1998.[151]
Apostolis I. Bournias is also noted as Apostolos.

From the main chart – right side by year of birth.

Apostolis Bournias was the son of Ioannis "Yangos" A. Bournias born 1872.

He was a Greek lawyer wrote about 150 legal and political studies, articles, and even literary works and poems using pseudonyms: Emil, Aimos, etc. or simply A.I.M., in Greek and written in various languages of foreign magazines and newspapers.

He initially worked as counsel to public companies.

In the elections of 1964, he was elected Political Minister (MP) of Evia.

He was a member of the Greek Institute for International and Foreign Law, Comparative Company Law Paris, the Evia Studies Company and the Literary Society of "Parnassos". He represented Greece repeatedly at international legal conferences.

He was buried at the First Cemetery of Athens.

I met with his spouse, but she did not provide any additional information.

Some legal works of Apostolis I. Bournias in Greek are (titles translated into English):[152]
- The concept of the office
- Beyond justice, injustice ends
- Transferable nature of possession by the Civil Code (1947)

---

151 Wikipedia Απόστολης Ι. Μπουρνιάς
https://el.wikipedia.org/wiki/%CE%91%CF%80%CF%8C%CF%83%CF%84%CE%BF%CE%BB%CE%BF%CF%82_%CE%9C%CF%80%CE%BF%CF%85%CF%81%CE%BD%CE%B9%CE%AC%CF%82
152 Biography and books
https://el.wikipedia.org/wiki/%CE%91%CF%80%CF%8C%CF%83%CF%84%CE%BF%CE%BB%CE%BF%CF%82_%CE%9C%CF%80%CE%BF%CF%85%CF%81%CE%BD%CE%B9%CE%AC%CF%82

Loukas D. Bournias (Λουκας Δ. Μπουρνιας), 1922 - 1942

Loukas D. Demetrios Bournias was born 1922 in the area of Vrontados Chios.

From the main chart – left side by year of birth.

He was executed by the Nazis during the occupation of Chios during WWII according a declassified CIA, OSS collection document regarding Nazi War Crimes and Atrocities under the heading AEGEAN ISLANDS stating that he was arrested and executed in Chios in April 1942 for possessing a weapon.[153]

During WWII, the Germans placed restrictions on the islanders and, one of the restrictions was the possession of weapons, as well as a curfew.
I spoke with his niece Maria Spyrakis-Karnieris, her mother was Katina D. Bournia.
Maria informed me that her uncle Loukas was thinking about escaping from the island, so Loukas and a few others thought that they could get off the island using a small boat.

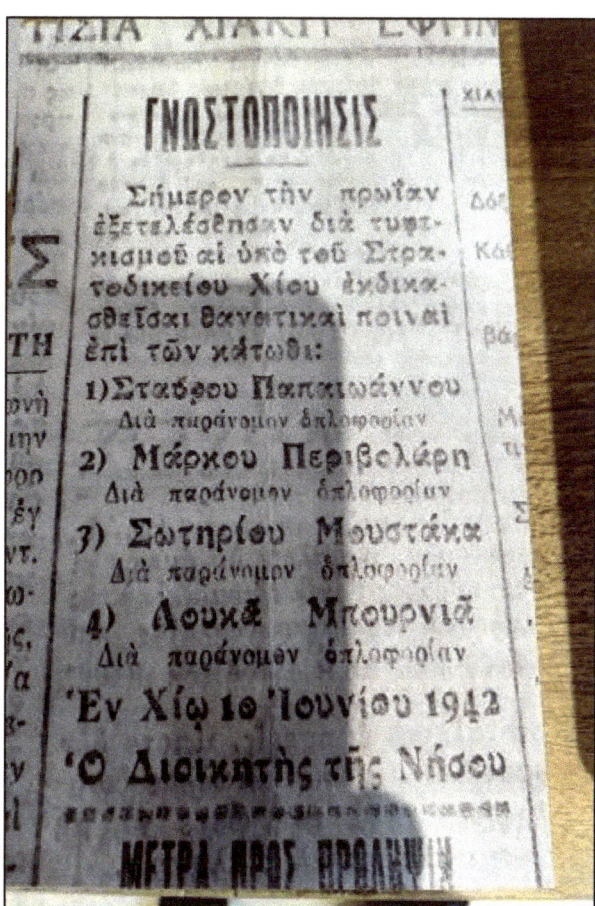

Chios, 10 June 1942, The Commander of the island

They took their hunting shotguns with them but while trying to get the boat past the shore waves, the boat was pushed back toward the beach. The Germans discovered them trying to escape and caught them with their weapons.
This sealed their fate as the Germans executed them.

The newspaper clipping translates as follows:
Announcements
This morning, today they executed by rifle under the military court in Chios (under the German's) for the penalty of death the following mentioned below:
1) Stavros Papaioannos for the illegal possession of a weapon
2) Markos Pervolaris for the illegal possession of a weapon
3) Sotirios Moustakas for the illegal possession of a weapon
4) Loukas Bournias for the illegal possession of a weapon

Image credit: Internet / Facebook, author and newspaper unknown.

---

153 Document id 1315, Atrocities #42, "CIA-GREEK HELLENIC INFORMATION BULLETIN_0008.pdf," January 1944, page 17, actual page number is page 13.

Ioannis P. Bournias (Ιωάννης Π. Μπουρνιάς), 1930 - 2021
Ioannis P. Bournias a.k.a. Ιωάννης Π. Μπουρνιάς a.k.a. John Bournias

From the main chart – left side by year of birth.

Ioannis P. Bournias was born in Vrontados Chios December 2, 1930. He died on 28 March 2021 in Corinth, Greece due to COVID19. His parents were Pantelis P. Bournias and Zabella A. Varia.

He completed grammar school and the equivalent of about the tenth grade. He took a job as a sailor aboard a ship and sailed as far as China and the USA. When he reached New York City, he never returned to the ship, he "jumped ship," as did thousands of others, and entered New York illegally without any immigration documents around 1950.

He met and married Maria C. Martinez, born Sept. 1924 Mayaguez Puerto Rico, married Nov. 1951, died Dec. 1996 Manhattan New York and attained his American citizenship.

They had two sons, my brother and myself the author.

Some years after, they divorced and he married his second wife.

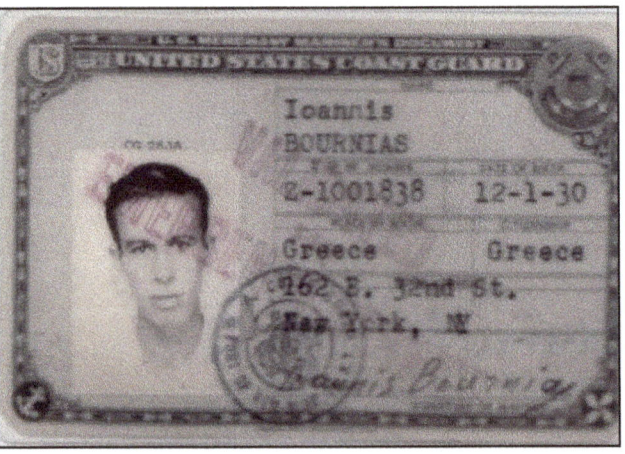

He once told me that he was supposed to finish school to become a ship captain but that he never wanted to be a sailor. Even though he didn't want to be a sailor, ironically he managed to work shortly with the U.S. Coast Guard.

After that, he worked at a restaurant in Brooklyn N. Y. as a dishwasher and learned to cook. He then worked as a short order cook until he saved enough money to open a grocery store in Harlem.

JOHN BOURNIAS CLEANS UP THE MESS
Lenox Ave. Grocer Found His Store a Shambles
Journal-American Photo by Sheldon Gottesman

His first grocery store was on 126 street and Lenox Avenue.[154]

From that one, he then opened a second store on 136 street and 7th Avenue.

The store was destroyed during the Harlem Riots in 1964[155] but he repaired it and re-opened it shortly after.

Around 1980, he sold the businesses and ventured into the Taxi and Limousine business until he returned to Greece in 1990.

Image credit: Journal - American Photo Sheldon Gottesman, New York, July 1964.

On the right, a photograph of his first store in the magazine The Voice, 1964.

Image credit: The Voice, Vol. 2, Number 6, August 1964, New York City.

---

[154] https://en.wikipedia.org/wiki/Lenox_Avenue
[155] https://en.wikipedia.org/wiki/Harlem_riot_of_1964

Maritsa P. Bournia(s) (Μαρίτσα Π. Μπουρνιά) 1933 - 2022

Maritsa P. Bournia(s) a.k.a. Maritsa I. Vagia(s) was born in Vrontados Chios in Sept. 1933.

From the main chart – left side by year of birth.

Maritsa was a kindhearted and loving person who lived the traditional Greek life of a woman brought up to marry, have children, and care for her home. Maritsa was a typical Greek homemaker, taking care of her family, an excellent cook, and she liked to joke. She always tried to do what she could for everyone.

She passed away on Feb. 26, 2022 at a hospital in Queens, New York.
Her parents were Pantelis P. Bournias and Zabella A. Varia.

Maritsa married Ioannis Vagias, a ship captain from Chios. Ioannis Vagias a.k.a. John Vagias died in Queens, New York. They had two daughters.

She worked in the family dry-cleaning business and as a seamstress for many years.

Maritsa spoke Greek and never made a great effort to learn English comfortably even though she lived in the Astoria area of Queens for over 30 years.

One of the best deserts that Maritsa made was the Greek Tsoureki a sweet bread, made during Easter.

Maritsa, on the left as a young woman in the central square of Hora the capital of Chios.

I believe that she may have been around 16 years of age in this photograph.

Image credit:
P. Bournias, family photo,
Maritsa P. Bournia about 1949.

Captain Adamantios P. Bournias (Αδαμάντιος Π. Μπουρνιάς), 1936 - 2001

Adamantios P. Bournias a.k.a. Diamantis P. Bournias, born in Vrontados in 1936. He died in December 2001 in New York and returned to his final resting place on Chios.

From the main chart – left side by year of birth.

His name Adamantios in its shorter form is Diamantis that translates to Diamond in English, which is what other Greek Diaspora use as a first name.
His parents were Pantelis P. Bournias and Zabella A. Varia.
He was married with three children.

Adiamantios as a young man, attended grammar school and high school in Chios and then continued his studies to become a ship captain. Adiamantis enjoyed Greek dancing and good conversation.

He was a extremely serious person and I believe that was due to the nature of his work commanding the crew of cargo ships and the responsibilities of the lives of his crew.

When I was around the age of 10, I remember going with my father to the seaports in New Jersey to meet and pickup my uncle when he disembarked. He gave me a tour of the ship from the top to bottom including the engine room where I saw and heard the roar of the huge ship engines, something unforgettable.

Image credit: Captain Adamantios P. Bournias, P. Bournias, family photo 1961.

Bournias from Spartounta to Koroni, Kalamata, and Texas

I researched many individuals and found that they were originally from Spartounta and Evia, and that many ventured into Asia Minor. During the period leading to and after the Catastrophe of Asia Minor, many of them re-settled in the areas outside of Koroni including Kompi (Κόμποι, παλαιότερα και ως η Κόμπη), Charokopio (Χαροκοπιό), and Vounaria (Βουνάρια), Messinia. Vounaria, Kompi, Charokopio are located in the area of Kalamata in the curvature on the map with Koroni facing east to the Gulf of Messinia.

The villages in this region are on hillsides and are plentiful with floricultural. The land is a similar terrain as that in the area of Spartounta and is used as farmland. Many families still have homes in these areas while others moved to the center of Kalamata or other places.

Attempting to verify and connect the individuals from Spartounta, Texas, and others that I have not been able to link what I have named **the chart of Texas** to my **main chart** but these two charts are currently the largest in my research. Although I have recorded family members from Spartounta from 1815 with a gap to 1850, it is an ongoing challenge.

Although I have discovered various individuals dating to 1815, I cannot link them without further information. The information provided by other individuals related to the families of Spartounta have conflicts that cannot be verified or crosschecked with existing historical information. Sadly, many of the family elders that might have provided more clues are now deceased.

I have not been able to attain birth or family status records through the Greek municipal services, not for the lack of trying, even though the individuals are deceased. This would normally provide the verification necessary to justify linking them with their ancestors.

Some of the information from the electoral lists has errors regarding the year of birth for individuals, as well as misspelling of the surnames.
As an example, I have received information regarding Stamatios Bournias, born about 1830 to 1840 that conflict in the difference in years between the births of the next born child. I have listed information regarding Stamatios and Stylianos that I found on the next page. Another conflict occurs with Stylianos Bournias regarding the middle initial, the dates of birth, and spouses.

There are also conflicts in the father's names of Georgios or Gregoris (Γεώργιος ή Γρηγόρης) as both have the same middle initial of the Greek gamma "Γ" for some individuals.

All of these discrepancies have prevented the completion of the chart of the Bournias family from Spartounta to connect to the main chart, including the fact that many to areas of Asia Minor and were then relocated or moved to the areas of Messinia, or Drama, while others emigrated to Canada, Australia, and the USA.

Translation of the Electoral List Municipality Chios 1930

I am providing a selection of names of individuals pertaining to the families of Spartounta, their fathers, and years of birth as noted from the electoral lists of the archives but a more complete list of individuals are displayed toward the end of this book.

#*	Spartountos 1928 Electoral List (sorted by YOB, then grouped by father)						
	surname	first name	father	YOB (abt.)	age**		
19	Bournias	Mihail	Stylianos	1840	89	Μιχαήλ	Στυλιανός
20	Bournias	Nikolaos	Stylianos	1846	83	Νικόλαος	Στυλιανός
20	Bournias	Nikolaos	Stylianos	1883	46	Νικόλαος	Στυλιανός
19	Bournias	Mihail	Stylianos	1889	40	Μιχαήλ	Στυλιανός
23	Bournias	Stylianos	Stamatios	1863	66	Στυλιανός	Σταμάτιος
23	Bournias***	Stylianos	Stamatios	1866	63	Στυλιανός	Σταμάτιος
	* line number from electoral list						
	** approximate age = 1928 - year of birth or age						
	*** There is a probability that this individual is from a different grandfather.						

Another analysis of the Electoral List of Chios for 1930 is shown in the pages below.

Stamatios Bournias (Σταμάτιος Μπουρνιάς), 1830 to 1840

From the chart of Texas and Messinia.

According to another source, Stamatios Bournias was born about 1830 to 1840, and died about 1913. He was married to Maria Heila (Μαρία Χειλά) who was probably from Pirama or Kourounia (Πυραμά ή Κουρούνια) Chios.[156]

I have not discovered any information from any of the archive materials pertaining to this person although the first name is common to those from Spartounta.

Based on the information from the above table and using an approximate average number of years between births, I can only estimate that the father Stamatios Bournias was born about 1838 to 1841 based on the births of Stylianos shown above using an average difference between births of about twenty-five (25) years.

The record has the same sequence number and therefore it is unclear as to whether or not this is the same person or if there are two individuals from different grandparents.

---

[156] Κουρουνια Ιστορία (Kourounia History), "Kourounia Travel into its History" by Christos Apostolou, Athens, Mar 22, 2013, page 43. See https://issuu.com/christosapostolou3/docs/

Stylianos S. Bournias (Στυλιανός Σ. Μπουρνιάς) a.k.a. Stanley A. Bournias

Stylianos S. Bournias is a pivotal individual for both the left and right sides of the chart of Texas and Messinia.

From the chart of Texas and Messinia.

Stylianos S. Bournias may be known as Stelios – Στέλιος.
One of the names in the table above is Stylianos S. Bournias, the "S" for Stamatios.

I first learned about Stylianos A. Bournias of 1830 and Panagiotis Bournias of 1842 from the Bournias-Kousakis Memorial Site and then from communications with Billie Marion Sneed Bournias of Texas who was kind enough to share additional information.[157]

Although I documented him on the chart of Texas and Messinia, I had reservations about the dates of birth due to information from the electoral lists and submission of information by multiple individuals.
I have noted his birth as 1840 or 1846 based upon the births of the next generation.

As an example, I received the following from Billie Marion Sneed Bournias wrote in a document that Stylianos Bournias was Stanley A. Bournias, based on verbal information from a relative. Of course, Stylianos "adopted" the name Stanley in English when he emmigrated to the USA but the middle initial of "A" does not conform to the father's name Stamatios in accordance with the time-period.
She also noted that the name of his spouse was Joanna surname unknown, which was most likely changed from Ioanna to Joanna after immigrating to the USA.

I received information from two other persons about Stylianos S. Bournias noting a year of birth of 1871 and another noting 1866 or 1871.
One source states that he died in 1915 while the other in 1949.
The second source of individuals noted that the name of his spouse was Maria Kassou.
According to the Bournias-Kousakis Memorial web site, he may have married 2 times.
Again, this created a conflict, as the years of birth for children on both charts appear to overlap.

The second group of persons did not notice that the first sibling from their information was about 1880. This birth could be possible in that time-period at the mother's age of fourteen assuming 1866 but not for 1871. Everything must be cross-checked.

No fault can be assigned to anyone attempting to document Greek ancestry because it is confusing and many find themselves having to accept that it cannot be completed.
I believe there are more records in the municipalities that have not been released, and will precariously deteriorate before anyone is allowed to see them but these are the consequences of inefficiency and apathy of government.

---

157 Dates of birth were recorded by Billie Marion Sneed Bournias based on verbal discussion with a relative, the documentation was recorded as Descendants of Stellianos aka Stanley Bournias.

While writing this book, I realized that the Bournias families of the northern areas of Chios, Pirama, Parparia, Spartounda, were prosperous as they propagated and raised many children.

The Bournias families of Spartounda were not rich, they were farmers living and working in a toilsome environment for their own survival, planting their crops on mountainous slopes, wherever plots of land allowed, and became the foundation for many of the families that exist today.

While visiting Spartounda in September 2016, I took some photographs of the area. Here is one to show what the environment looks like. I was not able to photograph a cave on the mountain above the village. This is where many from the area hid during the revolutionary war.

The village of Spartounta hidden in the hills and greenery.

Image credit: P. Bournias, September 2016

Researcher note:
The area of Spartounta is also problematic for research verification due to the lack of documentation and because many of the family members moved to Asia Minor and returned through Crete to Messinia, Chios, Athens or elsewhere.

Pantelis G. Bournias (Παντελής Γ. Μπουρνιάς), 1860

A booklet from Pantelis G. Bournias, born in Spartounta Chios.

From a chart of Spartounta.

Pantelis G. Bournias (Παντελής Γ. Μπουρνιάς) born about 1860 wrote about the local folk songs of Spartounta that was published in Chios in 1995.

This is an image that I received from Anna Katos on FB regarding her great grandfather. From this booklet, I was able to extract some family member names from Spartounta.

Anna Katos noted:
He was unable to read and right but he spoke in poetic verse and was an accomplished musician.

He was well known for his witty poems that in 1995 a book was produced that highlighted his poems.

He was a poet a musician, and he played the Lute.

Pantelis was married to Anna Kattou who was born in 1887.

Front cover translation:
IOANNOU MARKELLOU POULI, PRIEST VICAR OF CHALKI - CHIOS

PANTELIS G. BOURNIAS
AND HIS SONGS
FROM SPARTOUNTA CHIOS
CHIOS 1995

Photo of the church (Parish)
THE PROPHET ILIAS,
SPARTOUNTA CHIOS

Image credit: Anna Katos

Lineage of the Bournias Ancestry chart of Texas and Messinia

A synopsis of the family as depicted on the <u>left side</u> of the genealogical chart ordered by dates of birth.

First Tier

Stylianos S. Bournias
    Spouse Ioanna or Maria Kassos (in Greek Kassou for the female gender)

Second Tier – BOURNIAS_Texas_GR_1

Peter S. "Gus" Bournias
    Spouse Styliania Vassiliki

George S. Bournias
    Spouse Calliope Hilas
        Panagiotis G. Bournias
        Alexandros G. Bournias
        Kyriaki G. Bournia(s)

James Stanley "Jim" S. Bournias
    Spouse Vasiliki N. "Bessie" Tsirolia
        Stanley James N. Bournias
        Nola "Nellie" N. Bournias

Nicholas "Andrew" S. Bournias
    Spouse Helen Kandis (Capogiannis)
        Peter N. Bournias
        Jane N. Bournias
        Stanley N. Bournias
        William N. "Billy" Bournias

Michael S. Bournias
    Spouse Paraskevi Kassos (in Greek Kassou for the female gender)
        Mary M. Bournia(s) .a.k.a. Mary Filipos

Asimine "Minnie" S. Bournia(s) *
    Spouse Christos Kamarinopoulus (Kamas)

Ruby or Roubini or Roubinia S. Bournia(s) *

Mary S. Bournia(s) *
    Spouse Haravopoulos, first name unknown

Figelia S. Bournia(s) *

* Names unordered due to unknown dates of birth.

The children of Stylianos S. Bournias a.k.a. Stanley A. Bournias were:

Peter S. "Gus" Bournias, (first name may have been for Panagiotis),
b. about 1878 in Messinia, Greece, married Styliania Vassiliki.
His nickname was "Gus" otherwise it would mean that his father was Georgios. [158]

George S. Bournias, (Georgios) b.1880 Harakopio, Messinia, Greece
b. about 1862 per 1910 census in Brenham, Washington Co., TX., USA.

He sailed from Kalamata on SS Athinai on 30 Sept 1913, and arrived in NY 20 Oct 1913. The ship manifest shows George (age 45) profession clerk, destination Brenham, TX., USA, along with Vassiliki Tsirolia (age 22) destination Brenham, TX., USA, and travelled with her sister Styliani Tsirolia (age 18).

Married **Calliope Hila**(s) (Καλλιόπη Χίλα), dates unknown.

One of the charts for Spartouda Chios shows an individual as Calliope Hilas and a Maria Hilas.
The Hilas family were from the area of Parparia Chios as evidenced by an Electoral Catalog of 1928 for Chios.

Their children were: Panagiotis, Alexandros, and Kyriaki.

James "Jim" S. Bournias, (Demetrios) born 26 Oct 1882 in Kambos, Messinia, Greece and emigrated to the USA about 1902.
Married Vasiliki N. "Bessie" Tsirolia on 31 Oct 1913.
He died 16 June 1972 in Houston, Harris County, TX., USA.
Bessie was born 14 May 1893 in Koroni (Κορώνη) Messinia, Greece,
She emigrated to the USA 1913, and died 1 Jan 1963 in Washington Co., TX., USA.
They are both buried in Brenham, TX., USA.

Their children were:
  a) Stanley James N. Bournias, b. 29 Nov 1914 in Washington Co., TX., USA, d. 21 Sep 1968 in Harris Co., TX., USA., married Voula Zarafonetis, b. 19 Nov 1923 in Corsicana, Navarro Co., TX., USA, d. 29 June 1989 in Harris Co., TX., USA. Both are buried at Veteran Cemetery in Houston, TX., USA. They had two children.

  b) Nola "Nellie" (Annoula) N. Bournias, b. about 1917, Washington Co., TX., USA, d. 26 June 1964 in Harris Co., TX., USA. She married Author G. Dowdy (b. 15 Oct 1926) around 1947. They had one known child.

---

[158] His name "Peter" was most likely Panagiotis or Pantelis, and although his nickname is "Gus," it is not associated with Konstantinos.

Nicholas "Andrew" S. Bournias, (Nikolaos)

Nicholas S. Bournias was also known as Andrew (possibly from Andreas) Bournias. According to the information from Koroni, Messinia, Greece, he was born 15 Oct 1886 in Koroni, Messinia, Greece although his WWI Draft Card showed that he was born 15 Oct 1884. He died 6 Jan 1942 in Victoria, TX., USA. Nick married Helen Kandis (Capogiannis) about 1914, she was b. 25 Oct 1893, d. 29 Mar 1965 in Victoria, TX., USA. There is a possibility that he was previously married but no information is available to verify this.

Image credit: Billie Marion Sneed Bournias

Their children were:
a) Peter N. Bournias, b.11 Oct 1915 Brenham, TX, d. 11 Oct 2009 Bexar Co., TX., USA. Peter married Estell Callins b abt. 1915 in Greece. They had two children.
b) Jane N. Bournias, b. 25 Aug 1917 Brenham, TX., d. 28 July 1999, 1930 Census age 12, 1992 U. S. Pub. Records 802 N Craig St., Victoria, TX., USA.
c) Stanley N. Bournias, b. 3 June 1919, d. 29 Apr 2003 Victoria, TX., USA., married about 1947 Matina "Tina" Kousakis. Matina "Tina" Kousakis, b. 11 Dec 1921, d. 23 Apr 2005 in Victoria, TX., USA. They had four children.
d) William N. "Billy" Bournias, b. 1 Jan 1921 East Molene, Illinois, USA, d. 1 Dec 1991 Victoria, TX., USA. WWII enlistment 22 Sept 1942 in Victoria, TX., USA.

Michael S. Bournias, (Mihalis) b. 1889, Chios, Greece, d. 22 May 1998, age 109.
Married Paraskevi Kassos and they had one child Mary M. Bournia(s) with the surname Filipos.

Asimine "Minnie" S. Bournia(s), (Ασημένια) b. 15 June 1891, Vounaria, Messinia, Greece, (Ticket #8695 National Steam Navigation Ct. LTD of Greece) , d. 1958 in Baynard, Nebraska at a family gathering. Minnie married 21 July 1917 in Brenham to Christos Kamarinopoulus (Kamas) (b. 14 Dec 1895 in Greece, d. 1956 Nebraska, USA). According to a ship manifest, Christos Kamas was born 1884 in Sparta, which correlates in age with Asiminie and arrived in New York in 1934. They had eight children.

Ruby or Roubini or Roubinia S. Bournia(s), dates unknown
Unknown and unusual name in Greece, most likely female, it appears that the name maybe of Genovese origin or as reference to the gem stone.

Mary S. Bournia(s), (Maria) dates unknown, married a Haravopoulos (Χαραβόπουλος).

Figelia S. Bournia(s), dates unknown.
Figelia was most likely a female due to "a" ending, unknown and unusual name in Greece. The name Figalia was an ancient Arcadian city in the area of Zacharo, Elias, and Peloponnese.

James S. Bournias and Nicholas S. Bournias opened a business named **Candy Kitchen**, located on the corner of East Alamo Avenue and South St. Charles Street Brenham, Texas, where they made homemade ice cream and candy.

The Candy Kitchen operated in downtown Brenham, Texas from the 1920's into the 1960's.

Image credit: Nick S. Bournias, 16 Jul. 2006, via email.

Lineage of the Bournias Ancestry chart of Texas and Messinia

A synopsis of the family as depicted on the <u>right side</u> of the genealogical chart ordered by dates of birth.

First Tier

Panagiotis Bournias
  Spouse Eleni Maria Dareiotaki

Second Tier – BOURNIAS_Texas_GR_2

Georgios P. Bournias
  Spouse Angelina Halvatsioti
    Panagiotis, a child that died
    Anna G. Bournias
    Eleni G. Bournias
    Thanasis (Athanasio) G. Bournias
    Ioannis G. Bournias
    Anastasio "Tasos" G. Bournias
    Sophia G. Bournias
    Panagiotis G. Bournias

Demetra P. Bournia(s)
  Spouse Petros Balsounis
  Spouse Balasis or Valasis

William Pete "Bill" Bournias
  Spouse Evgenia "Virginia" Pontiki(s)
    Fannie W. Bournias
    Helen Elaine W. Bournias
    Athanasia or Anastasia "Tacia" W. Bournias
    Sam Bill W. Bournias, Sr.
    Panayiota "Teetsa" W. Bournias
    Bessie W. Bournias

Evgenia P. "Vangelio or "Vieno" Bournia(s)
  Spouse Panagiotis Mthiopoulos a.k.a. Peter Mathos

Konstantinos P. "Gus" Bournias
  Spouse Margaret Kandis
    Peter G. Bournias
    Mary G. Bournias
    Sam "Gus" G. Bournias
    James "Gus" "Jim" G. Bournias
    Nick G. Bournias

Efthymia P. Bournia(s)
    Spouse Panagiotaras, first name unknown

Fotis a.k.a. Frank P. "Fotis" Bournias
    Spouse Regina "Virginia" Valko
        Helen P. Bournias
        Nicoletta "Edith" P. Bournias
        Peter P. Bournias
        Athena "Edna" P. Bournias
        Larry P. Bournias
        Nicholas P. Bournias

Anastasios P. "Ernest" Bournias
    Spouse Katerini Palas
        Athanasia or Anastasia A. Bournias

Panagiotis Bournias (Παναγιώτης Μπουρνιάς), 1842 - 1920

Panagiotis Bournias, father unknown, born about 1842, and his spouse Eleni Maria Dareiotaki, birth and location unknown, from the area of Koroni, Messinia Greece.

From the chart of Texas and Messinia – right side by year of birth.

I was not able to find any vital records for Panagiotis Bournias but found some of his relatives.

Whether he was born on Chios or in Messinia is unknown and as records are not centralized, they can only be located by reading documents.

The first relative that I spoke with was Panagiotis G. Bournias, one of his grandchildren.

Panagiotis G. Bournias introduced me to his niece Irene Frangou.

They informed me that Panagiotis Bournias was born about 1842, as they did not have any of his vital records. Then they provided me with a photograph, date unknown, of him and his wife Eleni Maria Dareiotaki who was from the area of Koroni Messinia based on my research.

Image credit: Irene Frangou

I believe that this family originated from Spartounda, Chios based on the commonness of the first name of Panagiotis.

The children of Panagiotis Bournias and Eleni Maria Dareiotaki were:

Name in Greek	Name Latinized	Year of birth and death
Γεώργιος Π. Μπουρνιάς	Georgios P. Bournias	b. abt. 1880, d. 1944
Δήμητρα Π. Μπουρνιά	Demetra P. Bournia	Unknown
Ευάγγελος Π. Μπουρνιάς	Evangelos a.k.a. William Pete "Bill" Bournias *	b. 1883, d. 1951
Ευγενία Π. Μπουρνιά	Evgenia P. Bournia or "Vangelio or "Vieno" Bournia	b. abt. 1880 or 1884, d. 1950
Κωνσταντίνος Π. Μπουρνιάς	Konstantinos P. "Gus" Bournias	b. 1885, d. 1974
Ευθυμία Π. Μπουρνιά	Efthymia P. Bournia	Unknown
Φώτης Π. Μπουρνιάς	Fotis a.k.a. Frank P. "Fotis" Bournias	b. 1891, d. 1972
Αναστάσιος Π. Μπουρνιάς	Anastasios P. "Ernest" Bournias	b. 1893, d. 1925

Demetra P. Bournia(s), dates unknown, married Petros Balsounis, dates unknown. They divorced, dates unknown. She married, dates unknown, a Balasis or Valasis who was from an area outside of Koroni, Messinia, Greece.
Demetra P. Bournia and her second spouse had two children, Antonios, and Georgios.

Evgenia P. "Vangelio or "Vieno" Bournia(s), b. abt. 1880 or 1884, d. 1950 Charakopio, Messinia, Greece.
She married Panagiotis Mathiopoulos a.k.a. Peter Mathos, b. 15 Aug. 1874, d. 1 Jun. 1919 or 1921, and later married in Oct. 1923 Mr. Perivolarakis a.k.a. Thomas Pappas, b. Aug. 1874, d. June 1919.

Their children were:
a) Ruby "Rubini" Mathos, b. 5 Feb. 1903 or 1905 Charakopio, Messinia, Greece, d. 22 Oct 1987 Bridgeport, Nebraska, USA.
b) Irene Mathos, b. abt. 1908 Charakopio, Messinia, Greece, died in California, USA.
c) Two children, names unknown, from the second marriage.

Efthymia P. Bournia(s), dates unknown. She married a Panagiotaras (Παναγιωταράς).

Researcher note:
The above names are unordered as dates of birth unknown.

* Evangelos is also known as Vangelis, and this name is commonly translated to William with a nickname of Bill or Billy.

Georgios P. Bournias (Γεώργιος Π. Μπουρνιάς), 1880 –1944

From the chart of Texas and Messinia – right side by year of birth.

Georgios P. Bournias was the first son of Panagiotis Bournias, and as the first-born, he was entitled to inherit the small family farm and house.

He was born about 1880 in Messinia, Greece and married Angeliki Halvatsioti (Αγγελίκη Χαλβατσιώτη), born about 1886, died about 1958; they were married around 1913 or 1914. Georgios P. Bournias died from consumption in March 1944, aged 63, in Harakopio, Messinia.

Georgios and Angeliki had eight children. The children were Panagiotis, Anna, Eleni, Athanasios (Thanasis), Ioannis, Anastasios (Tasos), Sophia, and Panagiotis.
The first child Panagiotis died as a baby.

In 1916, after the birth of his second daughter, he emigrated to USA where he worked in train railway construction in San Antonio, Texas, but due to family circumstances, he returned to Harakopio where he worked in seasonal jobs such as making ceramics and farming.

Photo around 1916 with Georgios P. Bournias with his sister Eugenia "Vangelio" Mathiopoulou nee Bournia(s) with her four children.

Image credit: Panagiotis G. Bournias of 1929, son of Georgios P. Bournias.

Researcher note:
Panagiotis P. Bournias and Irene Frangou provided additional information regarding the family.

William Pete Bournias, 1883 – 1951

William P. Bournias was born in 1883 Charokopio (Χαροκοπιό), Messinia, Greece.

Evangelos a.k.a. William "Bill" Pete Bournias

From the chart of Texas and Messinia – right side by year of birth.

He emigrated to the USA arriving at Ellis Island in in 1904, lived in Illinois and died in Galveston, Texas, USA on May 10, 1951.

This beautiful historical photograph was kindly sent to me via email in September 2014 by Billie Marion Sneed.

Billie Marion Sneed is the spouse of Sam Bill Bournias, of the Bournias family of Texas.

Titles added for each person by P. Bournias.

Image credit: Billie Marion Sneed Bournias

There are a few first names for William P. Bournias in Greek, as I have not been able to locate a vital record for him.

The names are Evangelos, Vangelis, and Vassilis or Basil (Ευάγγελος / Βαγγέλης / Βασίλης Παναγιώτης Μπουρνιά).

His middle name Pete is a common translation from his father's name Panagiotis.

In the above photograph is William P. Bournias with his spouse Evgenia "Virginia" Pontiki(s), and two of their children Helen Elaine Bournias, and Sam Bill Bournias.

Evgenia "Virginia" Pontiki(s), born April 29, 1886, Koroni, Messinia, Greece. Died July 22, 1972, Bryan, Brazos Co., Texas, USA. Evgenia Virginia Pontikis, was on the ship Caroline that docked at Ellis Island on June 17, 1910.

William P. Bournias and Evgenia Virginia Pontikis had six children:

a) Fannie W. Bournias, born 1910, died 5 months old in 1910, Rock Island, Co., Illinois, USA.

b) Helen Elaine W. Bournias (most likely named Eleni, to honor her grandmother) was born 4 June 1911, and died Mar. 5, 2004 in Austin, TX, USA. She married Philip Athanasios Arhos. Philip Athanasios Arhos, born 15 Sept 1894, Tripoli, Greece, died 4 Aug 1981, Bryan, TX, USA. They had one child, Billy Philip Arhos, born 3 Nov 1934, died 11 Apr. 2015.

c) Athanasia or Anastasia "Tacia" W. Bournias, born 1912, Rock Island, Co., Illinois, USA, died age 2 ½ years old in 1914.

d) Sam Bill W. Bournias, Sr. was born 10 Nov 1915 New Braunsfels, Comal Co., TX, USA, died 16 Feb. 1960, Teague, Freestone Co., Texas, USA. He married Helen Irene Cain Cavanaugh, born 28 Oct 1921, died 21 Aug 1985. Sam Bill Bournias, Sr. and Irene Cain Cavanaugh had two children.

e) Panayiota "Teetsa" Bournias (Panagiota) W. Bournias, born 25 May 1922, died 29 July 1964. Panayiota "Teetsa" Bournias married Aristotle Tally Paras, born 12 Aug 1924, died 4 Nov 1998, Okeechobee, Florida, USA.

f) Bessie W. Bournias, b. Navasota, TX, USA, died in 1923 Navasota after living 10 months 17 days old.

Panayiota "Teetsa" Bournias
(Panagiota) W. Bournias

A Greek passport photograph of
Virginia (Pontikis) Bournias

JAMES BOURNIAS

A native of Greece, James Bournias came to the United States in 1902 and settled in Oshkosh, Wisconsin, where he resided for three years.

Leaving Oshkosh, Mr. Bournias came to Brenham in 1905 and opened the Candy Kitchen, which he has operated continuously for almost 37 years.

From the Who's Who in
Brenham, Texas of
James Bournias,
publish date unknown

Konstantinos P. "Gus" Bournias

Images credited to: Billie Marion Sneed Bournias

Konstantinos P. Bournias, (Κωνσταντίνος Π. Μπουρνιάς) 1885 - 1974

Konstantinos P. "Gus" Bournias was born 3 June 1885 Greece, and died 3 Jan 1974 Victoria, TX, USA.

Konstantinos P. Bournias married Margaret Kandis, b. 3 Oct 1889, d. 30 Nov 1963 Bexar Co., TX, USA.

Their children were:
a) Peter G. Bournias, b. 15 Feb 1914, d. 13 Oct 1997, married Fofo Chickenis, (Φωφώ Τσιγκένη), b. 6 Aug 1919 Komboi, Messinia, Greece, d. 1 July 1996 Houston, TX, USA.

b) Mary G. Bournias, b. 1 Feb 1916, d. 21 Dec 2007.

c) Sam Gus Bournias, b. 26 Apr 1917, d. 14 June 1935.

d) James Gus "Jim" Bournias, b. 26 Jan 1919, d. 10 Dec 1939.

e) Nick G. Bournias, b. 18 Apr 1921, d. 3 Nov 2003, married Norma Rita Ann Duplantis, b. 6 Feb 1927, d. 6 Feb 2004.

Frank P. Bournias, (Φώτης Π. Μπουρνιάς) 1891 - 1972

Frank "Fotis" P. Bournias, (Φώτης Π. Μπουρνιάς) was born 13 May 1891 in Harokopio, Messina, Greece. He died on 16 Aug 1972 in Frenchtown, Hunterdon, New Jersey, USA.

He travelled to the USA as single arrived on 20 Nov 1908 on the La Provence. Frank P. Bournias married Regina "Virginia" (Ρεγγίνα) Valko, b. 1892, Harokopio, Messina, Greece, d. abt. 1974, Frenchtown, Hunterdon, New Jersey, USA. They had five children.

Their children were:
a) Helen P. Bournias, b. 1914, d. 1940, married Frank Mentis.
b) Nicoletta "Edith" P. Bournias, b. 1915, married George Maliangos.
c) Peter P. Bournias, b. 5 July 1917, d. 13 July 1986.
d) Athena "Edna" P. Bournias, b. 30 Apr 1919, married Leo Peter Munger. Edna, her husband Leo, and family operated the Cavalier Restaurant and the L&N on Jefferson Street in Roanoke, Virginia, USA. She served as Hollins University's snack bar director until her retirement in 1981.
e) Larry P. Bournias, b. 13 July 1921, d. 25 Oct 2010, married Eva Gertrude "Trudy" Lavender, b. 30 Jun. 1933 of Neshanic Station, NJ, USA, d. 17 Nov. 2017.
f) Nicholas P. Bournias, b. 2 Aug. 1923, Wilmington, d. 27 Dec. 2020, Maryland, USA., married Maria Charuhaus (Μαρία Τσαρούχα).

Anastasios P. Bournias, (Αναστάσιος Π. Μπουρνιάς) 1893 - 1925

Anastasios "Ernest" P. Bournias, (Αναστάσιος Π. Μπουρνιάς) was born 3 Jul.1893, and died on 17 Feb.1925.

He married Katerini "Katina" Palla(s) (Αικατερίνη "Κατίνα" Παλλα), b. abt. 1895, d. 30 Apr 1969.

He served in WW1 until the time of his death in 1925 (from complications of being gassed in 1918).

Inscription on tomb stone:
HERE RESTS ERNEST BOURNIAS BORN JULY 3, 1893 DIED FEB. 17, 1925
ΕΝΘΑΔΕ ΚΗΤΕ ΑΝΑΣΤΑΣΙΟΣ Π. ΜΠΟΥΝΙΑΣ ΕΚ ΧΟΡΙΟΥ ΧΑΡΑΚΟΠΙΟ
ΔΗΜΟΥ ΚΟΛΟΝΙΔΟΝ ΟΠΕΒΙΟΣΕ 17 ΦΛΕΒΑΡΙΟΥ 1925 ΕΤΩΝ 32

Image credit: Billie Marion Sneed Bournias

Military Registration WWI
"Texas, World War I Records, 1917-1920," database with images, *FamilySearch* (https://familysearch.org/ark:/61903/1:1:QV18-D3FT : 9 March 2021), Ernest Bournias, 28 Apr 1918; citing Military Service, New Braunfels, , Texas, United States, Texas Military Forces Museum, Austin.

Ioannis G. Bournias (Ιωάννης Γ. Μπουρνιάς), 1923 - 1949

Ioannis G. Bournias was born 26 Jun. 1923 in Messinia. An alternate name for Ioannis is Giannis.

From the chart of Texas and Messinia – right side by year of birth.

From the newspaper, "*MESSINIAKOS LOGOS, Searching the Heroes of the National Resistance: Our Brother Giannis,*" MARCH 10 2005, written by Sophia Bournia – Frangou.
The article refers to his mother Angeliki and siblings (the family from Messinia):
Anna, Eleni, Koula, Tasos, and Sophia with her daughter Rena (Irene).[159]

It states that because he participated in the National Resistance to the German occupation as a member of EAM and ELAS. In October 1945, he escaped to Athens to avoid arrest and death by tagmatasfalites of Messinia. When he went to the National Army to fullfil his conscription, he was sent to Makronissos.[160]
He was executed in Alexandroupolis, Northern Greece on 31 March 1949 because he did not inform his superiors that some soldiers deserted.

Based upon unverified facts, it appears that Ioannis G. Bournias was executed "without good cause" by order of the British. I refer to that phrase in the continuing pages.

Ioannis Bournias (name shown as Giannis) was executed by the Greek Military on March 31 1949 in Alexandroupolis as ordered by the British military.[161]
Image credit: Irene Frangou

---

[159] Newspaper: Μεσσηνιακός Λόγος, 10 Μαρτίου 2005, Bournias-Ioannis-National-Resistance-Messiniakos-Logos-2005.jpg
[160] https://en.wikipedia.org/wiki/Makronisos
[161] https://www.theguardian.com/world/2014/nov/30/athens-1944-britains-dirty-secret

According to his brother Panagiotis G. Bournias, Ioannis and Athanasios "Thanasis," joined the resistance while his brother Anastasios were in the Greek military fighting the Germans during WWII.

Ioannis was in the resistance and Anastasios in the Navy but during the Greek civil war, the three brothers were treated as traitors for their anti-royalist beliefs and for those who went to Egypt to reorganize their fight against the Germans. The Greek Army was similarly known as the Democratic Army of Greece[162] and the National Army treated them as traitors.

I believe that the British and the Greek government associated leftist Democrats and Communism with Nazism during that time-period to be the same.

In this photograph taken about 1948, Ioannis is an imprisoned soldier with his fellow combatants still wearing their military uniforms on the island of Makronissos, near Cape Sounio until they were sent to Alexandroupoli, were they either died, or were freed.[163]

Image credit: Irene Frangou

---

162 https://en.wikipedia.org/wiki/Democratic_Army_of_Greece
163 https://en.wikipedia.org/wiki/Makronisos

Why do I write that Ioannis G. Bournias was executed "without good cause"?

I use the phrase **"without good cause"** as a "legal expression," that implies unjustly. This is because royalty is in essence equal to aristocracy, which in a developing country like Greece in those days equated to servitude.

During this time-period, many Greeks were anti-royalists. I state this to explain how and why people like Ioannis G. Bournias an anti-royalist were categorized as communists even though they may not have been.[164]

"The British soldier did not take long to find out the truth of the words written by a former Greek Minister in London, commenting on a sonnet of Rupert Brooke's too famous to need quoting, 'Greek soil is not foreign for the British.'"[165]

After WWII, Britain and the Great Powers at the time feared that Greece would become another country joining forces with Russia resulting in a loss of the Balkan area of Europe.[166]

Additionally, the royalty that came to power from 1832 were not Greek but German, and were forced upon the Greeks by England, France, and Russia as they too had royalty as their government and leadership until France, and Russia dissolved the royal powers.

During the early 1900's, political differences created the National Schism that negatively displayed the alliance with Germany by King Konstanine I while disagreeing with the Prime Minister Eleftherios Venizelos. This affected Greece through the numerous wars of the 20th century.[167]

It wasn't until King Konstanine II[168] acceded his father to the throne in Greece that created the events that historically followed including the junta.[169]

Greece abolished the monarchy on June 1, 1973 ending with the House of Glücksburg.

Lastly, the British military made a decision to execute a foreign national without jurisdiction.

---

164 Sfikas, Thanasis D. "The Year of 'Doubt and Anxiety': 1948." In The British Labour Government and The Greek Civil War: 1945-1949, 205–40. Edinburgh University Press, 1994. http://www.jstor.org/stable/10.3366/j.ctvxcrcrc.9.
165 http://archive.spectator.co.uk/article/4th-november-1949/10/the-british-in-greece
166 https://en.wikipedia.org/wiki/Aftermath_of_World_War_II#Europe
167 National Schism, https://en.wikipedia.org/wiki/National_Schism
168 https://en.wikipedia.org/wiki/Constantine_II_of_Greece
169 House of Glücksburg, https://en.wikipedia.org/wiki/House_of_Gl%C3%BCcksburg

Nicholas F. Bournias (Νικόλαος Φ. Μπουρνιάς), 1923 - 2020
Nicholas F. Bournias was born on August 2, 1923 in Wilmington Delaware and passed away at the age of 97 on December 27, 2020.[170]

From the chart of Texas and Messinia – right side by year of birth.

His Greek immigrant parents were Frank (Φώτης Π. Μπουρνιάς 1891 - 1972) and Regina "Virginia" Bournias nee Valko 1892 - 1974. He was married to Maria Charuhaus (Μαρια Τσαρούχα).

After graduating high school, he enlisted in the U.S. marine Corp at the age of 18. Nick served in WWII, defending the United States on the island of Okinawa. After his honorable discharge, he attended Ryder College where he received a BS in Accounting.

Recipient of the 1979 Presidential Management Improvement Award
Nicholas was an auditor with the office of the Inspector General, in Washington, D. C., contributed to the reduction of fraud, abuse, and errors in the Medicaid program by developing a methodology for auditing billions of dollars spent under the program. After a 50 year illustrious career, which included Presidential Awards before he retired from the Government Accounting Office.

Maria and Nick Bournias
November 1994

Image credit: Billie Bournias.

Nicholas F. Bournias met Queen Elizabeth II during a WWII with fellow Legionnaires at a Memorial in Washington, D. C., May 9, 2007

---

[170] Obituary of Nicholas F. Bournias on the internet.

Anastasios G. Bournias (Αναστάσιος Γ. Μπουρνιάς), 1925 - 2015

A self-published book by Αναστάσιος "Τάσος" Γ. Μπουρνιάς a.k.a. Anastasios "Tasos" G. Bournias, born 1925 in Messinia, given to me by his brother Panagiotis G. Bournias in 2017. Anastasios passed away at the age of 90 on March 10, 2015.

From the chart of Texas and Messinia – right side by year of birth.

The book title is "ΤΟΤΕ ΠΟΥ ΠΟΛΕΜΟΥΣΑΜΕ" translated / interpreted "Then When We Fought," was written by Anastasios G. Bournias, who served in the Greek Navy from the age of twelve (12), until after WWII with the rank of commander.[171]

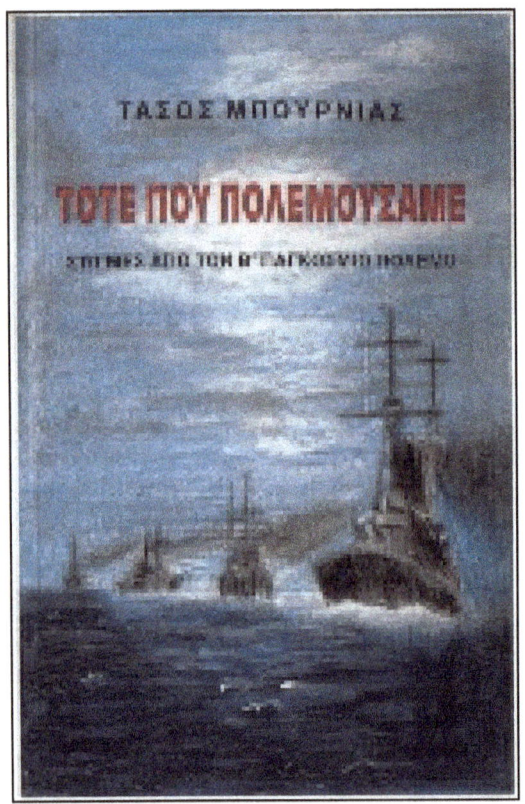
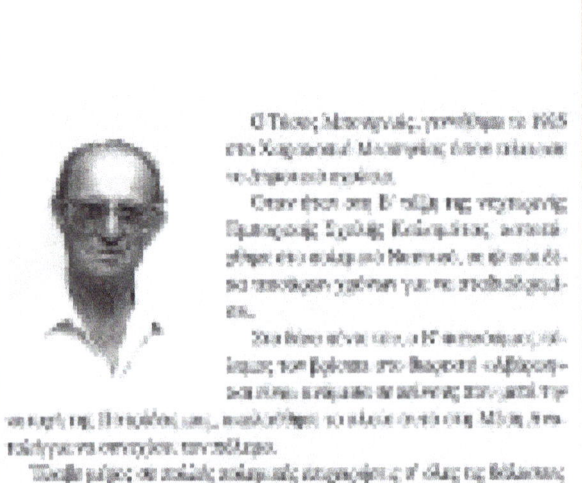

Although I was skittish about reading this initially because it is completely in Greek, I am happy that I did. Anastasios G. Bournias provides a detailed story of his life.

Beginning with entering into the Greek Navy at the age of twelve years old, serving on different ships, what he and his shipmates experienced, including the bombing of the Port of Piraeus in WWII by the German Luftwaffe[172], and through the torment and aggravation by the military that affected his personal career and life.

---

[171] The book ΤΟΤΕ ΠΟΥ ΠΟΛΕΜΟΥΣΑΜΕ, Στιγμές από τον Β' Παγκόσμιο Πόλεμο, 194 pages, Tasos Bournias, no date
[172] The German Air Force, https://en.wikipedia.org/wiki/Luftwaffe

In the book, he describes what happened in order to save the ship during the bombardment of Piraeus and the agony of the crewmembers as they faced the decision to agree or disagree with the captain about surrendering the ship to the Germans or disobeying the captain thereby committing mutiny. This decision had to be made to save the ship and escape to Egypt to regroup with other Greek Navy forces who managed to escape the sudden attack or to surrender.

Commander Anastasios G. Bournias

Με τη σύζυγο

Anastasios with his spouse Kyriaki.
Anastasios and Kyriaki had a son and a daughter.

Military ID (Greek Navy) at the age of twelve (12)

Image credit: photographs from his book, *ΤΟΤΕ ΠΟΥ ΠΟΛΕΜΟΥΣΑΜΕ*.

While I do not wish to encumber the reader with too much history, many do not know some of the finer details about Greece's history, it helps to clarify and understand the zeitgeist of the circumstances that the Greeks and family members endured.

During the 20th century there were more than 200,000 Greeks living in Alexandria, Egypt. Today there are less than five hundred.[173]

World War II began October 28, 1940 for Greece by the Italian invasion through Albania into Greece.

Prior to the German invasion, the Royal Family under George II with the remnants of the Greek government at the time moved first to Crete and then to Cairo to establish a temporary headquarter to continue the fight against the Germans.[174]

By April 6, 1941, Germany began their invasion into Greece through the borders of Bulgaria and Yugoslavia into Northern Greece and the Battle of Crete marking the beginning of the German Occupation.[175]

On April 24, 1941, the Greek Army in Epirus Northern Greece surrendered as did the remaining Greek government. Greek soldiers and sailors that managed to escape went to Cairo and Alexandria to regroup, and were watched by the British who were there too preparing their attack on the Germans.

In October 1944, the battleship "Georgios Averof" transported the exiled Greek government back to Greece.[176]

After the crew refused to surrender the ship, Anastasios along with others were marked as mutineers. This lead to confinement and imprisonment for him and crewmembers for a number of years. This separated him from the love of his life, Kyriaki, and affected his life afterwards. I found that the Navy Archives produced a book about a ship that he served on but did not include his name. Anastasios G. Bournias served on various naval ships during his wartime service.

Later in the 1980's the government of Pasok recognized the Greek resistance positively, and Anastasios's participation; he was promoted to his proper naval rank accordingly and received his military pension.

I believe that the above information, though a short snippet of history, clarifies the paradox that soldiers from the Greek Army and the Greek Navy who went to Egypt and continued fighting the Germans were considered traitors by the Greek government and Royal family.

---

[173] https://www.lifo.gr/videos/lifo-picks/oti-apemeine-apo-tin-alexandreia-ton-200000-ellinon
[174] Η ελληνική παροικία στην Αιγυπτίου και ο Δεύτερος Παγκόσμιος Πόλεμος, (The Greek Province in Egypt and the Second World War), 1981, Alexander Kitroeff, 32 Pages, see pages 4-5.
[175] The Greek version of this link provides additional information, https://en.wikipedia.org/wiki/World_War_II
[176] The battleship G. Averof History, https://averof.mil.gr/en/istoria-pliou/

Sofia G. Fragou nee Bournia(s) (Σοφία Γ. Μπουρνιά), 1926 - 2013

From the chart of Texas and Messinia – right side by year of birth.

Sofia was born on 15/9/1926 in Harakopio, Messinia. She was the 6th child of George and Angeliki Bournia.

She attended the primary school of Harakopio. She worked during her childhood on the family home and farm. Later she became an apprentice tailor in a nearby village.

During the German occupation she became a member of EAM, the National Liberation Front from 1941 to 1947, and participated in national resistance for the liberation of Greece.

For this reason, she was arrested by Tagmatasfalites[177] of the area, taken to Vounaria a village in Messinia, and beaten by the drunk Tagmatasfalites who came out of a tavern of the village.

Luckily, as she was the niece of the local priest, the cause of her arrest was documented that she went to the grocery shop of Harakopio during Martial Law[178] of circumscription.

After her arrest in 1946, she escaped from Harakopio. She found work in a textile factory for two years, the latter as a tailor for women's clothing.

In 1953, she married Filippos Fragos (b. 1920 - d. 2002) who moved to Athens in 1936 from Volos. Sofia was self-employed in dress making until the late 1960's when she opened a shoe store in Holargos, which she kept until her retirement in 1997. Sofia had a daughter and a son. Sofia passed away on 1/12/2013.

The above text was provided by Irene, her daughter.

Image credit: Irene Frangou, daughter of Sofia P. Bournias.

---

[177] https://en.wikipedia.org/wiki/Security_Battalions
[178] https://en.wikipedia.org/wiki/Martial_law

Panagiotis G. Bournias (Παναγιώτης Γ. Μπουρνιάς), 1929 - 2022

From the chart of Texas and Messinia – right side by year of birth.

Παναγιώτης "Τάκης" Γ. Μπουρνιάς a.k.a. Panagiotis "Takis and Pete" G. Bournias was born in 1929. He married Efstathia also known as Effie, and had two sons. He and his brother Ioannis worked making ceramics at a factory near Methoni Beach in the area of Methoni in Messinia, and in 1946, he studied to become a ship engineer. He spoke Greek and English.

I decided one day to make a few random phone calls to individuals with the surname Bournias. I called Panagiotis and explained who I was and what I was doing with regard to the family research. He offered to help provide information and I arranged a meeting with him in Kalamata. I met Panagiotis, who told me to call him by his nickname "Pete," in Kalamata Messinia. He made me feel like one of the family. He spoke about his grandfather, and about his brothers and sisters, and he provided me with a photograph of them.

Sadly, Panagiotis passed away at the age of 93, two days after I called him for his name day on August 17, 2022.

His brothers and sisters were:

The first Panagiotis, abt. 1900 dates unknown, died soon after birth.

Anna born about 1914 - 2017, age 103.

Eleni born about 1916 - 2021, age 105.

Athanasios (Thanasis) born about 1922 - 2008, age 86.

Ioannis born 1923 - 1949, age 26, previously mentioned.

Anastasios (Tasos) born about 1925 - 2015, age 90, previously mentioned.

Sophia born 1926 – 2013, age 87.

Panagiotis born 1929 was given the same name as the first child most likely because it may not have been baptized and therefore not officially recognized.

Image credit: His son, Ioannis P. Bournias

Bournias family members not linked on my Genealogy Charts

These are individuals that are not linked due to missing information or individuals that were discovered in Greece the USA, or elsewhere.

Ioannis Bournias (Ιωάννης Μπουρνιάς), 1885 - 1970 KALAMATA

Image credit: *Μπουρνιά Ιωαννης – Lifo Magazine*

The text on the image states:
"Old equipment of the Bournias ceramic factory donated to the Municipality of Kalamata".

The son of Ioannis Bournias was Charilaos I. Bournias (Χαρίλαος Ι. Μπουρνιάς) and he donated the factory that began operations in the early 1900's to the Municipality of Kalamata as evidenced by an email and website:
Μπουρνιά Ιωάννης δωρίζονται στο Δήμο Καλαμάτας - Messinia Live[179]
On another website, there is information written about a **Brounias** from the same area that may have been a typographical error by the publisher.

---

[179] https://www.messinialive.gr/palia-michanimata-tou-ergostasiou-mpournia-dorizontai-sto-dimo-kalamatas/

Tasos Spiliotopoulos wrote in an email:
I have a relation to the Bournias family and am glad that I even came across your website by accident. ***My grandfather Ioannis Bournias (1885 -1970) came to Kalamata in the early 20th century from Sifnos, and first started working in a local soap factory.***

He then started his own ceramic factory for the production of bricks, tiles and ceramics.

For the needs of the factory, he brought his cousins and compatriots from Sifnos, including my grandfather and his cousin Nikolaos Mariora (Μαριόρας), members of the Venios Bakery (αρτοποιών Βενιός) family and members of the Komis (Κόμης) family.

Nikolaos Marioras was my mother's grandfather (my grandmother's father).
Two years ago (2018) Ioannis Bournias' last child, Charilaos died at the age of 95.
He had donated the machinery of his father's factory to the Municipality of Kalamata, but to date it has not been utilized as a museum exhibit. I do not know if you have a relation to my grandfather, but if you have, I would like to inform you, because I make the pedigree of my tree and I'm looking for relatives and from where we are related and with which families. Let me also tell you that the ceramic tiles that my grandfather made (the photo has been published in Kalamata magazine), as he is referred to as **Brounias (Μπρουνιάς)**.

In addition, my grandfather Ioannis Bournias is responsible for the discovery of lignite deposits in the area that is today the PPC (power) plant in Megalopolis in the early 1950's.

He was looking for fuel for its factory furnaces and had managed to exploit the reserves until he lost them for various reasons (and economically) and when PPC seized them without giving him compensation.
I will be happy to receive your reply.
Τάσος Σπηλιωτόπουλος <via email - withheld> dated March 26, 2020.

Researcher note:
Ioannis Bournias (Ιωάννης Μπουρνιάς), about (1885 -1970), location unknown, was on the island of Sifnos according to the above information.

A suburb in Kalamata is known as Bournias.[180]

Charilaos I. Bournias (Χαρίλαος Ι. Μπουρνιάς), about (1923 – 2018), location unknown.

---

[180] An area named Bournias in Kalamata may have been named after this person.

Ariadni Bournia, (Αριάδνη Μπουρνιά) 1953 - 1972

Ariadni Bournia (Αριάδνη Μπουρνιά) was a teacher at the Second Boys High School of Athens, birth about 1953, father unknown, and location unknown.

I discovered this photograph of her on the Internet, as she was apparently loved by her students. Among the faculty, she is the fourth person from the left in the white skirt; her facial features are an obvious match to the Bournias family characteristics.

Image credit: Internet / Second Boys High School of Athens

Translation of the bus itinerary:
Bus #5 is designated as an excursion bus, probably for a student trip to Laconia in the Peloponnese.

Apostolos Bournias
A Soldier, birth and father unknown

Apostolos Bournias a Soldier at Fort Roupel at the Northern Border of Macedonia Greece.[181]

"The Battle of the Fort - Events that prove the Greatness of the Greeks!"
The incident of what transpired in Rupel on 6 April 1941.[182]
Written by Elias Kotridis - Lieutenant Colonel, author.

1st. The commander of the "Molon Lave" (a famous Greek phrase from Sparta meaning, come and take it if you can) brigade, Lieutenant Zachariadis Fotios, noted the continuing evening absence of soldier Apostolos Bournias.[183]

Investigating the absence, he was informed that the soldier was going to the Promachon's cafe and became inebriated.

He called Bournias to his office and reprimanded him. Bournias was an unruly, undiciplined man, pointed his weapon by threatening the commander of his speech, stressing at the same time that "if he wants to work, he must give him the cart".

The cart (carriage) was two-wheeled with a horse used to carry food and supplies from Sidirokastro (iron fort).

After a little thought, the lieutenant gave it to him. The next cart and horse was glistening with cleanliness, and the food was always on time in the fort.

A German motorcyclist with a machine gun managed to harass three of the machine gun emplacements. This soldier was also a protagonist during the battles.
Continuous machine guns and machine gun fire failed to neutralize him (the German).

At a meeting of the lieutenant with the officer Vakuftsis to find a solution to this problem, Bournias intervened and asked him to leave the fort at night.

He was allowed to, and at night, he crawled over a ditch outside the fort, armed with his faith, a knife, and rope, where he previously encountered a German the previous day.

He waited and when the German appeared again, he jumped on him, tied and bound him, put him in the "back" of the cart, and drove cart (carriage) himself up to the fort. Fortunately, he was not hit by friendly fire.

(End of segment regarding Bournias)

---

181 Fort Roupel, https://en.wikipedia.org/wiki/Fort_Roupel
182 Fort Roupel web site, https://www.roupel.gr/
183 Molon Labe, an Ancient Greek phrase of defiance meaning, "come and take it / them". https://en.wikipedia.org/wiki/Molon_labe

2nd. During a break in the fighting, soldier Seraphim Karavasilis with an observer came out of the fort in the trenches, holding some food in their canteens. At that moment two German planes were shooting at us, and knocked the food out of the observer's hands without the soldiers getting any. One plane returned and shot again tried to hit them. An angry observer positioned his machine gun and shot at the plane hitting it, sending it down in flames near the village of Koimimi. The locals "captured" the pilot and hosted him until the fighting ended. In return for their "hospitality," he gave them his decorated hat.

3rd. During the air strikes the soldiers were ordered to remove the machine guns and go down to the bunkers. The bombardments damaged interior doors, a machine gun, and promptly required the repair shop to repair the damage.
The latest bombings killed the two wonderful Greeks (Kyriakos Anthimos and Kon. Voulgaris).*

Two meters outside the entrance of the fort, and almost simultaneously, disobeying orders, a soldier named Zania takes a machine gun and begins shooting at the planes.

A nearby blast filled the interior of the machine gun with stones and dirt blinding Zania. Even in this situation, he was trying to identify the soldier replacing him while pointing out the "targets," telling the other "The tree in front and to the left is three hundred meters, the other to the right is four hundred and fifty."
Later, at a hospital in Athens Zania was visited by his commander, Lieutenant Zachariadis, who told him:
"Well, Zania, didn't I tell you to go down to the bunkers when they start bombing?"[184]

Researcher note:
Video Link in Greek with English subtitles:
Rupel Fortress - Their glorious history and the heroic Greek soldiers,
https://www.youtube.com/watch?v=E8O23zswRIg

* Kon is an abbreviation for Konstantinos.

---

[184] Translated text from this web site, http://defenceline.gr/index.php/history/item/2612-oxyra

THE BOURNIAS SURNAME IN THE UNITED KINGDOM

These individuals are not linked on my charts.

From the U.K. National Archives regarding military personnel.[185]
Apparently, these Bournias family members travelled to Tipperary[186] Ireland and joined the Irish Dragoon Guards. They may have been related even though they changed their names.

William Donahoe born BOURNIAS, born 1739
Reference: WO 121/25/102 [187]
Tipperary Served in **87th Foot Regiment; 105th Foot Regiment**[188]
Description: WILLIAM DONAHOE, Born BOURNIA, Tipperary[189]
Discharged aged 57, after 25 years of service
Date: 1796
Held by: The National Archives, Kew

Nathaniel Hurst born BOURNIAS, born 1809
Reference: WO 97/70/61 [190]
Tipperary Served in **4th Dragoon Guards** (Royal Irish)[191, 192]
Description: NATHANIEL HURST, Born BOURNIA, Tipperary[193]
Discharged aged 31
Date: 1827 - 1840
Held by: The National Archives, Kew, London, England

Image credit: Internet The National Archives, Kew, Richmond, U.K.

---

185 https://www.nationalarchives.gov.uk/
186 Tipperary, https://en.wikipedia.org/wiki/Tipperary_(town)
187 http://discovery.nationalarchives.gov.uk/details/r/C8878230
188 87th Foot Regiment, https://en.wikipedia.org/wiki/87th_(Royal_Irish_Fusiliers)_Regiment_of_Foot
189 https://discovery.nationalarchives.gov.uk/results/r?_q=William+Donahoe+Tipperary
190 http://discovery.nationalarchives.gov.uk/details/r/C8688679
191 Dragoon Guards, https://en.wikipedia.org/wiki/Dragoon_Guards
192 4th Dragoon Guards (Royal Irish), https://en.wikipedia.org/wiki/4th_Royal_Irish_Dragoon_Guards
193 https://discovery.nationalarchives.gov.uk/results/r?_q=Nathaniel+Hurst+Tipperary

There is no relationship to the individuals on the previous page in the above image.

Image credit: Internet U.K. National Archives

An archive photograph of the 87th Foot Regiment showing what the Irish Dragoon Guards looked like and their uniforms from the 1800's.

Rhetorical questions to ponder:
Were these individuals Bournihas from France or Bournias from Greece?
Was William Donahoe, born in 1739 related to Apostolos 1760?
Was Nathaniel Hurst, born 1809, related to William Donahoe?
Why did they choose to go to Ireland?
Why did they become soldiers of the Irish regiment?
Unfortunately, I do not have the answers.

SETTLEMENTS NAMED BOURNIAS

Based upon information from a history book published by the Greek newspaper the BHMA, Antonios Bournias served in Egypt Lieutenant Colonel in the French army under Napoleon went to Tripoli to request the assistance of Demetrios Ypsilantis to help in the liberation of Chios in April 1822. There is a small piece of land (in the area of Mirofillo, Pyli, Trikala) that may have been given the name Bournias in honor of him.[194]

The following information has been extracted from the BHMA Encyclopedia, a Greek published edition in cooperation with Papyros Larous Bretanica.

Trikala
Trikala is a city of western Thessaly, the capital of Trikala Regional Unity and the Trikala Municipality. The city is crossed by the river of Lethaios, which is a tributary of Pinios.

Myrofyllo or Mirofillo in the area of Pyli, Trikala - GOOGLE map
Myrofyllo is a mountainous village in the prefecture of Trikala located in the southwest of the prefecture on the border with the prefecture of Arta. It is built at an altitude of 700 meters on the eastern slopes of Tzoumerka.[195]

When you look at the map, remember that Antonios Bournias would have to sail from Chios to the area of beaches to the right of Larissa and then cross by foot, donkey, or horse to get to Trikala, and then return to Chios to begin the revolution.

A settlement or plot of land with the name Bournias in Kalamata
In the municipality of Kalamata in the prefecture of Messinia, there is a settlement or suburb located about 1 kilometer west of Kalamata that has the name Bournias.

Bournias and the island of Samos

I discovered this information on the Internet but have not found any historical reason as to why this mountain area was named Bournias. It could have been done by the Simians' because they fought on Chios with Antonios Bournias during the Greek revolution.[196]

---

194 The area of Bournias in the Peloponnese
https://www.google.com/maps/place/%CE%9C%CF%80%CE%BF%CF%85%CF%81%CE%BD%CE%B9%CE%AC%CF%82+420+33/@39.3574627,21.3441282,14z/data=!4m5!3m4!1s0x13594e8f08f5a6af:0xa9d1ee862fd4e06b!8m2!3d39.3655734!4d21.3401505

195 History of Mirofillo, https://dimospylis.gr/egkatastasi/mirofillo/

196 The hill of Bournias on the island of Samos
https://el.wikipedia.org/wiki/%CE%9C%CF%80%CE%BF%CF%85%CF%81%CE%BD%CE%B9%CE%AC%CF%82_(%CE%B2%CE%BF%CF%85%CE%BD%CF%8C)

HOMES OF SOME BOURNIAS FAMILY MEMBERS

The home of Antonios A. Bournias in Parparia Chios

At first you might think, what kind of a home is this but you may not have realized that what you are looking at is a newer home built on top of an older home. The original house that has been renovated during the time-period of the 19th century is the smaller area on the bottom left of the photograph.

If you look carefully, you will notice that there is a plaque on the wall next to a pipe, behind a column of the balcony. That wall and the rest of the lower house around the backside were the home of Antonios Bournias.

Image credit: P. A. Bournias

A PLAQUE ON THE HOME OF ANTONIOS A. BOURNIAS

Inscription of the plaque and a translation:
Here was born "X" (for Hatzi - Χατζή) Antonios Bournias, second in command of the revolution of 1822 with the leader Lykourgos Logothetis[197], and fought in Napoleon's army in Egypt.

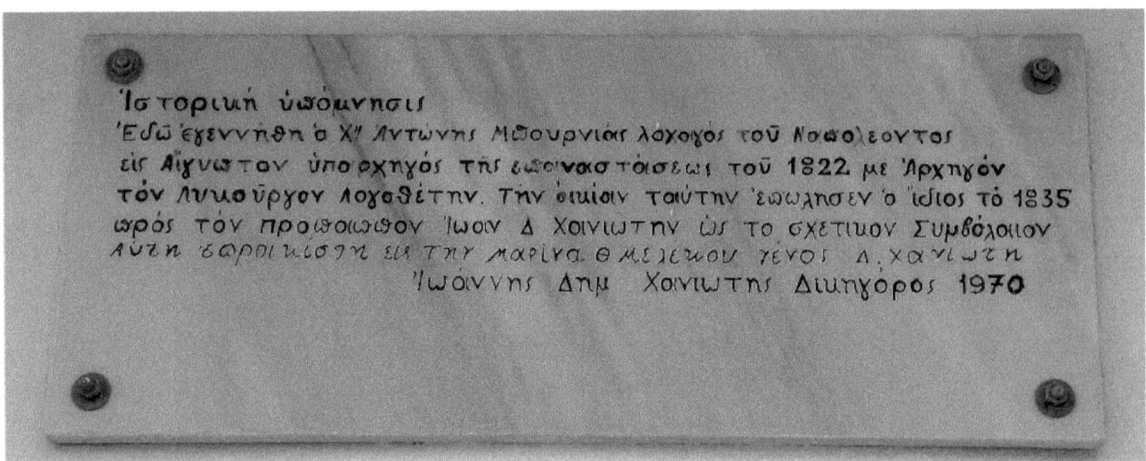

Translation of inscription:
This home was sold by the same (Antonios Bournias) in 1835 as a dowry for Ioannis D. Haniotis as noted in the related deed.
This dowry was for Marina Th. Melekou born (daughter) of D. Haniotis
Ioannis Dem(etrios) Haniotis, Lawyer 1970[198]

Image credit: P. A. Bournias

Ioannis Demetrios Haniotis was a Lawyer born in Chios in 1892. Ioannis Demetrios Haniotis or Chaniotis was elected to Parliament in 1936 as a member of the Independent Party.[199]
The Haniotis or Chaniotis family were related to the Bournias family because the maiden surname of their daughter was Haniotis and she was the spouse of Apostolos Bournias.

---

197 Lykourgos Logothetis, https://en.wikipedia.org/wiki/Lykourgos_Logothetis
198 Ioannis Demetrios Haniotis, https://el.wikipedia.org/wiki/%CE%9A%CE%B1%CF%84%CE%AC%CE%BB%CE%BF%CE%B3%CE%BF%CF%82_%CE%95%CE%BB%CE%BB%CE%AE%CE%BD%CF%89%CE%BD_%CE%B2%CE%BF%CF%85%CE%BB%CE%B5%CF%85%CF%84%CF%8E%CE%BD_(1936)
199 Liberal Party in Greece, https://en.wikipedia.org/wiki/Independent_Party_(Greece)

The home of Gregorios A. Bournias

In the historical Plaka area of Athens, the home of Gregorios A. Bournias exists today. Walking inside provide a glimpse into the past with various rooms, furniture, photographs, and paintings. It is now owned by the government, used as a community center, and is maintained by funds from the European Union and companies in Greece.

Sophia G. Bournia was the daughter of Gregoris Bournias and Areti.
Ersi-Alexia Hatzimihali was the great granddaughter of Sophia.
Their home exists in the Plaka area of Athens and is a museum.
This family is shown on the main chart of the Bournias Family.

The other house on the corner is now a museum that belonged to Angeliki Bournia Chatzimihali.

She was the daughter of a Sophia Bournia and Alexios Kolyvas.

Her grandfather was Gregorios A. Bournias.

Her second husband was Platonas Chatzimihalis.

This is a three floor home designed in 1924 and is a wonderful example of early modern architecture of the time and is decorated as it was providing ideas as to what is was like living in Athens.

The Mayor of Athens honored her by assigning the building with the street address of **Aggeliki Chatzimichall 6 Athens**, which makes it easy to find.

Here is a photograph of the home of Angeliki Bournia Chatzimihali.

Image credit: P. A. Bournias

This building diagonally on the next corner was the home of Gregorios A. Bournias.[200]

A similar house before renovations.

The next photograph is another building of the same generation that has probably been abandoned by the property owners to the procrastination of the city leaders.

Image credit:
P. A. Bournias

200
https://www.google.com/maps/place/37%C2%B058'20.1%22N+23%C2%B043'52.4%22E/@37.97226,23.7306595,19z/data=!3m1!4b1!4m6!3m5!1s0x0:0x0!7e2!8m2!3d37.9722596!4d23.7312083

TRAVELING ON A STEAMSHIP

It was a different period of time, one that the majority of us will never know even if we take a week long cruise on the Mediterranean sea or elsewhere.

If you have visited Greece, then you will know that most of us today jump on an airplane and fly anywhere from two to twenty hours to get to Athens or Thessaloniki Greece. We have the "luxury" of having a snack or lunch and maybe even dinner on the plane, and can easily take our almost anything we want to bring with us in our luggage.

Now jump back in time to early 1900 when there were no planes. You had to book a ticket at a shipping office normally at a port for the next ship leaving for the USA or wherever. In this context, I will mention the USA but it could have been anywhere.

How would you like to go, first class or third class? Well that depended on your economic status, which in the case of someone from Chios in the late 1800's or early 1900's, a poor island with little or no industry, clearly suggests that, it was probably third or dreadfully storage class. I will let you imagine what storage class is.

My trip to Chios was aboard a steamship in August 1973, smaller than those that crossed the Atlantic. My trip was a first time personal experience and I want to express what it was like from the point of view of a young person, eighteen at the time.

The trip from the Port of Piraeus to Chios was about a twelve to fourteen hour journey. There was essentially nothing to do, and whether you sat inside or outside the temperature was the same as there was no air conditioning. If you didn't smoke, then you wanted to be out on a deck because back then smoking was allowed everywhere and it was stifling.

Throughout the rest of the trip chit chatting about whatever was the social thing to do, whether that was with your family or if you could manage it with other travelers of the same language.

The ship had a lounge that served two meals lunch, and dinner, assuming again that you could pay for it, we could but this was 1973 not 1900. Back then, a traveler most likely carried some olives and a piece of bread, but this was normal then.

After dinner, we sat outside watching the waves of the sea, the setting of the sun, and the evening darkness setting upon us with the stars lighting above.

By ten o'clock, many were already heading towards the rooms. Don't get excited, third class rooms had anywhere from four to eight bunk beds and the men were separated from the women. We didn't have to worry about our belongings because anything we carried was most likely in one piece of luggage as the rest or our luggage was stored in the entrance area of the ship.

Upon arrival at Hora the central city of Chios, disembarking like embarking was a chaotic experience completely disorganized with people trying to get off the ship while others attempting to board the ship with whatever they were carrying.

Sadly, it is not so different today, as everyone scrambles to find transportation by taxi or someone from the family prearranged to collect the family members and to go wherever they will be staying.

This was a trip by a person whose destination was Chios but what if you destination was the USA. You had to be financially funded even to consider making the trip because first you would have to be able to buy a ticket. The trip would encompass travel to numerous ports of call from Chios to Piraeus, and then possibly to Marseille France then to England, and then to the port of New York in the USA.[201] After that, if your final destination was not New York you would have to use an alternate method of transportation.

Let's take a step back to arrange a trip in the past. Assuming that you still wanted to, you would need some money because you would have to eat. Lastly, you had to have a minimum amount as a surplus because in 1900 the immigration officers at Ellis Island in the USA could reject your entry into the USA if you were penniless.
This was especially applicable to those who were entering the USA without knowing having any relatives or knowing anyone who could guarantee their well-being.

Another method of attaining passage was that of working your way to the USA.
Many members of the Bournias family worked on ships, as Chios was known for its sailors and captains. There are quite a few who were on crewmember lists in the archived documents.

Men would leave their families for the risk of the opportunity of a better life by using their family connections to attain a job aboard a ship. This would provide them with passage and a minor amount of money that they could earn. The amount was miniscule because most of the shipping agencies knew that the men would do anything for the work and that they would most likely not return to Chios.

The men that sailed to opportunity entered into the USA either through immigration at Ellis Island in New York Harbor or by "jumping ship" and becoming an illegal alien.
They entered the Port of New York and simply disappeared establishing their new lives, and then writing their families and sending them money to leave their homeland.

My father who was single when he came to the USA "jumped ship" but received his American citizenship after he married my mother who was an American by birth.
Many single men and women from Greece and other countries used this method to attain American citizenship.

---

[201] From 1820 to 1950, there were five (5) U.S. Ports of Call: Boston, New York, Philadelphia, Baltimore, and New Orleans. https://www.genealogybranches.com/arrivalports.html

THE SS PATRIS

The SS Patris, one of the many ships that carried Greeks immigrating to the USA.

The trip usually took about 10 days as the ships travelled along the coasts and crossed the Atlantic at the most northern closest points between Europe and North America.

Image credit: Internet / Wikipedia

The steamship "*Patris*" ("Homeland" in English), formerly the French "*Saint Rémi*," sank in the early hours of June 15, 1927, after being rammed by the steamer "*Moschanthi Toya*," formerly the British yacht "*Catania*," due to a navigational error.[202]

"At 22:50 hrs on June 14, 1927, "Patris," with a total of 16 people on board sailed from Piraeus, with final destination the island of Naxos. At 1:30 on June 15, she was sailing on the opposite direction of "*Moschanthi Toya*" and "Tinos" steamships, which were on their way from Syros Island to the port of Piraeus. At a short distance behind these two ships, another steamer, the "*Angeliki*," followed for safety. The "Patris" tried to avoid the collision and turned to the left, exposing her right side to "Moschanthi Toya." The latter rammed "*Patris*" and immediately after, with her engines full astern, left a gaping hole in "Patris," which sank in a few minutes with ten people lost forever in the deep blue sea."[203]

---

[202] https://en.wikipedia.org/wiki/SS_Paris_(1916)

[203] http://www.ww2wrecks.com/portfolio/steamship-patris-sitting-upright-on-the-seabed-for-89-years/

Conclusion of Research

I have been known to say that everyone with a Bournias surname is connected to the family and I now provide you with the culmination of my research.

It has been a very long time since I was enrolled as a student at the university but I believe that a conclusion is necessary to provide a synopsis of what I hope you found in this book.

From all of the genealogy research data that I have discovered, I have been able to complete the majority of the main chart of the family that clearly indicates the origin of the Bournias family on the island of Chios with connections from families everywhere.

I have also educated you to the challenge of Greek genealogy and shown you some techniques to cross check the work to avoid such errors if you do your own.

Although I have not been able to connect many families to the main chart, I maintain numerous charts and hope that more data emerges or that family members reading this book might be encouraged to reveal details prior to 1900 that may help to populate them.

I provided supplementary information about the Bournias family suggesting that they may have originated in France. After searching the French archives, newspapers, and social media it appears that the family name of Bournihas will soon be remembered only in the archives of France as the families disappear.

I have provided some history of who Antonios A. Bournias was and what he attempted to accomplish, the consequences, and that the family name was exonerated by the Greek government.

I have shown how and where the Bournias family ventured, and how some returned to Chios or other areas of Greece, and other countries.

Therefore, I conclude that this effort has been a positive experience, and hope that you found it rewarding as well.

I hope that it will provide you and your families with the pride that I have found in my ancestors.

FAMILY RECORDS

I have translated the details of the Greek records that I found for those of you who wish to see examples, if you are searching for information about your own relatives.

I have noted reference numbers of file names with the ending ".jpg" without any image because some of the records are from ledger books and are the size of A3 paper.

A Birth Certificate of Ioannis P. Bournias of 1930

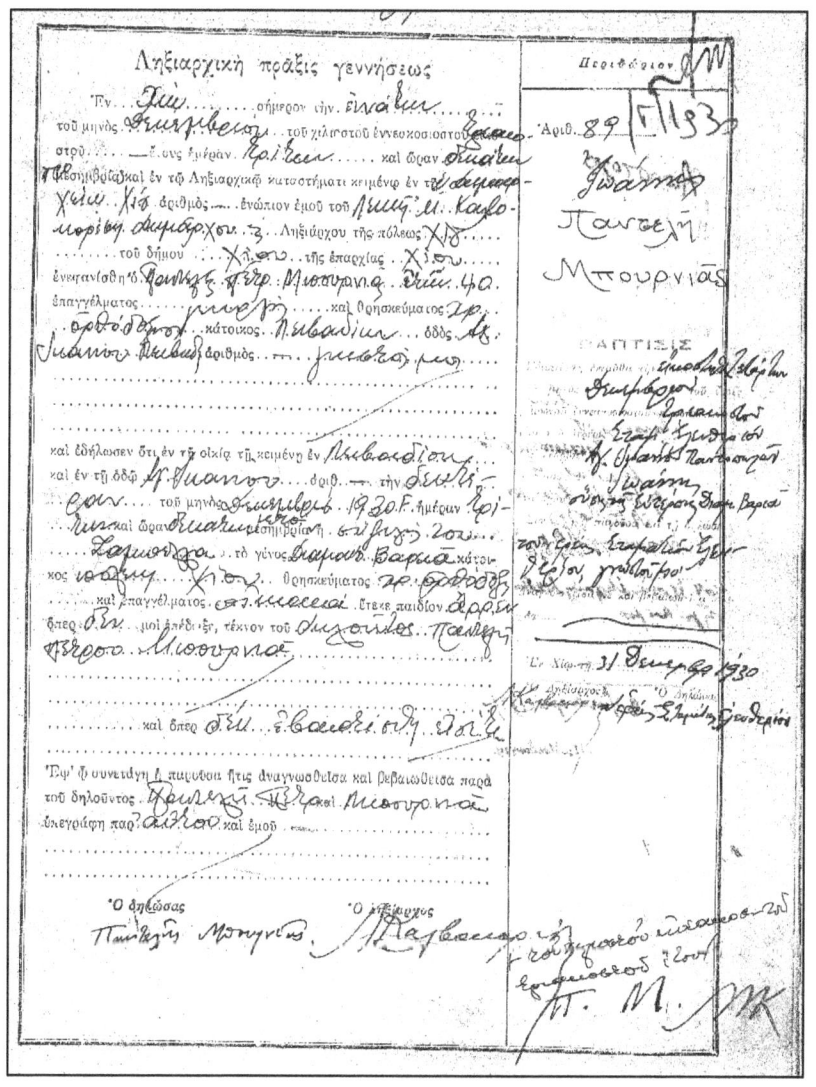

Municipality of Chios Registry of Births

I am including some images of various certificates from the time-period to show what they look like and what was written on them.

Punctuation on original documents are similarly reproduced.

This is the from the Registry of Birth for Ioannis P. Bournias of 1930.

Image Reference: Scanned by P. Bournias
Municipality of Chios, Registry of Births including the Baptism,
File: Bournias-P-Ioannis-Certificate-Birth-1930.jpg

REGISTRY OF BIRTH	MARGIN
In **Chios** today the **9th** of the month **December** of the year of **(1930) nineteen hundred thirty**, Tuesday at the time of **15:00** at the Registry of birth, marriage, and death of the **Municipality of Chios** located at **street (blank) number (blank)** in the presence of **L. Kalvamar** the of the **mayor and registrar** of the city and **Municipality of Chios** of the **Prefecture of Chios** Mr. **Pantelis Petros Bournias age 40** profession **farmer** and religion **Christian Orthodox** resident of **Livadia, Ag. Ioannou** number **illegible/unreadable** (blank lines) Declare that in the house of the above in **Livadia** and at the street **Ag. Ioannou** number **blank** on the day of **second** (day) of the month of **December 1930** on **Tuesday** at the time **15:00** p.m. **the spouse of Zavella from the family name of Eleftherios Diam. Varia** a resident of **illegible/unreadable Chios** and religion **Christian Orthodox** profession **illegible/unreadable** godparent of a **male** child of the declarer **Pantelis Petros Bournias** (blank lines) The child has not been baptized yet. This document or presence was recognized and certified by the declarers **Pantelis Petros Bournias** who signs this and myself. **The declarer** (Signature of) **Pantelis Bournias** **Registrar / Town Clerk** (Signature of) **L. Kalvamar**	**Number: 89 / Γ / 1930** (Hand Written) **Ioannis** (Hand Written) **Pantelis** (Hand Written) **Bournias** (Hand Written) *Stamp regarding BAPTISM* On this day of the 24th of December of (1930) nineteen hundred thirty by the priest Stamatios Eleftherios of the Parish Ag. Tama Pantelemonon baptised Ioannis by the spouse of Eleftherios Diam. Varia In the presence of and as witnesses the priest Stamatios Eleftherios, second name illegible/unreadable In Chios on the 31 December 1930 **The Registrar** L. Kalvamar (signature Hand Written) **The declarer** Priest Stamatios Eleftherios (signature Hand Written)

The above translation / interpretation of the birth and baptism certificate of my father Ioannis (John) P. Bournias. It combines both certificates.

The Marriage Certificate of Pantelis Petros Bournias 1928

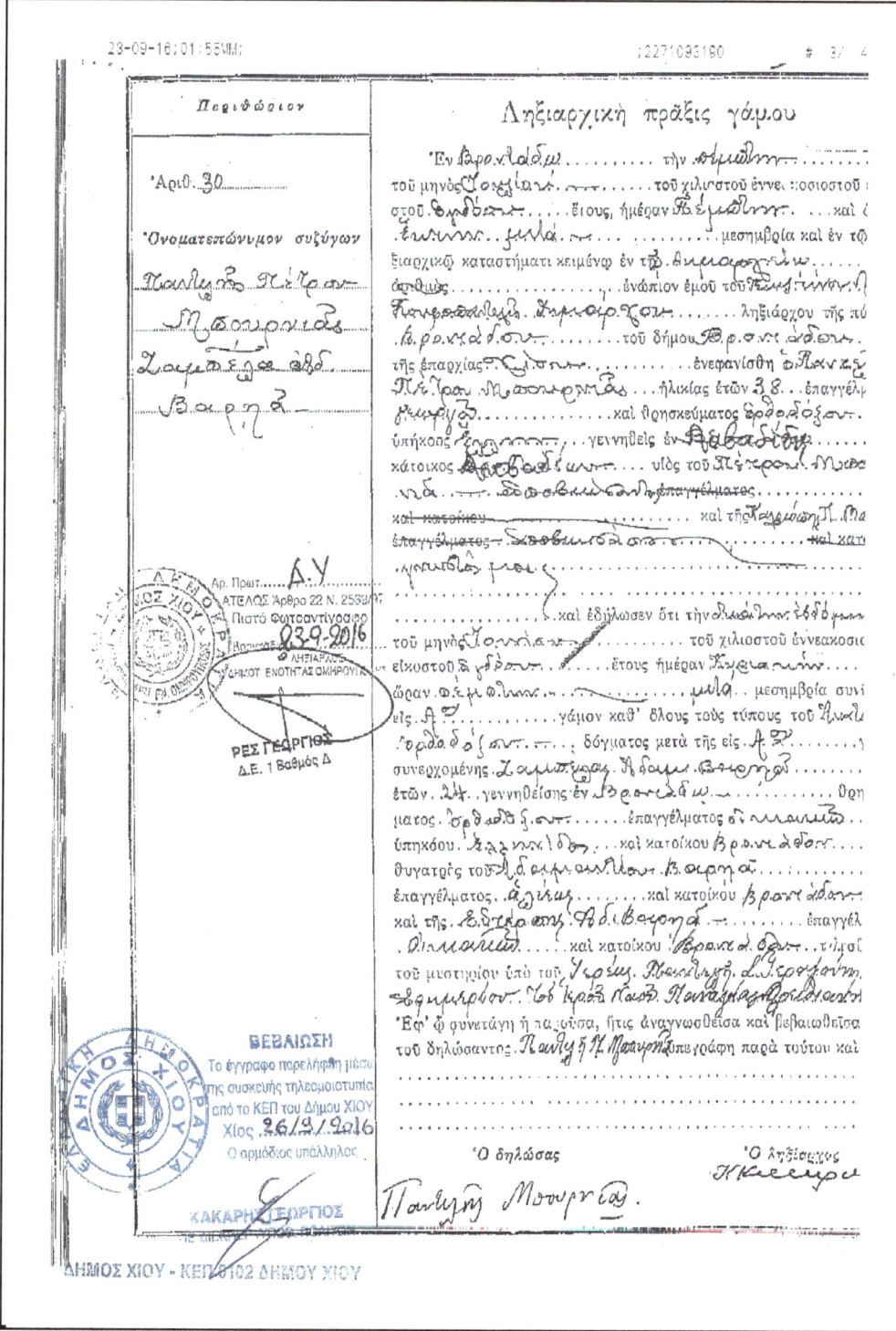

Municipality of Chios, **Registry of Marriages**

File: Bournias-P-Pantelis-Certificate-Marriage-1928.jpg

Image Reference: Scanned by P. Bournias

MARGIN	REGISTRY OF MARRIAGE
Number: 30 (Hand Written) **Complete names of spouses** Pantelis Petros Bournias Zabella Adamantios* Varia * Father's first name, female maiden name truncates the ending character of the maiden surname. STAMP / SEAL **GREEK REPUBLIC** **Municipal Section of CHIOS** Protocol # D. Y Not taxed Article 22 Law 2539/97 **Exact duplicate photocopy of the original act found in our files.** Vrontados 23-9-2016 (Hand Written) Registrar of the Municipal Section of OMIROUPOLIS Signature Illegible/unreadable Stamp of The Registrar of Birth, Marriage, Death **Res, Georgios** Municipal Section Rank D **CERTIFIED** STAMP / SEAL **GREEK REPUBLIC** **Municipal Section / District of CHIOS** 26/9/2016 (Hand Written) **KEP 0102 Municipality of CHIOS** Stamp of The Registrar of Birth, Marriage, Death **Kakaris, Georgios** **Civil Employee**	In **Vrontados** today the **Thursday 5**th of the month **July** at 6:00 p.m. of the year **nineteen hundred twenty-eight** (**1928**), **Thursday** at the time of **blank** at the Office of the Municipality ~~number~~ **(blank)** in the presence of myself **Konstantinos Koufopantelis** Mayor and Registrar of **Vrontados** and **Municipality of Vrontados** of the Province of **Chios** appeared **Pantelis Petros Bournias** age **38** profession **farmer** and of the religion **Christian Orthodox**, a **Greek** citizen born in **Livadia** and a resident of **Livadia** son of **Petros Bournias** who has died ~~profession~~ **(blank)** ~~and a resident of~~ **(blank)** and of **Kalliopi P. Ma? (surname truncated)** profession **who has died** declared that in the month of **June** of the year **nineteen hundred twenty-eight** (**1928**) on the day of **Sunday** at the time of **5:00 p.m.** of their **first marriage** of the **Christian Orthodox doctrine** after the first continuous marriage to **Zabella Adamantios Varia** age **24** born in **Vrontados** of the religion **Christian Orthodox** profession housewife, a **Greek** citizen and a resident of **Livadia** daughter of **Adamantios Varias** profession **fisherman**, a resident of **Vrontados** and **Efterpis Adamantios Varias** profession **housewife**, a resident of **Vrontados** fulfilled the sacred ceremony of marriage by the Priest Pantelis Iergounis at the Holy Parish of the sacred **church of Agios Panagias Erithianis** By reason of the presence of those who legally recognize and certify that the declarers signature of this and to me. **BLANK LINES** **The declarer**　　　　　　**Registrar / Town Clerk** (Signature of)　　　　　　(Signature of) **Pantelis Bournias**　　　　**K. Kalliopi**

THE GAK OF CHIOS

Electoral List Municipality Chios by local churches

Re-edited 556/1930 decision by the first court of Chios

Αὔξων ἀριθμός	Ἀριθμός μητρῴου ἀρρένων ὑφ' ὅν φέρεται	ΤΟΥ ΕΚΛΟΓΕΩΣ					
		Ἐπώνυμον	Ὄνομα	Ὄνομα πατρός	Ἔτ. γεν. Ἡλικία	Ἐπάγγελμα	Ἐνεστῶσα διαμονή
10		Κουτσουράδης	Νικόλαος	Κωνσταντίν.	1902	γεωργός	
11		Κουκιάς	Γεώργιος	Δημήτριος	1877	παντοπώλης	
12		Καραμαούνας	Θεόδωρος	Στέφανος	1856	γεωργός	
13		Καραμαούνας	Μιλτιάδης	Θεόδωρος	1902	»	
14		Κοκαλίδης	Δημήτριος	Κωνσταντίν.	1872	ἄεργος	
15		Λαγούρος	Ἰωάννης	Νικόλαος	1895	ἁλιεύς	
16		Δευκάκης	Ἐλευθέριος	Γεώργιος	1872	ναυτικός	
17		Μῶρος	Νικόλαος	Ἀλέξανδρος	1886	ἐργάτης	
18		Μοσχούργης	Νικόλαος	Ἰωάννης	1880	ἔμπορος	
19		Μ μίδης	Ἰωάννης	Παντελῆς	1860	γεωργός	
20		Μαυρίδης	Πέτρος	Κωνσταντίν.	1880	ταπητοπώλης	
21		Μπουρνιάς	Νικόλαος	Πέτρος	1878	ἔμπορος	
22		Μοσχούργης	Ἀλέξανδρος	Ἰωάννης	1901	γεωργός	
23		Μυλωνάδης	Γεώργιος	Λεωνίδας	1900	εἰσοδηματίας	
24		Μιμίδης	Παντελῆς	Ἰωάννης	1903	γεωργός	
25		Μπουρνιάς	Παντελῆς	Πέτρος	1893	»	
26		Σπυράκης	Μάρκος	Κωνσταντίν.	1899	»	
27		Στουπάκης	Ἰωάννης	Ἀντώνιος	1885	»	
28		Τζούμας	Ἀλέξανδρος	Νικόλαος	1887	δικηγόρος	
29		Τσακμάκας	Γεώργιος	Ἰωάννης	1864	ἁλιεύς	
30		Τσικούρας	Νικόλαος	Κωνσταντίν.	1900	»	
31		Φλάμος	Σταμάτιος	Γεώργιος	1880	γεωργός	

Image Reference: GAK Chios, line #21, Bournias, Nikolaos, Petros, 1878, commerce.

Name and area of the local churches - parishes, followed by

#	Surname	First	Father	Birth (Abt.)	Profession
Enoria Ag. Ioannou Pantopolon (Leivadion)					
21	Bournias	Nikolaos	Petros	1878	commerce
Enoria Ag. Ioannou Pantopolon (Leivadion / Leivadia)					
25	Bournias	Pantelis	Petros	1893	farmer
Enoria Ag. Louka (Leivadion)					
81	Bournias	Demetrios	Petros	1894	worker
86	Bournias	Georgios	Petros	1884	Παντοπώλης - shop owner

Enoria Ag. Ioannou Theologou

104	Bournias	Georgios	Apostoolos	1872	Lawyer

Enoria Ag. Marinis Kaloplitou

155	Bournias	Demetrios	Leonidas	1865	worker
196	Bournias	Nikolaos	Demetrios	1908	designer

Enoria Ag. Mathaiou Kofina

95	Bournias	Mihail	Pantelis	1878	farmer
96	Bournias	Haralambos	Mihail	1899	farmer

Frouriou Chiou

277	Bournias	Kyriakos	Leonidas	1866	μικροπωλητης - street seller

Panagias Latomitisis (Leivadion)

60	Bournias	Georgios	Antonios	1899	saddle maker
75	Bournias	Loukas	Antonios	1903	painter

??? – Unreadable / illegible name of the church

182	Bournias	Antonios	Leonidas	1875	money changer
217	Bournias	Christos	Pantelis		1892 farmer

Enoria Panagias Tourlotis - Παναγιασσ Τουρλωτης

129	Bournias	Emmanouil	Georgios	1905	foreman

Electoral List Municipality Chios re-edited 245/1933 decision by the first court of Chios

506	Bournias	Stamatios	Antonios	1911
942	Bournias	Christoforos	Demetrios	1910
70	Bournous*	Ioannis	Georgios	31	farmer, Αίγυπτος (Egypt)

* Μπουρνούς, I include this surname because there were errors in some names recorded even though a family with the surname Bournous does exist on Chios.

Researcher note:
Enoria = Parish.
Bournias Extracted Voters by Parish Chios 1930.txt, P. Bournias

Election List Chios Spartounta 1930

The following list may not be complete, as I have discovered other individuals born about 1815 but without enough information to publish them.

# *	surname	first	father	YOB (abt.)	age**	Όνομα	Όνομα Πατέρας
17	Bournias	Mihail	Panagiotis	1864	65	Μιχαήλ	Παναγιώτης
18	Bournias	Konstantinos	Demetrios	1854	75	Κωνσταντίνος	Δημήτριος
19	Bournias	Mihail	Stylianos	1840	89	Μιχαήλ	Στυλιανός
19	Bournias	Mihail	Stylianos	1889	40	Μιχαήλ	Στυλιανός
20	Bournias	Nikolaos	Stylianos	1846	83	Νικόλαος	Στυλιανός
20	Bournias	Nikolaos	Stylianos	1883	46	Νικόλαος	Στυλιανός
21	Bournias	Demetrios	Pantoleon ***	1849	80	Δημήτριος	Πανταλέων ***
21	Bournias	Demetrios	Pantoleon ***	1880	49	Δημήτριος	Πανταλέων ***
22	Bournias	Christoforos	Demetrios	1848	81	Χριστόφορος	Δημήτριος
22	Bournias	Christoforos	Demetrios	1881	48	Χριστόφορος	Δημήτριος
23	Bournias	Stylianos	Stamatios	1863	66	Στυλιανός	Σταμάτιος
23	Bournias	Stylianos	Stamatios	1866	63	Στυλιανός	Σταμάτιος
24	Bournias	Christoforos	Pantoleon ***	1841	88	Χριστόφορος	Πανταλέων ***
24	Bournias	Christoforos	Pantoleon ***	1888	41	Χριστόφορος	Πανταλέων ***
25	Bournias	Mihail	Pantoleon ***	1855	74	Μιχαήλ	Πανταλέων ***
25	Bournias	Mihail	Pantoleon ***	1874	55	Μιχαήλ	Πανταλέων ***
26	Bournias	Ioannis	Mihail	1857	72	Ιωάννης	Μιχαήλ
26	Bournias	Ioannis	Mihail	1872	57	Ιωάννης	Μιχαήλ
27	Bournias	Nikolaos	Georgios	1840	89	Νικόλαος	Γεώργιος
27	Bournias	Nikolaos	Georgios	1889	40	Νικόλαος	Γεώργιος
28	Bournias	Alexandros	Georgios	1843	86	Αλέξανδρος	Γεώργιος
28	Bournias	Alexandros	Georgios	1886	43	Αλέξανδρος	Γεώργιος
29	Bournias	Ioannis	Georgios	1850	79	Ιωάννης	Γεώργιος
29	Bournias	Ioannis	Georgios	1879	50	Ιωάννης	Γεώργιος
30	Bournias	Pantelis	Panagiotis	1850	79	Παντελής	Παναγιώτης
30	Bournias	Nikolaos	Panagiotis	1865	64	Νικόλαος	Παναγιώτης
31	Bournias	Ioannis	Nikolaos	1841	88	Ιωάννης	Νικόλαος
31	Bournias	Ioannis	Nikolaos	1888	41	Ιωάννης	Νικόλαος
32	Bournias	Pantelis	Panagiotis	1879	50	Παντελής	Παναγιώτης
Noticed doubling of record numbers and names. It could be those with erroneous YOB from the electoral lists or it could be from electoral lists of different years shown as 1930.							
The individuals in this case are those with minor differences in YOB and age.							
There is a very small probability that this individual is from different grandfathers.							
* line number from electoral list							
** approximate age = 1928 - year of birth							

A list of Bournias from the Municipality of Kardamyla, Chios dated 1928

Election List Chios Spartounta 1930

The following list is a slightly skewed image of individuals that I have extracted the information originating from the electoral listings of Kardamyla from February 16, 1928 from Spartounda. There are sixteen Bournias surnames, one of which is misspelled as Mournias (#18 Μουρνιάς).

		Spartountos 1928 Electoral List (grouped by father, then by YOB)				
#	# *	surname	first	father	YOB (abt.)	Age **	Όνομα Πατέρας
1	18	Bournias	Konstantinos	Demetrios	1854	75	Δημήτριος
2	22	Bournias	Christoforos	Demetrios	1881	48	Δημήτριος
3	29	Bournias	Ioannis	Georgios	1879	50	
4	28	Bournias	Alexandros	Georgios	1886	43	Αλέξανδρος
5	27	Bournias	Nikolaos	Georgios	1889	40	Γεώργιος
6	26	Bournias	Ioannis	Mihail	1872	57	Μιχαήλ
7	31	Bournias	Ioannis	Nikolaos	1888	41	Ιωάννης
8	30	Bournias	Pantelis	Panagiotis	1850	79	Παντελής
9	17	Bournias	Mihail	Panagiotis	1864	65	Παναγιώτης
10	27	Bournias	Nikolaos	Panagiotis	1865	64	Παναγιώτης
11	25	Bournias	Mihail	Pantoleon	1874	55	Πανταλέων ***
12	21	Bournias	Demetrios	Pantoleon	1880	49	Πανταλέων ***
13	24	Bournias	Christoforos	Pantoleon	1888	41	Πανταλέων ***
14	23	Bournias	Stylianos	Stamatios	1866	63	Σταμάτιος
15	20	Bournias	Nikolaos	Stylianos	1883	46	Στυλιανός
16	19	Bournias	Mihail	Stylianos	1889	40	Στυλιανός

* Line number from electoral list.
** Approximate age = 1928 - year of birth or age.
*** The father's name Pantoleon is Pantelis.

Image Reference:
GAK Chios & the Korai Library, Bournias-Dimos-Karystos-Evia.jpg, 2014

Researcher note:
Election List Chios Spartounta 1930.txt, P. Bournias.
Bournias Extracted Voters by Parish Chios 1930.txt, P. Bournias.
Registered-Voters-on-Chios-Island-1930-ΕΚΛΟΓΙΚΟΣ-ΚΑΤΑΛΟΓΟΣ-ΣΤΗ-ΝΙΣΟΥ-ΧΙΟΥ-1930-Εγγεγραμμένοι-ψηφοφόροι-στη-Χίο-το-1930. txt, P. Bournias.

THE GAK OF ERMOUPOLI SYROS AND MYKONOS

This is an example of the online records from the website of IMS.

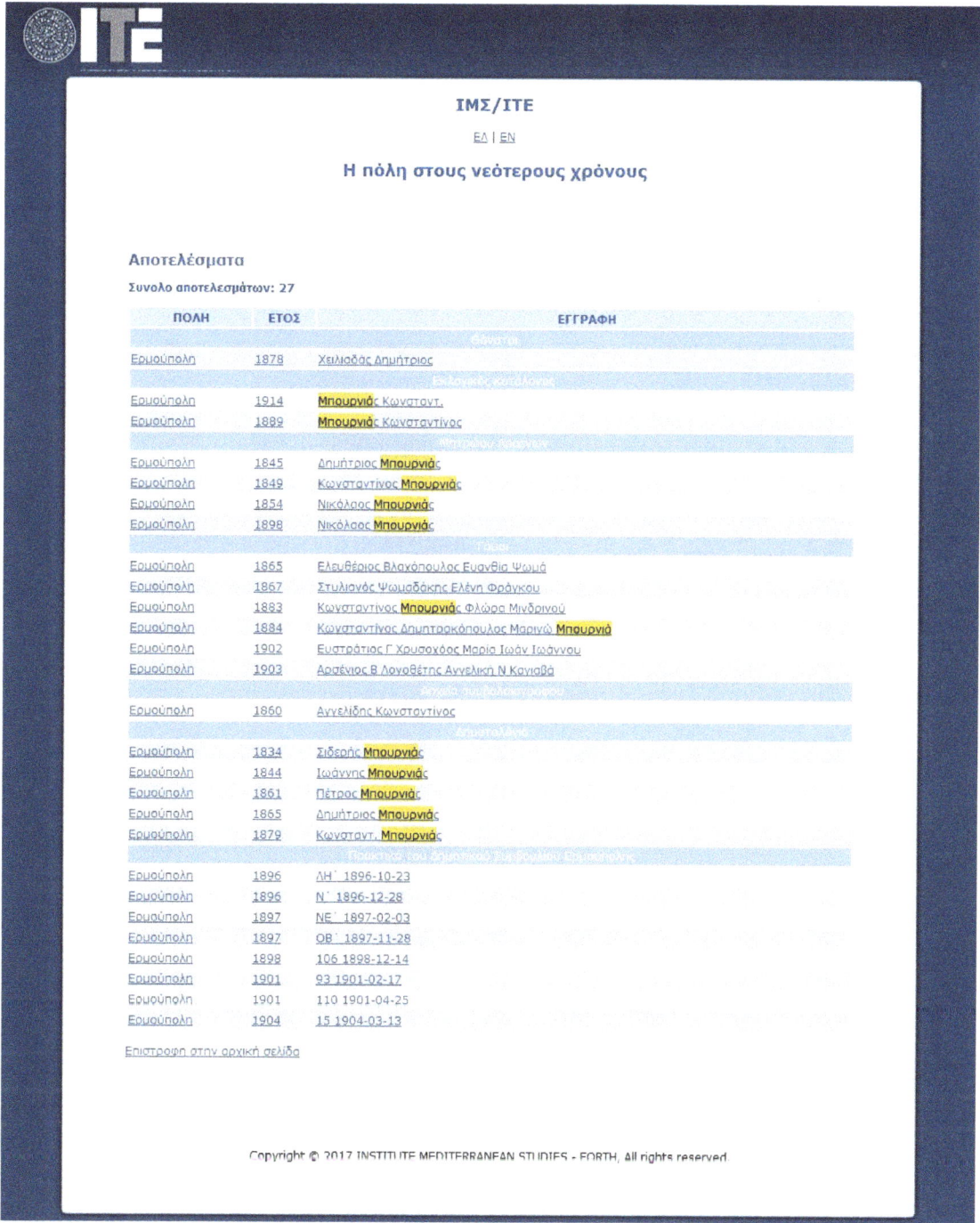

Image Reference: Institute of Mediterranean Studies – Forth.

Translation of the extracted documents from the GAK Syros for Ioannis Bournias 1844

Researcher note: Punctuation on original documents are similarly reproduced.

1ˢᵗ page

Ermoupolis Police
... that they have truth (???) ....
the following days...
Ermoupolis on May 15, 1844

The Policeman

(signature)

To the mayor's office
Syros Ermoupolis

The undersigned wishes to become a citizen of Ermoupolis in order to enjoy the right to be a Greek citizen, I hasten to bring to your attention the following ....

My name is Ioannis Bournias
I was born in Chios, I am 45 years old.

The profession of security guard, I live in the Municipality....
Since 1822 I have lived independently, I took the oath of submission to the Kingdom today in this City Hall.

The obedient for the uneducated
Ioannis Bournia

Th. Fokas
(name of the person who wrote the document)

1ˢᵗ page

Η Αστυνομία Ερμούπολεως
... ότι εχουσιν αληθείας (???) ....
τις παραυοης ....
Ερμούπολη τις 15 Μαΐου 1844

Ο Αστυνόμος

(υπογραφή)

Προς το δημαρχεύον
Σύρου Ερμούπολη

Ο υποφαινόμενος επιθυμώ να γινώ δημότης Ερμούπολης δια να απολαύσω το δικαίωμα τον πολίτων Έλληνος σπεύδω να θέσω υπόψιν σας των εξής ....

Ονομάζομαι Ιωάννης Μπουρνιάς
εγεννηθην εν Χίου, είμαι ετών 45.

Το επάγγελμα φύλακας κατοικώ εις τον Δήμο ....
Από το 1822 ζω ανεξάρτητος έδωκα τον όρκον της υποταγής εις τον Βασιλεία σήμερον εις το Δημαρχείο τούτο.

Ο Ευπειθέστατος
δια τον αγγράμματον
Ιωάννη Μπουρνιά

Θ. Φωκάς

2nd page **Number 1061** **805** (???) **5411** (letters, possible initials)	**The Mayor of Syros** **Certifies** That Mr. Ioannis Bournias, aged 45, married, Orthodox Christian, by profession a security guard, resident of the Municipality of which we are the head, and (???) registered in the census from October 28, 1840 under the number. ~~3584~~ 5411 according to the Constitutional oath, he is a Greek enjoying the right of Greek Citizenship because he has the right to immigrate.... in Greece in the year 1824, and complied with the terms of the protocol (???) of June 16, 1830. **Ermoupolis, April 10 1857** **The Mayor (signature)** **To the Prefecture** I am sending attached the Certificate of Ioannis Bournias, Issued a right (???) under number 11422 by the local Port Authority ... which I ask the Prefecture to send (???) wherever he sees fit. **Same day** **The Mayor (signature)**

2nd page **Αριθμός 1061** **805** (???) **5411**	**Ο Δήμαρχος Σύρου** **Πιστοποιώ** Ότι **Ο Κος. Ιωάννης Μπουρνιάς**, ετών 45, έγγαμοι, χριστιανό ορθόδοξος, το επάγγελμα φύλακος κάτοικος του Δήμου τούτου του οποίου προϊστάμεθα, και (???) εγγεγραμμένος εις το δημοτολογίου από την 28 Οκτώβριου 1840 υπό τον αριθμό. ~~3584~~ 5411 ως τον Συντάγματος όρκον, είναι Έλλην απολαυων του δικαιρωματος της Ελληνικής Ιθαγένειας διότι έχει το δικαίωμα του μεταναστεύσεως .... εις την Ελλάδα το 1824 έτος, και συνεμμορφώθη με τους ορούς του πρωτοκόλλου (???) της 16 Ιονίου 1830. **Ερμούπολης** **10 Απρίλιου 1857** **Ο Δήμαρχος** (υπογραφή) **Προς την Νομαρχών**

	Αποστέλλω συνημμένων το Πιστοποιητικόν του Ιωάννη Μπουρνιά,
	Εκδοθεί δικαίωμα (???) του υπο αριθμό 11422 εγγράφον του ενταύθα Λιμεναρχειου ...
	το οποίον παρακαλώ ινα η Νομαρχία επιθυμώ και αποστείλει (???) οπού δει.
	Αυθημερόν
	Ο Δήμαρχος (υπογραφή)

Researcher note:
Ioannis Bournias, age 45, religion Christian Orthodox, resident Municipality of Ermoupoli, profession Port / Coast Guard, he was married, and uneducated.

A handwritten record from the Registry of Citizens of the Municipality of Ermoupoli, GAK Syros-Ioannis-Bournias-1844.pdf, as translated by P. Bournias shows that that he moved from Chios to Ermoupoli Syros escaping from the results of the revolution in 1822.
In the same document is his request to become a Greek citizenship again.

Ellipsis and/or question marks refer to text that is illegible / unreadable.

Electoral List Municipality Syros 1871

#	Surname	First name	Father	Age	Profession	Location
2942	Bournias	Demetrios	Isidoros	45	Sailor	Ermoupoli
3396	Bournias	Konstantinos	Sideris	40	Boiler-maker	Ermoupoli

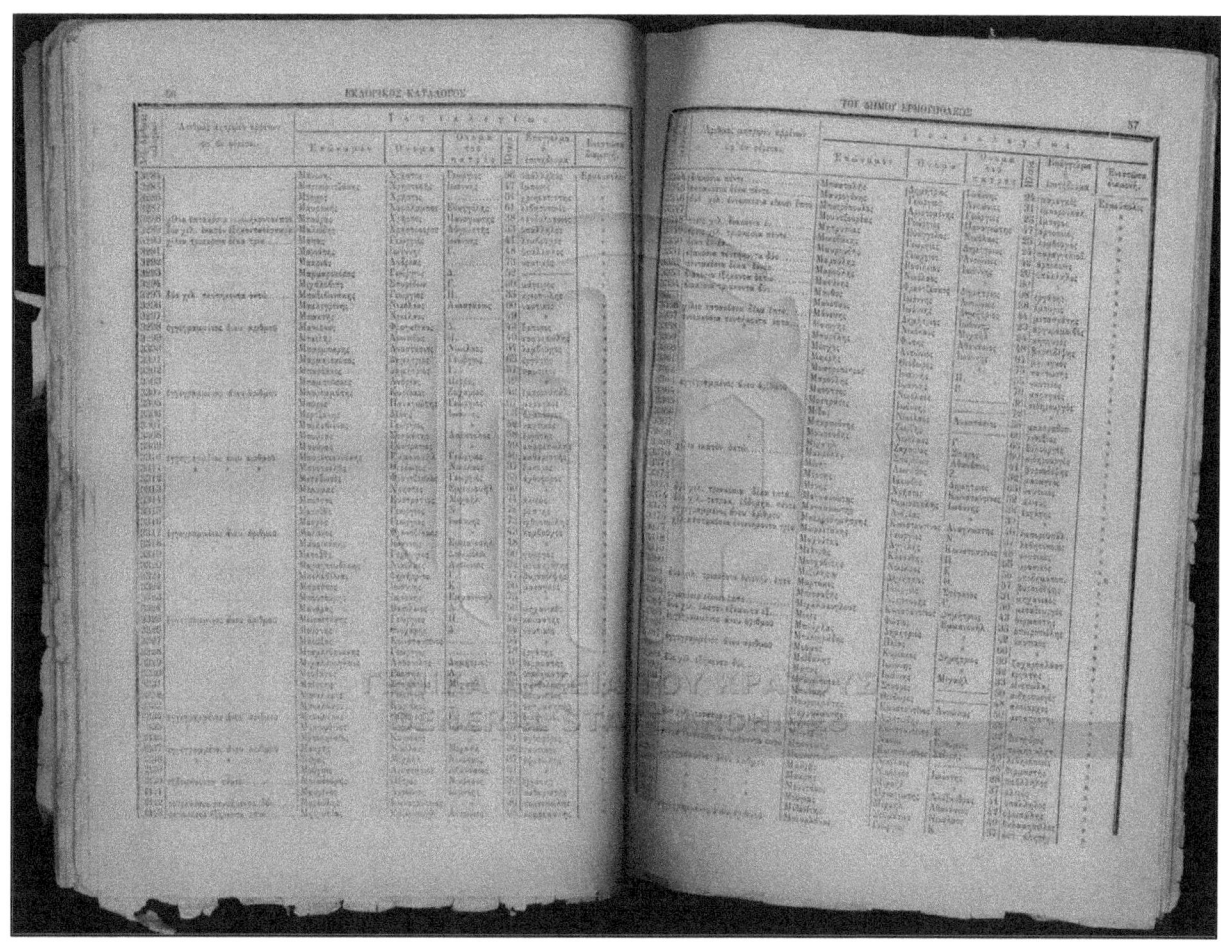

Image Reference: GAK Syros

Various Registries

The following data was extracted from the IMS and GAK Syros website. It is unclear as to which registries the websites originated. Some have births and marriages.

540001
Dimitrios Bournias - Angelika Gialadena   343

540003
Ekaterina Sideris Bournia   201
Ekaterina, daughter of Sideris Bournias and Marouka Kavathakena (201/1839) IMS

540004
George Isidoros Bournias Maria   290; July 3;
It does not look like the info is on the same line.
George, son of Isidoros Bournias and Maria (253/1835) IMS

540006
Konstantinos Sideris Bournias   ???
It does not look like the 85 is on the same line.
Constantine, son of Sideris Bournias and Marouka (53/1845) IMS

540007
Marigo 78 Sideris Bournia Kalliopi;
Numbers are in the fold of the book.
Marigo, daughter of Sideris Bournias and Marouka Nikolaou (254/1847) IMS

540009
8 ??? Ioannis Bournias   ???   1844 15 13 October

540010
96 Sofia Antonios Bournia Despina Giannari
It does not appear that the information is on the same line.
Sofia, daughter of Antonios Bournias and Despina Giannari (364/1839) IMS
Antonios, son of Dimitrios Bournias and Angelika Gialadena (343/1829) IMS

540011
Finareti   Petrou Bournia   Fotini Athanassiou   47   1858   City   Hall   900
Finareti, daughter of Petros Bournias and Fotini Athanassiou   (47/1858)   IMS

110001
???   Isidoros   Bournia   Marouka   1837   62 or 67   6 or 12 March
It does not appear that the information is on the same line.
Aggerou, Daughter of Isidoros Bournias and Marouka   (67/1837)   IMS

110002
12   Dimitrios Sideris Bournias Marigos Kokkinou   142 or 147
Dimitrios, son of   Sideris   Bournias and Marigos Kokkinou   (147/1842)   IMS

110003
Nikolaos Isidoros Bournias   Maria Kalouta ???   296   9 October
Nikolaos, son of   Isidoros Bournias and Maria Kalouta   (296/1849)   IMS

Researcher note:
Ellipsis and/or question marks refer to text that is illegible / unreadable.

GAK ERMOUPOLI SYROS AND MYKONOS

Various Registries and Electoral lists

Death registers
Showing 1-1 of 1 item.

#	Fullname	Father	Mother	Age of	Disease	Date	Area
	of Deceased	of Deceased	of Deceased	Deceased		of death	
1367	Cheiliadas Dimitrios	Dimitrios Chiliadas	Marigo Bournia	03	drakos	1878-08-19	Hermoupolis

Electoral catalog or registers
Showing 1-2 of 2 items.

#	Name	Surname	Father	Age	Occupation	Year	Area
38528	Constant.	Bournias	Sideri	65	Boiler maker	1914	Hermoupolis
53930	Konstantinos	Bournias	Sideris	40	Boiler maker	1889	Hermoupolis

Male Registry
Showing 1-4 of 4 items.

#	Name	Surname	Father	Birth Year	Area
108	Dimitrios	Bournias	Sideris	1845	Hermoupolis
1137	Konstantinos	Bournias	Isidoros	1849	Hermoupolis
2612	Nikolaos	Bournias	Konstantinos	1854	Hermoupolis
20898	Nikolaos	Bournias	Michael	1898	Hermoupolis

Marriage Registries
Showing 1-6 of 6 items.

#	Cert. #	Name	Name	Marriage	Year	Area
937	18	Eleftherios Vlachopoulos	Evanthia Psoma	1865-01-17	1865	Hermoupolis
1339	87	Stylianos Psomadakis	Eleni Frangou	1867-07-30	1867	Hermoupolis
3591	146	Konstantinos Bournias	Flora Mindrinou	1883-11-10	1883	Hermoupolis
3686	61	Konstantinos Dimitrakopoulos	Marigo Bournia	1884-04-22	1884	Hermoupolis
5898	83	Efstratios C Chrysochos	Maria Ioan Ioannou	1902-10-28	1902	Hermoupolis
5946	24	Arsenios B Logothetis	Angeliki N Kagiava	1903-02-16	1903	Hermoupolis

Notaries
Showing 1-1 of 2 items.

#	Act	Notary	Name	Date	Year	Area
3688	18298	Epitropiko	Angelidis Konstantinos	09/09/1860	1860	Hermoupolis

Municipal rolls
Showing 1-5 of 5 items.

#	Name	Surname	Father	Age	Year	Area
11858	Sideris	Bournias		27	1834	Hermoupolis
16003	Ioannis	Bournias		45	1844	Hermoupolis
20537	Petros	Bournias		30	1861	Hermoupolis
22016	Dimitrios	Bournias	S.	22	1865	Hermoupolis
25836	Constant	Bournias	Sid.	32	1879	Hermoupolis

Proceedings of the Town Council
Showing 1-8 of 8 items.

#	Session #	Chronology	Year	Area
1387	ΛH΄	1896-10-23	1896	Hermoupolis
1399	NY	1896-12-28	1896	Hermoupolis
1405	NE΄	1897-02-03	1897	Hermoupolis
1422	OB΄	1897-11-28	1897	Hermoupolis
1458	106	1898-12-14	1898	Hermoupolis
1484	93	1901-02-17	1901	Hermoupolis
1501	110	1901-04-25	1901	Hermoupolis
1579	15	1904-03-13	1904	Hermoupolis

Male Records Catalog

#	Name	Father	Year	Area
108	Dimitrios Bournias	Sideris	1845	Hermoupolis
1137	Konstantinos Bournias	Isidoros	1849	Hermoupolis
2612	Nikolaos Bournias	Konstantinos	1854	Hermoupolis
20898	Nikolaos Bournias	Michael	1898	Hermoupolis

Proceedings of the Town Council: # 15 / 1904-03-13
City Hermoupolis
Year 1904
Number 109
Session Number 15
Chronology 1904-03-13

Abstract Text The minutes of the 12th, 13th and 14th sittings are ratified.
the mayor is instructed to file a lawsuit against unknown persons for the theft of the lights of the City Hall.
Of the Council, we are asking for 720 drachmas from arrears.
The proposal of P. Katsimantis to make an appeal regarding the abolition of the position of librarian.
It is decided to make an appeal and of the decision of the prefect for reduction of the subsidy to the Association "Philomousos of Syros". It is proposed to set the subsidy at 2000 drachmas.

GAK ATHENS
Election Lists

| # | Name | Surname | Father | Age | Occupation | GAK reference | Year | Area |

0195-Antonios-Bournias-Gregorios-age-46-notary-2066985.w.1200-voters-1907-Athens.jpg
0450-Mournias-Georgios-Ioannis-age-30-commerce-2066989.w.1200-voters-1907-Athens.jpg
0615-Emmanuel-Bournias-age-35-fisherman-2065870.w.1200-voters-1867-Aegina.jpg
0615-Emmanuel-Pournias-Antonios-age-35-fisherman-voters-1867-Aigina-2065870.w.1200.jpg
0986-Georgios-Bournias-Gregorios-age-51-customs-agent-2066998.w.1200-voters-1907-Athens.jpg
1005-Demetrios-Bournias-Emmanuel-age-54-barber-2066998.w.1200-voters-1907-Athens.jpg
1858-Ioannis-Bournias-Vasilios-age-30-employee-2067013.w.1200-voters-1908-Athens.jpg
2215-Konstantinos-Bournias-Vasilios-age-29-employee-2067018.w.1200-voters-1910-Athens.jpg
2801-Emmanouel-Bournias-Ioannis-age-30-commerce-2067028.w.1200-voters-1912-Athens.jpg
5706-Nikolaos-Bournias-Mihail-age-23-sailor-2067074.w.1200-voters-1922-Ermo.jpg
6039-Antonios-Bournias-Emmanuouil-age-67-shop-2067080.w.1200-voters-1922-Aegina.jpg
6040-Emmanouil-Bournias-Demetrios-age-22-student-2067080.w.1200-voters-1922-Aegina.jpg
6067-Dionysios-Bournias-Panagiotis-age-40-upholsterer-2067080.w.1200-voters-1922-Letrinon-Pyrgos.jpg
6349-Konstantinos-Bournias-Apostolos-age-58-lawyer-2067085.w.1200-voters-1922-Karystos.jpg
6826-Loukas-Bournias-Apostolos-age-30-potery-2067092.w.1200-voters-1923-Skouasi-Karystos.jpg

Electoral-List-1864-1925-Athens-1005-Bournias-Demetrios-Emmanouil-age-54-barber-2066998.w.1200.jpg
Electoral-List-1864-1925-Athens-195-Bournias-Antonios-Gregorios-age-46-Symvouliografos-2066985.w.1200.jpg
Electoral-List-1864-1925-Athens-624-Bournias-Periklis-Gregorios-age-40-civil-servant-2066992.w.1200.jpg
Electoral-List-1864-1925-Athens-986-Bournias-Georgios-Gregorios-age-51-customs-agent-2066998.w.1200.jpg

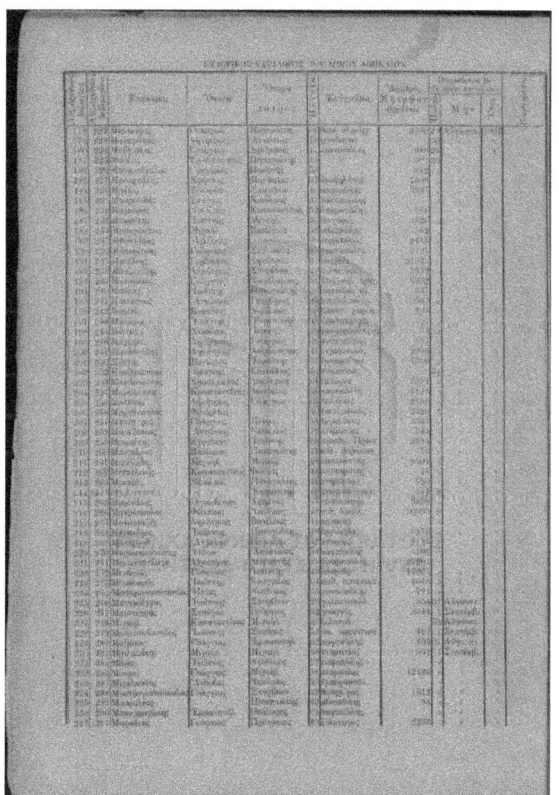

Image Reference: GAK Athens

GAK KALAMATA
Municipality Records Koroni

School Record of Student Grades

Student Grades from the first grade of a school in Koroni.
The layout of the book shown on the **left side of the page:**
Sequence number, a student number, student surname and first name, area, age, conduct, profession of the parent

Right side of the page: Average grades for the lessons in:
Greek, Mathematics, Religion, History, Geography, Gymnastics, Calligraphy.
Some classes taught Latin, French, and Physics, and teachers remarks.

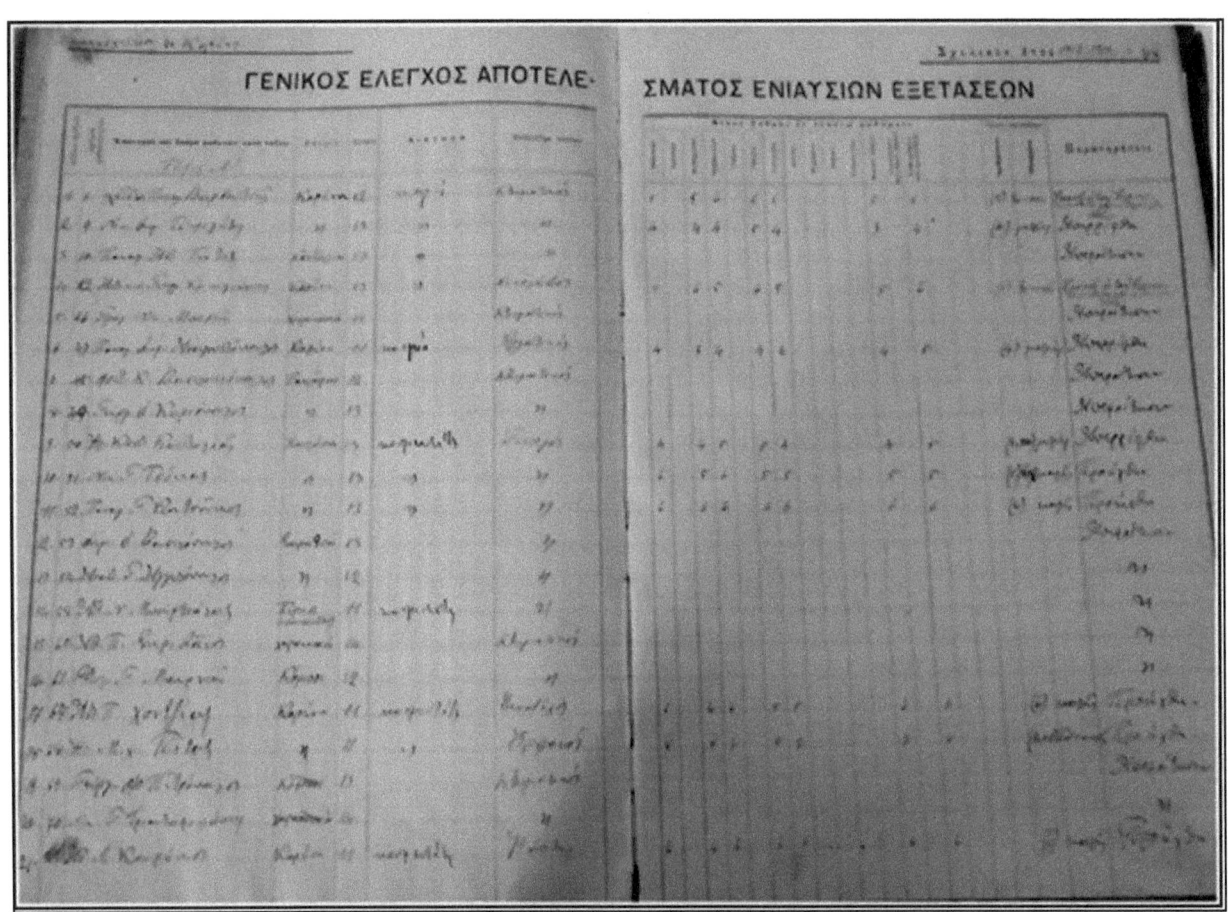

016-Bournias-xxxxx-Georgios-age-12-Koroni-school-record-1913.jpg

Image Reference: GAK Kalamata

Researcher note: The "xxxxx" in the image file name indicates no father shown.

GAK KALAMATA
Municipality Records Koroni
Records of the Registry of (Boys) Males

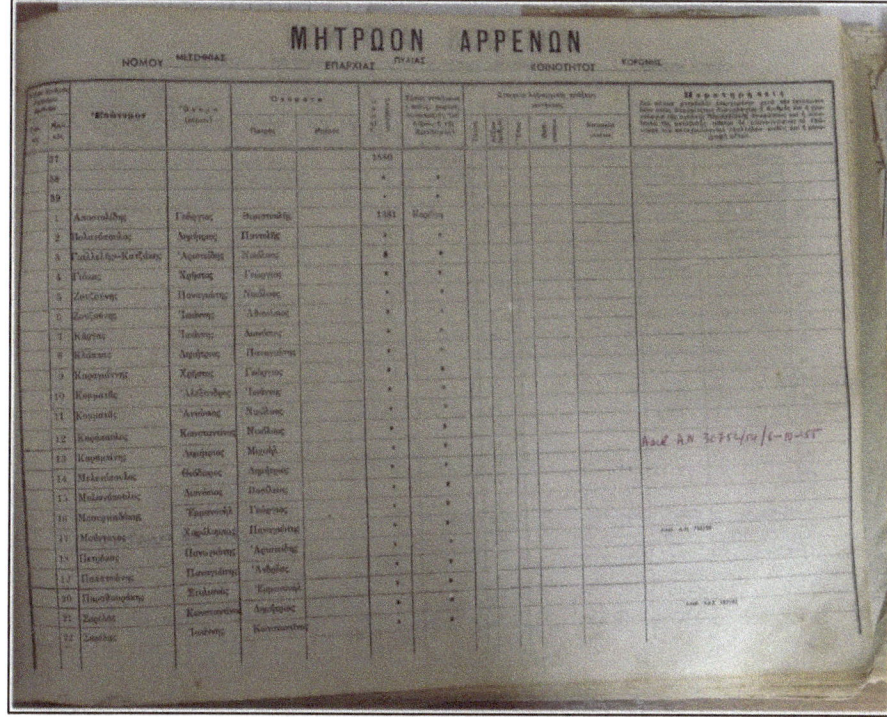

Reference:
Dsc_1523-Bourniadakis-Emmanuel-Georgios-1881-Koroni-Mitroo-Arenon.jpg

Dsc_1524-Bournias-Demetrios-Stylianos-1882-Koroni-Mitroo-Arenon.jpg

Dsc_1527-Bournias-Demetrios-Georgios-1884-Koroni-Mitroo-Arenon.jpg

These records were provided to the military and recorded in a ledger for the year that the boys reach the age for induction.

Image Reference: P. Bournias

MUNICIPALITY RECORDS OF KARYSTOS EVIA

This image is a list of Bournias family members with dates of births from 1861 to 1926 from the Registry of (Boys) Male Records, separated by the father's name.

#	Surname	name	father	year of birth
1	Bournias	Antonios	Apostolos	1861
2			Konstantinos	1864
3			Michail	1866
4			Leonidas	1868
5			Georgios	1870
6			Panagis	1872
7			Ioannis	1877
1	Bournias	Apostolos	Antonios	1888
2			Nikolaos	1889
3			Andreas	1893
1	Bournias	Apostolos	Leonidas	1895
2			Georgios	1903
1	Bournias	Apostolos	Panagis	1907
2			Demetrios	1908
3			Georgios	1910
4			Ierotheos	1913
5			Ioannis	1926

Text translated at bottom of the image:
This chart displays the men who are recorded in the Registry of Boys of the Municipality of Karystos with the surname Bournias and separated by the family (most likely brothers, with the same father).

Image credit:
Facsimile from Municipality of Karystos Evia, Bournias-Dimos-Karystos-Evia.jpg

Researcher note:
The following image was sent to me by fax from the Municipality of Karystos Evia. I used it to calculate and verify the years of birth and cross-reference with ages, and the differences between age groups.

The first series of names are the children of the second son of Apostolos, Antonios Bournias born about 1835 in Karystos Evia.

The name Panagis originates from the name Panagiotis, and Takis is used as a nickname.

I have discovered some names of the female siblings, but I was not able to find their years of birth.

GREEK ORTHODOX CHURCH BAPTISM AND MARRIAGE RECORDS

Greek Orthodox Church baptism and Marriage Records of Chios are available but were not digitized when I visited the office of the Metropoli. I informed them about my research, and why I wanted to see them, and they finally agreed to allow me to photograph part of the archive.

File names of my photographs are shown instead of the photographs for those with information about family members from the Baptisms

The information on the pages may vary depending on who wrote them, when they were recorded, usually with the following details:
- Page number
- Sequence or line number
- Date recorded may be the same as the year of birth
- Village local church
- Name at birth
- Baptism name (used if different)
- Gender of child
- Date of Birth (may or may not be 100% accurate)
- Father's name and surname
- Mother's name and spouse's surname
- Godparent
- Name of the Priest
- Date Baptized
- Village
- Remarks

Researcher note:
In some cases, individuals may have been baptized much later, depending on where they lived. Question marks or X's may be used to indicate unknown or illegible data.
You may see repeating photograph numbers if there are more than one Bournias family member on a page.

Photo # Baptism Line # Child Father Mother YOB Date Baptized
Dsc_1010-Baptism-0382-Georgios-Petros-Kalliope-Bournias-1882-June-1886.jpg
Dsc_1017-Baptism-1212-Konstantinos-Demetrios-Stamatia-Bournias-June-1923.jpg
Dsc_1018-Baptism-1216-Kalliopi-Georgios-Zenovia-Bournias-Aug-1923.jpg
Dsc_1019-Baptism-0145-Antonios-X(Christos)-Kon. Avgousti-Bournias-March-1924.jpg
Dsc_1020-Baptism-0483-Markella-Antonios-Chrysanthi-Bournias-March-1919.jpg
Dsc_1021-Baptism-0517-Xristoforos-Stylianos-Maria-Bournias-June-1923.jpg
Dsc_1023-Baptism-0994-Katina-Demetrios-Stamatia-Bournias-March-1924.jpg

Photo #   Baptism Line #   Child   Father   Mother   YOB   Date Baptized

Dsc_1024-Baptism-0995-Georgios-Nikolaos-Despoina-Bournias-July-1924.jpg
Dsc_1024-Baptism-0999-Xristina-Georgios-Zenovia-Bournias-Jan-1925.jpg
Dsc_1026-Baptism-2047-Vasilios-Haralambos-Maria-Bournias-Sept-1925.jpg
Dsc_1029-Baptism-0739-Georgios-Demetrios-Eleni Kontari-Bournias-Aug-1910.jpg
Dsc_1029-Baptism-0741-Anitsa-Nikolaos-Despoina Axioti-Bournias-Jan-1926.jpg
Dsc_1029-Baptism-0743-Hleias-Ioannis-Eugenia-Bournias-Aug-1910.jpg
Dsc_1029-Baptism-0744-Irini-Stylianos-Maria-Bournias-Dec-1910.jpg
Dsc_1030-Baptism-0825-Xristos-Demetrios-Fotini-Bournias-Jan-1910.jpg

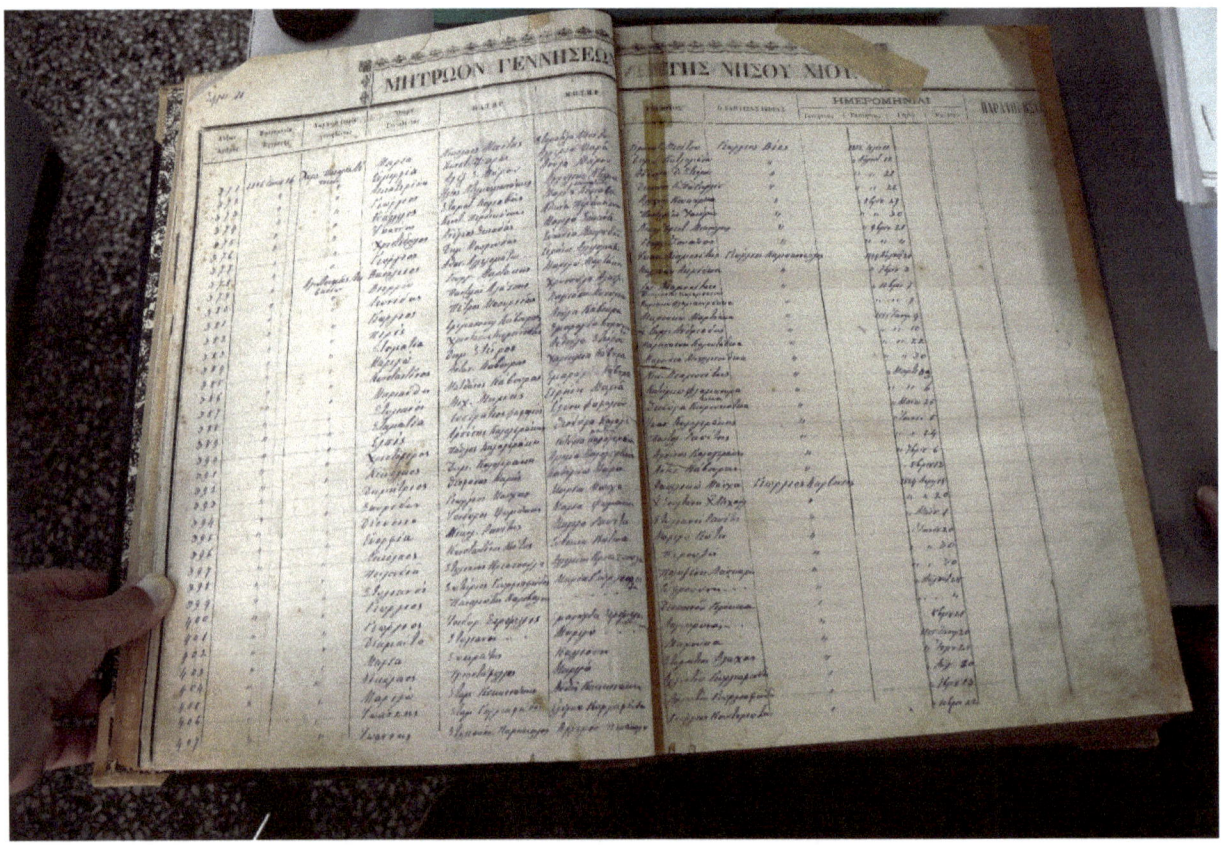

A page (reduced in size) from the baptismal records of the "Mitropoli" of Chios

Image credit: P. A. Bournias

CEMETERIES

Cemeteries where Bournias family members may be remembered and revered

Documentation from various Cemeteries are available to direct line family members.

I have over the years collected obituaries of Bournias family members as part of the research effort, and have photographed some graves. The purpose of doing this is to be able to extract the names and chronologies of the individuals and their families for historical purposes.

Additionally, I have taken photographs of the graves at some Greek cemeteries that I have visited. No obituaries or photographs are shown in this document to respect those who may not wish to see them. I have included references to the information and images of those that have been linked to the various trees on my charts.

Some Cemeteries listed here have been visited while others have not due to limitations of time and resources. Each has an office either within the cemetery or outside in a building.

Each municipality has its own cemetery and there are major and minor cemeteries in every city, and many are listed on GOOGLE maps.

The First Cemetery of Athens is known as the A (proto) Kimitirio Dimou Athineon from 1838.

The Second Cemetery of Athens is known as the B (deftero) Kimitirio Dimou Athineon from 1849.

The Third Cemetery of Athens is known as the "Γ" (gamma) Kimitirio Dimou Athineon from 1934.

There are about four (4) major and about twenty (20) minor cemeteries on Chios.

Gravesites only exist if a family member or someone pays for the yearly maintenance fees to the municipality otherwise; the grave is exhumed for the use by others.
When a grave is exhumed, the bones of the deceased are usually placed into boxes and stored for an annual fee.
I have not found any references regarding the indexing of the individuals at a gravesite.

From a legal viewpoint, I have learned from my lawyer Magda Tazedaki that the office at the cemetery should have a copy of the death certificate, and that it may be requested by a family member.
This assumes that the clerk at that office is willing to do that.

The death certificate may provide valuable historical health information regarding how the person died, in addition to family information.

GREEK ARMY RECORDS
BOURNIAS FALLEN IN ACTION

From the Greek army online records, I discovered the following Bournias who fell in action.

Note that indented information is a sub-record. Ordered by year of death.

Bournias Charalambos	Bournias Leonidas, A.
Father's name: (unknown)	Father's name: Athan. (Athanasios)
Rank: Soldier	Rank: Soldier
Period: Balkan Wars	Period: World War I 1914 - 1919
Bournias Charalambos	Bournias Leonidas
Father's name	Father's name Athan.
Weapon ---	Birth county of Achaia and Ilidos
Birth of Artis	OTA birth of Livartziou
OTA birth of Artaeans	Birth settlement Livartzi Achaia
Birth settlement Arta	World War I period 1914 - 1919
County of death -	Date of death 13/10/1918
OTA of death -	Place of death 6th Military Hospital Athens
Settlement of Death -	https://en.wikipedia.org/wiki/Livartzi
Grave County -	
OTA burial -	
Grave settlement -	
Balkan Wars Period	
Unit -	
Date of death 17/1/1913	
Place of death Veria Military Hospital	
Bournias Basil – Vasilios, K.	**Bournias Ioannis, V.**
Father's name: Const. (Konstantinos)	Father's name: (Basil) Vasileios
Grade: Soldier	Grade: Captain
Period: World War I 1914 - 1919	Period: Asia Minor Campaign 1919 - 1922
Bournias Basil	Bournias Ioannis
Father's name Const.	Surname Basil
OTA birth	Weapon Artillery gun
World War I period 1914 - 1919	Birth Attica
Date of death 25/7/1918	OTA birth of Athenians
Place of death Nafplio Military Hospital	Birth settlement Athens
	Asia Minor Campaign Period 1919 - 1922

Other Bournias family members discovered have been added to the various charts or noted on a **Chart of the Unknowns**.

PESONTES OF THE GREEK ITALIAN WAR OF 1940 AND 1941

The northern border of Greece with Albania.

Pesontes in Greek means fallen in action.

Demetrios Mihail Bournias, (Δημήτριος Μιχαήλ Μπουρνιάς)
Soldier, died 12-01-1941,
Kleisoura, Kastoria, Macedonia (Κλεισούρα, Καστοριάς της Μακεδονίας).

Georgios Konstantinos Bournias, (Γεώργιος Κωνσταντίνος Μπουρνιάς)
Soldier, died 8-03-1941,
Boularati, West of Kakavias (Μπουλαράτι, Δ. Κακαβιάς).

Researcher note:
Demetrios Mihail Bournias, Rank - Βαθμός 16ου, Σ. Π., page 28
PESONTES_GREEK-ALBANIAN-WAR-1940-Kathimerini20151028.pdf, as translated by P. Bournias.

Georgios Konstantinos Bournas, Rank - Βαθμός 11ου, Σ. Π., page 29
PESONTES_GREEK-ALBANIAN-WAR-1940-Kathimerini20151028.pdf, as translated by P. Bournias.

THE PARLIAMENT LIBRARY COLLECTION

The Parliament Library Collection for Bournias

The following information can be seen at the Library of the Parliament regarding Antonios and other Bournias using the Greek references. I translated the references into English but the documents are in Greek.

181.
The great men of humanity [Athens]: Bible Publishing House, 1952-1953.

Collection.	Reference	No.	Copy	Status
Benakeios Library	Collection Bournia	BOP 1440	v9	Available
Benakeios Library	Trikoupi Collection	TPI 1100	1 (Series 1)	Available
Lenorman	Closed Collection	C40 67	v1	Available

182.
Greek novelists: Dionysios Solomos [et al.] Under Harris, Petros, 1902-1998. [Athens]: Bookstore of "Estia," [1963-]

Benakeios Library	Collection Bournia	MPO 2222	v4	Available
Lenorman	Closed Collection	C40 93/96	v2	Available
Lenorman	Closed Collection	C40 93/96	v1	Available

184.
The generation of '30 under Tsakonas, Dimitrios Gr., 1921-2004. Athens: Cactus, c1989.

Benakeios Library	Collection Bournia	BOP 1402	Available
Lenorman	Closed Collection	C40 544	Available

Βιβλιοθήκη της Βουλής Συλλογή Μπουρνιά
Original references provided in Greek.

181.
Οι μεγάλοι άνδρες της ανθρωπότητας [Αθήνα] : Εκδοτικός Οίκος Βίβλος, 1952-1953.

Συλλογή	Ταξιθ.	Αρ.	Αντίτυπο	Κατάσταση
Μπενάκειος Βιβλιοθήκη	Συλλογή Μπουρνιά	ΜΠΟ 1440	v9	Διαθέσιμο
Μπενάκειος Βιβλιοθήκη	Συλλογή Τρικούπη	ΤΡΙ 1100	1 (Σειρά 1η)	Διαθέσιμο
Λένορμαν	Κλειστή Συλλογή	Γ40 67	v1	Διαθέσιμο

182.
Έλληνες πεζογράφοι : Διονύσιος Σολωμός [κ.α.] υπό Χάρης, Πέτρος, 1902-1998. [Αθήνα] : Βιβλιοπωλείον της "Εστίας," [1963-]

Μπενάκειος Βιβλιοθήκη	Συλλογή Μπουρνιά	ΜΠΟ 2222	v4	Διαθέσιμο
Λένορμαν	Κλειστή Συλλογή	Γ40 93/96	v2	Διαθέσιμο
Λένορμαν	Κλειστή Συλλογή	Γ40 93/96	v1	Διαθέσιμο

184.
Η γενιά του '30 υπό Τσάκωνας, Δημήτριος Γρ., 1921-2004. Αθήνα : Κάκτος, c1989.

Μπενάκειος Βιβλιοθήκη	Συλλογή Μπουρνιά	ΜΠΟ 1402	Διαθέσιμο
Λένορμαν	Κλειστή Συλλογή	Γ40 544	Διαθέσιμο

CENSUS RECORDS OF GREECE

While the first population census shows that it has been recorded since 1828, information is sparse or not available for many areas including Chios. The census information is in Greek.

Links to the Population Census of 1959, and the Population Movement for the year 1860 are shown but I did not perform any further research using this data as most of it pertains to mainland and some of the Cyclades (group of island in the Aegean) in Greece.

Researcher note:
The following data is available online through the Internet.

Census Data and Years in Greek
https://el.wikipedia.org/wiki/%CE%95%CE%BB%CE%BB%CE%B7%CE%BD%CE%B9%CE%BA%CE%AE_%CE%B1%CF%80%CE%BF%CE%B3%CF%81%CE%B1%CF%86%CE%AE_1834-1836

Hellenic Statistical Authority
https://www.statistics.gr/en/home/

Hellenic Statistical Authority - Population Census 1959
http://dlib.statistics.gr/Book/GRESYE_02_0101_00102.pdf

Hellenic Statistical Authority - Population movement for the year 1860
http://dlib.statistics.gr/Book/GRESYE_02_0102_00081.pdf

Greece Census familysearch.org
https://www.familysearch.org/en/wiki/Greece_Census

SHIP MANIFESTS

The Statue of Liberty - Castle Garden Ellis Island Foundation

Ellis Island Passenger Manifest

Here is an Ellis Island record for a Georgios, age 37, who arrived in NY, which would mean that he was born about 1879. He travelled to the USA as married arriving on 24 May 1916 on the Steam Ship Patris.

I have extracted a list of Bournias family members, male, female, and newborn children, who entered the United States as immigrants, and were processed before 1920. The list that I extracted from the archive in May 2001 contains fourteen pages of information about the individuals, in my files known as Ellis_Island_Bournias.doc.[204]

While the use of the Internet makes searches easier, misspelled names and surnames through some of the websites requires an understanding and flexibility of modifying the searches to accommodate the inaccuracies.

Image Reference: The Ellis Island Foundation, Bournias-Georgios-ship-manifest-USA.jpg

---

[204] https://www.statueofliberty.org/ellis-island/
The Ellis_Island_Bournias.doc are records extracted from the Ellis Island Manifest archives on May 27, 2001 by P. Bournias.

Ship manifests for travelers from Greece to the USA including port hubs and ship names sorted by year. Year is the arrival in the USA.
These are for males and females up to 1928.[205]

Full name	Year	Departure Port	Ship
Bournias, Demetrios	1902	Pyrus	La Touraine
Bournias, Nicoloos	1903	Piree	La Bretagne
Bournias, Nicolas	1906	Coutreva	La Bretagne
Bournias, Fotis	1908	Curapocio, Greece	La Provence
Bournias, Panagiotis	1909	Vounaria, Greece	Patris
Bournias, Constantin	1910	Zaferoglis, Greece	Caroline
Bournias, Evgenia	1910	Zaferoglis, Greece	Caroline
Bournia, Anastassio	1911	Haracopio/Greece	Themistocles
Bournias, Apostolos	1911	Carystos, Greece	Patris
Bournia, Sofia	1912	Carystos, Greece	Macedonia
Bournias, George	1913	Coroni, Greece	Athinai
Bournias, Michail	1913	Chios, Greece	Ioannina
Bournia, Asimina	1914	Caroni	Themistocles
Bournias, Johannis	1915	Spartounta, Greece	Vasilefs Constantinos
Bournia, Crini	1916	Hios, Greece	Themistocles
Bournias, Antonios	1916	Livadia, Greece	Patris
Bournias, Charalabis	1916	Spartounta, Greece	Patris
Bournias, Georgios	1916	Harokopis, Greece	Patris
Bournias, Georgios	1916	Spartounta, Greece	Patris
Bournias, Maria	1916	Chio, Greece	Giuseppe Verdi
Bournias, Mihail	1916	Spartonta, Greece	Patris
Bournias, Stamatios	1916	Hios, Greece	Themistocles
Bournias, Stileanos	1916	Chio, Greece	Giuseppe Verdi
Bournias, Spiridon	1920	Patmos, Italy	Themistocles
Bournias, Ioannis	1921	N/A	Megali Hellas
Bournias, Ioannis	1921	N/A	Megali Hellas
Bournia, Marie	1928	Greek	Patria

Researcher note:
Some first names are spelled incorrectly, e.g. Nicoloos is actually Nicholaos, as well as area names are spelled incorrectly, e.g. Pyrus and Piree is Pireaus, etc. because of the incorrect pronunciation and clerical errors at the time.
Johannis is more correctly Ioannis in English.
Nicoloos is more correctlly spelled in English as Nikolas or Nicholas.
Spiridon can be spelled more correct in English as Spyridon or Spyros.
Stileanos is more correctlly spelled in English as Stylianos.

---

[205] Steamship Passenger Lists (the 1870s through the 1960s), https://www.gjenvick.com/index.html

First Name : Anastassio	First Name : Ioannis
Last Name : Bournia	Last Name : Bournias
Nationality : Greece, Greek	Nationality : Greece, Greek
Last Place of Residence : Haracopio/Greece	Date of Arrival : December 1st, 1921
Date of Arrival : December 12th, 1911	Age at Arrival : 44y
Age at Arrival : 18y	Gender : Male
Gender : Male	Ship of Travel : Megali Hellas
Marital Status : Single	Port of Departure : Constantinople
Ship of Travel : Themistocles	Manifest Line Number : 0028
Port of Departure : Calamata	
Manifest Line Number : 0008	
First Name : Crini	First Name : Ioannis
Last Name : Bournia	Last Name : Bournias
Nationality : Greece, Greek	Nationality : Greece, Greek
Last Place of Residence : Hios, Greece	Date of Arrival : October 1st, 1921
Date of Arrival : December 12th, 1916	Age at Arrival : 41y
Age at Arrival : 12y	Gender : Male
Gender : Female	Ship of Travel : Megali Hellas
Marital Status : Single	Port of Departure : Piraeus
Ship of Travel : Themistocles	Manifest Line Number : 0028
Port of Departure : Piraeus, Greece	
Manifest Line Number : 0006	
First Name : Sofia	First Name : Johannis
Last Name : Bournia	Last Name : Bournias
Nationality : Greece, Greek	Nationality : Greece, Greek
Last Place of Residence : Carystos, Greece	Last Place of Residence : Spartounta, Greece
Date of Arrival : April 20th, 1912	Date of Arrival : July 12th, 1915
Age at Arrival : 27y	Age at Arrival : 37y
Gender : Female	Gender : Male
Marital Status : Single	Marital Status : Single
Ship of Travel : Macedonia	Ship of Travel : Vasilefs Constantinos
Port of Departure : Piraeus, Greece	Port of Departure : Piraeus
Manifest Line Number : 0004	Manifest Line Number : 0023

First Name : Antonios	First Name : Maria
Last Name : Bournias	Last Name : Bournias
Nationality : Greece, Greek	Nationality : Greece, Greek
Last Place of Residence : Livadia, Greece	Last Place of Residence : Chio, Greece
Date of Arrival : May 24th, 1916	Date of Arrival : January 6th, 1916
Age at Arrival : 37	Age at Arrival : 40y
Gender : Male	Gender : Female
Marital Status : Single	Marital Status : Married
Ship of Travel : Patris	Ship of Travel : Giuseppe Verdi
Port of Departure : Piraeus	Port of Departure : Naples
Manifest Line Number : 0011	Manifest Line Number : 0027
First Name : Apostolos	First Name : Michail
Last Name : Bournias	Last Name : Bournias
Nationality : Greece, Greek	Nationality : Greece, Greek
Last Place of Residence : Carystos, Greece	Last Place of Residence : Chios, Greece
Date of Arrival : July 14th, 1911	Date of Arrival : November 28th, 1913
Age at Arrival : 17y	Age at Arrival : 16y
Gender : Male	Gender : Male
Marital Status : Single	Marital Status : Single
Ship of Travel : Patris	Ship of Travel : Ioannina
Port of Departure : Piraeus	Port of Departure : Piraeus
Manifest Line Number : 0019	Manifest Line Number : 0017
First Name : Charalabis	First Name : Mihail
Last Name : Bournias	Last Name : Bournias
Nationality : Greece, Greek	Nationality : Greece, Greek
Last Place of Residence : Spartounta, Greece	Last Place of Residence : Spartonta, Greece
Date of Arrival : May 24th, 1916	Date of Arrival : May 24th, 1916
Age at Arrival : 13	Age at Arrival : 39
Gender : Male	Gender : Male
Marital Status : Single	Marital Status : Married
Ship of Travel : Patris	Ship of Travel : Patris
Port of Departure : Piraeus	Port of Departure : Piraeus
Manifest Line Number : 0007	Manifest Line Number : 0006

First Name : Constantin	First Name : Nicolas
Last Name : Bournias	Last Name : Bournias
Nationality : Greece, Greek	Nationality : Greece, Greek
Last Place of Residence : Zaferoglis, Greece	Last Place of Residence : Coutreva
Date of Arrival : June 17th, 1910	Date of Arrival : October 8th, 1906
Age at Arrival : 24y	Age at Arrival : 20y
Gender : Male	Gender : Male
Marital Status : Single	Marital Status : Single
Ship of Travel : Caroline	Ship of Travel : La Bretagne
Port of Departure : Havre	Port of Departure : Havre
Manifest Line Number : 0022	Manifest Line Number : 0018
First Name : Demetrios	First Name : Nicoloos
Last Name : Bournias	Last Name : Bournias
Nationality : Greece, Greek	Nationality : Greece, Greek
Last Place of Residence : Pyrus	Last Place of Residence : Piree
Date of Arrival : April 19th, 1902	Date of Arrival : October 18th, 1903
Age at Arrival : 2oY	Age at Arrival : 18y
Gender : Male	Gender : Male
Marital Status : Single	Marital Status : Single
Ship of Travel : La Touraine	Ship of Travel : La Bretagne
Port of Departure : Havre	Port of Departure : Havre
Manifest Line Number : 0015	Manifest Line Number : 0030
First Name : Evgenia	First Name : Panagiotis
Last Name : Bournias	Last Name : Bournias
Nationality : Greece, Greek	Nationality : Greece, Greek
Last Place of Residence : Zaferoglis, Greece	Last Place of Residence : Vounaria, Greece
Date of Arrival : June 17th, 1910	Date of Arrival : June 2nd, 1909
Age at Arrival : 26y	Age at Arrival : 32y
Gender : Female	Gender : Male
Marital Status : Married	Marital Status : Married
Ship of Travel : Caroline	Ship of Travel : Patris
Port of Departure : Havre	Port of Departure : Piraeus
Manifest Line Number : 0021	Manifest Line Number : 0026

First Name : Fotis	First Name : Spiridon
Last Name : Bournias	Last Name : Bournias
Nationality : Greece, Greek	Nationality : Italy, Greek
Last Place of Residence : Curapocio, Greece	Last Place of Residence : Patmos, Italy
Date of Arrival : November 21st, 1908	Date of Arrival : December 15th, 1920
Age at Arrival : 20y	Age at Arrival : 18y
Gender : Male	Gender : Male
Marital Status : Single	Marital Status : Single
Ship of Travel : La Provence	Ship of Travel : Themistocles
Port of Departure : Havre	Port of Departure : Piraeus
Manifest Line Number : 0002	Manifest Line Number : 0023
First Name : George	First Name : Stamatios
Last Name : Bournias	Last Name : Bournias
Nationality : Greece, Greek	Nationality : Greece, Greek
Last Place of Residence : Coroni, Greece	Last Place of Residence : Hios, Greece
Date of Arrival : October 19th, 1913	Date of Arrival : December 12th, 1916
Age at Arrival : 45y	Age at Arrival : 11y
Gender : Male	Gender : Male
Marital Status : Married	Marital Status : Single
Ship of Travel : Athinai	Ship of Travel : Themistocles
Port of Departure : Calamata	Port of Departure : Piraeus, Greece
Manifest Line Number : 0012	Manifest Line Number : 0005
First Name : Georgios	First Name : Stileanos
Last Name : Bournias	Last Name : Bournias
Nationality : Greece, Greek	Nationality : Greece, Greek
Last Place of Residence : Harokopis, Greece	Last Place of Residence : Chio, Greece
Date of Arrival : August 18th, 1916	Date of Arrival : January 6th, 1916
Age at Arrival : 36 y	Age at Arrival : ...0y
Gender : Male	Gender : Male
Marital Status : Married	Marital Status : Married
Ship of Travel : Patris	Ship of Travel : Giuseppe Verdi
Port of Departure : Piraeus	Port of Departure : Naples
Manifest Line Number : 0007	Manifest Line Number : 0026

First Name : Georgios	
Last Name : Bournias	
Nationality : Greece, Greek	
Last Place of Residence : Spartounta, Greece	
Date of Arrival : May 24th, 1916	
Age at Arrival : 37	
Gender : Male	
Marital Status : Married	
Ship of Travel : Patris	
Port of Departure : Piraeus	
Manifest Line Number : 0008	

Description:
The SS Patris was built in England in 1909 by the National Greek Line founded in 1908 by the Embiricos Brothers. On her first voyage, the SS Patris left Smyrna (Ismir) on March 27, 1909 and then went to Piraeus on March 29th on her way to New York.

As with other passenger ships sailings were drastically curtailed by 1916 during World War I and Patris did not resume sailing until June 1920. Her last trans-Atlantic voyage began in Dec. 1920.

The Ports of Call generally consist of Azores, Belfast/Greenock, Boston, Bremerhaven, Cobh, Genoa, Halifax, Le Havre, Lisbon, Liverpool, Malta, Messina, Montreal, Naples, New York, Piraeus, Quebec, and Southampton.

Collection: Remembering Newark's Greeks: An American Odyssey

Link: https://rucore.libraries.rutgers.edu/rutgers-lib/10803/
This link states that the ship was from Andros, which is in error.
Sailing from the ports of Piraeus and Patras, Greece 4 October 1912
Arriving in New York, New York, 22 October 1912
Latter Day Saints Family History Center, Microfilm # 1,400,644. (National Archives and Records Administration Film T715, Reel 1572, Volume 3463.)
https://www.immigrantships.net/v6/1900v6/patris19121022.html

Citation
National Greek Line ship named Patris. Retrieved from https://doi.org/doi:10.7282/T3S75HTH

Ship Crew Lists

Crew lists are another source for documenting your ancestors and are available through many of the genealogical websites. I prefer to use familysearch.org and have found records of family members that worked on ships and emigrated to the USA from Greece.

Georgios Mpournias or Bournias
Principal
California, San Francisco Passenger and Crew Lists of Vessels Arriving, 1954 - 1957
Immigration 1956, San Francisco, San Francisco, California, United States
Birth Greece
He is listed on line number 31.
Other information may be available according to the column headings.

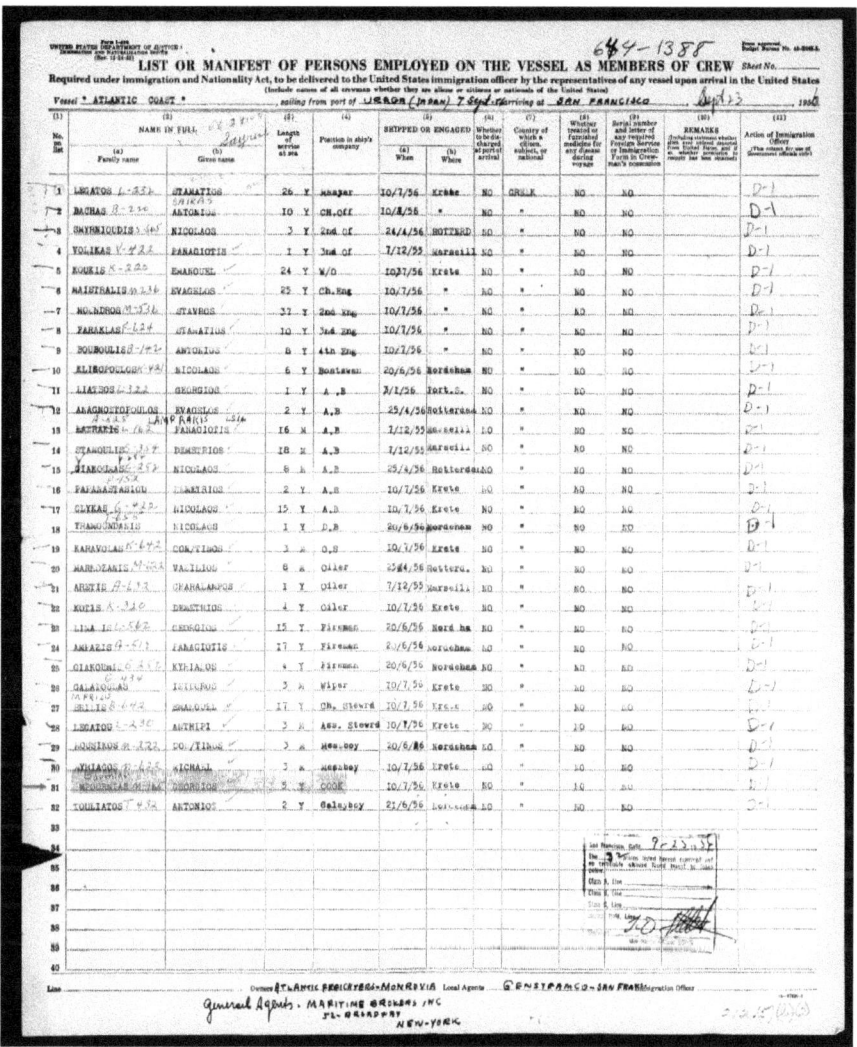

Image credit: familysearch.org

BNF GALLICA FRANCE ARCHIVE

This is information from the Historical BNF Gallica Archive of France. They have done an incredible job of scanning their images with the ability to do a search of the text within the images.

Many Chiots and other Greeks travelled to **Marseille France** and either to move there or to go to other countries in Europe or the USA. Some stayed there and this is what I have noted regarding some Bournias family members.

Researcher note:
Noted text in French with a translation in English, and some show the Internet links to the original reference. https://gallica.bnf.fr

Page 1, 25
ARTILLERIE - ARTILLERY - Jan. 1, 1893
Bounias (Léon), gardien de batterie de 1re classe 6 à 1 la direction de batterie de 16 ans de services
Bounias (Léon), 1st class battery guard 6 to 1 16 years service battery direction
Journal_officiel_de_la_République_Jan_1893.pdf

page 7346
VAUCLUSE, FRANCE - Nov. 6, 1900
Mention honorable. — M. Bounias Pascal, ouvrier à l'Isle-sur-Sorgue; 15 aout 1900
Honorable mention. - Mr. Bounias Pascal, worker at Isle-sur-Sorgue; August 15, 1900
Journal_officiel_de_la_République_Nov_1900.pdf

July 1950
BOURNIAS Apostolos, Avocat à la Cour de Cassation, 46, rue du Pirée, ATHENES (Grèce). — HELLENIQUE
BOURNIAS Apostolos, Attorney at the Court of Cassation, 46, rue du Piraeus, ATHENS (Greece). - Hellenic
BNF-Gallica-3.png, BNF-Gallica-3a.png, BNF-Gallica-3b.png.

La Terre de Bourgogne : La Bourgogne agricole et La Bourgogne rurale réunies : organe de la Fédération des associations agricoles et viticoles de la Côte-d'Or, du Syndicat de défense paysanne, de l'Office agricole départemental et des services agricole
Vendeurs : Clermont-Fcrraud : Maison Fauconnct.— Vertaizon : Delorme-Mondanel. — Courpière : Bournilhas frères. — Ambert : Jean-Pierre Fonlupt. — Seychalles : Guillon-Bonnet

The Land of Burgundy: Agricultural Burgundy and Rural Burgundy together: organ of the Federation of Agricultural Associations and Vineyards of the Côte-d'Or, the Union of Farmers' Defense, the Departmental Agricultural Office and Agricultural Services
Vendors: Clermont-Fcrraud: House Fauconnct.- Vertaizon: Delorme-Mondanel. - Courpière: Bournilhas brothers. - Ambert: Jean-Pierre Fonlupt. - Seychalles: Guillon-Bonnet

L'Echo d'Alger : journal républicain du matin - 1912-1961
Arrestation - Hier soir, a onze heures, l'agent Bournias a arrete, rue Marengo, le nomme Chenionni Areski ben Said, journalier, sans domicile fixe, inculpe de vol au prejudice de Thefat Mohamed ben Hamou, demeurant rue Medee 5.
BNF-Gallica-4.png, BNF-Gallica-4a.png.

The Echo of Algiers: republican newspaper of the morning - 1912-1961
Arrest - Yesterday evening, at eleven o'clock, the agent Bournias stopped, street Marengo, named Chenionni Areski ben Said, every day, homeless, accused of theft to the prejudice of Thefat Mohamed ben Hamou, residing street Medee 5.

L'Ouest-Éclair (Rennes) - 1899-1944 - December 1909
dans l'étude du notaire Bournias pour y dresser un acte exigé par la loi chaque foie qu'un fidèle de la reli-l gion schismatfque épouse un catholime ou un protestant, et cet acte n'est ni ufl contrat de mariage ni même un contrat de fiançailles il règle très sagement la condition religieuse des enfants à venir du futur marriage.
BNF-Gallica-5.png

West Éclair (Rennes) - 1899-1944
In the study of the notary Bournias to draw up an act required by law, every time a faithful of the schismatical religion marries a catholic or a protestant, this act is neither a marriage contract nor even a engagement contract it wisely regulates the religious condition of the future children of the future marriage.

Le Figaro (Paris. 1854) - 1854
Bournias présidence du conseil M. Maccas gouverneurs généraux de Macédoine M. Gonatas Thrace M. Florias.
The Figaro (Paris, 1854) - 1854
Bournias Presidency of the Council Mr Maccas Governors General of Macedonia Mr Gonatas Thrace Mr Florias.

La Lanterne : journal politique quotidien 1918-01-29
Une maison s'est subifement effondree au village de chamerlat **Puy-de-Dome**.
Deux jeunes filles, **Mlles Marie et Jeanne Bournihas**, âgées de 25 et 28 ans, ont été tuées.
Le pere et la mere ont ete assez grievement blessees.

A house has collapsed in the Chamerlat **Puy-de-Dome** village.
Two young girls, **Miss Marie and Jeanne Bournihas**, 25 and 28 years old, were killed
The father and the mother have been severely injured.

References:
Search terms used: Bournias / Bournia / Bournihas,
from the website https://gallica.bnf.fr/ark:/12148/cb34378481r/date?rk=85837%3B2

https://gallica.bnf.fr/services/engine/search/sru?operation=searchRetrieve&version=1.2&startRecord=0&maximumRecords=15&page=1&collapsing=disabled&query=arkPress%20all%20%22cb34378481r_date%22%20and%20%28gallica%20all%20%22Bournias%22%29#resultat-id-1

Census Records of the United States

Census Records for the USA are available through many of the genealogical websites. I prefer to use https://www.familysearch.org and have found numerous records of family members that emigrated to the USA from Greece.

Here is another example of a spelling error in the name recorded at the time:
Gosteis Bournias – most likely Kostis and officially Konstantinos
Principal
United States Census, 1940
Census 1940
Detroit Ward 18, Detroit, Wayne, Michigan, United States
Birth 1892
Greece
Spouses Angeline Bournias
Children Jim Bournias, William Bournias
They are listed on line numbers 36 to 39. Other information may be available according to the column headings.

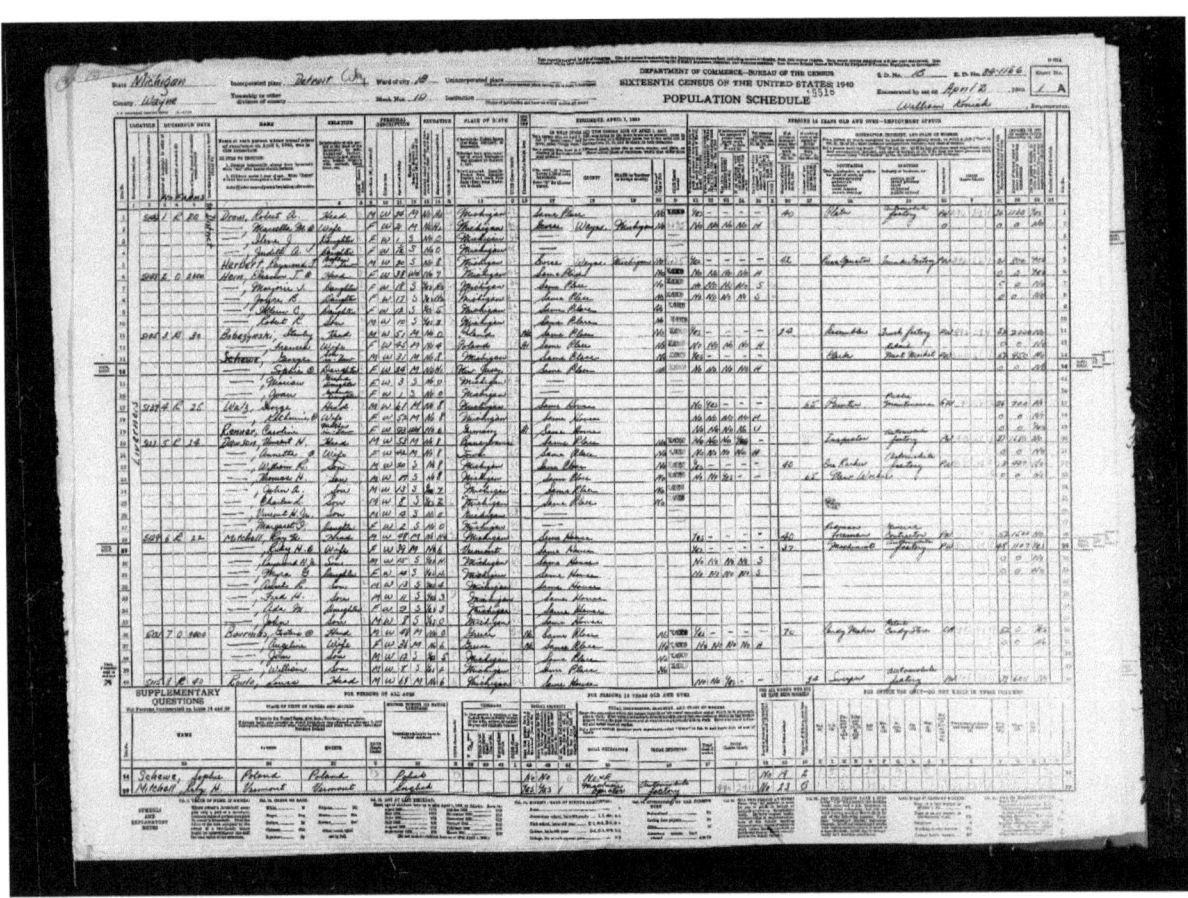

Image credit: familysearch.org

Voting Records of the United States

There are 48 voter registration records for Bournias online that provide details about related records, age, location, political party, and more.

The information attained belongs to younger groups of individuals in the USA and are therefore under the protection of privacy laws of the USA.

I will note that the information that I discovered is freely available on the Internet and that individuals should be aware of it.

Due to the privacy laws of the EU, Greece, and the USA, personal data is restricted for publication of living individuals.

Researcher note:
Bournias has 48 Voter Records, from the website: https://voterrecords.com/
Bournias Voter Records - 1 - voterrecords.com.pdf
Bournias Voter Records - 2 - voterrecords.com.pdf
Bournias Voter Records - 3 - voterrecords.com.pdf
Bournias Voter Records - 4 - voterrecords.com.pdf
Bournias Voter Records - 5 - voterrecords.com.pdf

GENEALOGY CHARTS

Genealogical Charts have the names of the individuals born in Greece in Greek with their corresponding names in English, along with various analytical information, vital records e.g. birth, marriage, death, locations, parishes, and any additional information that has been discovered.

The descendant chart begins with Apostolos Bournias born about 1760.

I have created the lineage on the charts to provide visually similar time-periods across the families for an easier view of the periods.

The chart provides additional information and more tiers of ancestors that are allowed in accordance with the privacy laws for historical purposes.

Incomplete charts are not provided. If you believe that you have useful information, e.g. regarding missing family members, you may correspond with me if you wish to help add information to or complete a chart. I give credit where credit is due and will provide the acknowledgement directly on the chart, especially for the Bournias from Spartounta.

All individuals are in their order of birth year, and each line of years provide a clear view of the progression of each of the families.

Many of the charts that I have created are up to four (4) meters by 60 centimeters (about 12 feet by 24 inches) length x height in size and could not fit within the size of this book.

Unfortunately, I could not find a publisher that could satisfy the printing of the book with a chart as an insert.

For anyone that purchases this book, copies of the **Main Chart** or the **Texas Chart** are available. **Both charts consist of two parts**, a left and a right side due to the size of the chart.

Please be aware that the chart I can only provide publicly the birth of individuals from about 1760 to about 1930 on the Main Chart and from about 1842 to 1930 on the Texas Chart.

If the reader is interested, I can provide the printed charts, both sides of each, at an additional charge for printing and shipping. Please contact me by post or email for details.

PHOTOGRAPHY AND HISTORY

I have asked various relatives of mine for photographs of my ancestors and have received some but of very poor quality most likely taken using odd cameras based on the size of the pictures.[206]

If you are searching for photographs of your ancestors, I would recommend that you ask all of your relatives because I have asked about photographic archives of the photographers that worked on Chios and they do not exist.[207]

The year of the first photograph taken in Europe was 1826 or 1827.[208]

The beginnings of photography in Greece was during the periods shown for each photographer of the times whose work was published: [209, 210]

Nicephore Piepce	1765 – 1833
William Fox-Talbot	1800 – 1877
Jacques Daguerre	1787 – 1851
Hyppolyte Bayard	1801 – 1887
Mary Paraskeva	1882 – 1951
Voula Papaïoannou	1898 – 1990
Elli Sougioultzoglou-Seraidari a.k.a. Nelly	1899 – 1998

First photography on Chios

Date unknown but based upon the photograph of Demetrios L. Bournias that was taken around 1912, I would guesstimate that photography on Chios began around 1890 to 1900.

On one of my trips to Chios, I inquired about photographic archives but unfortunately, the negatives of the photographic studios were not saved by the general archives or any other organization.

There were only a handful of photographic studios in the 1900's on Chios.
One of them was the photographic studio called **Photo Bournias (Φωτο Μπουρνιά)**.

I contacted the family to learn where they were from exactly and if they have any archive of family photographs from my family. I learned that they were from Spartounta but could not add a family photograph that was posted on Facebook due to the privacy laws. Unfortunately, the family and other photographic studios of Chios do not have any photographic archives.

---

[206] https://en.wikipedia.org/wiki/History_of_the_camera
[207] https://en.wikipedia.org/wiki/Photography_in_Greece
[208] https://en.wikipedia.org/wiki/Photography
[209] https://en.wikipedia.org/wiki/Photographer
[210] https://en.wikipedia.org/wiki/List_of_Greek_photographers

I have searched for other photographic archives on Chios and in Athens. Unfortunately, no photo studios that existed or exist on Chios have any archives.

If you have relatives on Chios, it would behoove you to ask to see them and even request to take them to a photocopier shop to have them scanned or copied.

I mention this because one of my cousins lost the entire family collection of photographs due to water damage and never took the opportunity to scan or copy them.

A photographic archive does exist in Athens but it does not have family photographs from Chios.

A wonderful photographer from Chios was Νικόλαος Χαβιάρας, (Nicholas Chaviaras), b. 1913 – d. 1985.

Many of his photographs had various themes, became postcards, and continue to circulate on the Internet, especially in posts by Greeks on Facebook.

First Women Photographers in Greece

Mary Paraskeva began to photograph around 1903.[211]
Elli Sougioultzoglou-Seraidari a.k.a. Nelly's began to photograph around 1924.[212]
Voula Papaïoannou began to photograph around 1940.[213]

Researcher note:
As many Chiots were sailors, I believe that the purchase of personal cameras became more available abroad after 1900.

Nelly's photographs can be seen at the Benaki Museum in Athens.

---

211 https://en.wikipedia.org/wiki/Mary_Paraskeva
212 https://en.wikipedia.org/wiki/Nelly%27s
213 https://en.wikipedia.org/wiki/Voula_Papaioannou

VRONTADOS CHIOS ABOUT 1930

I found this photograph showing the area of Vrontados Chios from about 1930 on Facebook.

This is the view of the time-period when my father Ioannis P. Bournias was born and lived down that road. The same road leads to the top of the mountains toward Spartounta and other areas.

Sadly, we cannot zoom in on this photograph, but if we could, we would see how undeveloped Chios was back then. Unpaved roads, no power lines, no cars, no buses, small homes, no stores, a small factory on the shore line, and one person walking on the road just before another set of windmills towards the end, like those of the famous Chioti landmark of the three (3) windmills just outside of the main city of Hora.

Image Reference: From the archive of George Moutsatsos (watermark in Greek) from Chios on Facebook

BIBLIOGRAPHY AND ONLINE BOOKS

Bibliography

Bournias, Peter A. *HISTORICAL TESTIMONIALS FOR ANTONIOS BOURNIAS.* 1.4. Edited by Peter A. Bournias. Translated by Peter A. Bournias. Athens, Attiki: Bournias, Peter A., 2013.

Viou, Stylianos G. *The Massacre at Chios, From the Mouth of the Chiotan People.* First Edition was published in 1922. Chios, Chios: Omiros Spiritual Center, Municipality of Chios, 1987.

Έρση, Χατζημιχάλη. *Περίπατος με την Αγγελική.* Μοντάζ: ΜΠΕΚΑΤΩΡΟΣ ΣΤΕΦΑΝΟΣ. Athens, Attiki: ΚΑΚΤΟΣ, 1999.

ΚΑΡΑΒΟΛΟΥ, ΕΙΡΗΝΗ. *ΣΥΜΒΙΩΣΗ ΕΛΛΗΝΩΝ ΚΑΙ ΟΘΩΜΑΝΩΝ ΣΤΗ ΧΙΟ ΠΡΙΝ ΑΠΟ.* ΙΩΑΝΝΙΝΑ: ΔΙΔΑΚΤΟΡΙΚΗ ΔΙΑΤΡΙΒΗ, DOCTORAL THESIS, 2019.

Τριανταφυλλίδης, Μανόλης. *Τα Μυστικά των Ονομάτων: Τα Οικογενειακά Μας Ονόματα.* Μοντάζ: Ε. Ε. Στάθης. Αθήνα, Αττική: Τα Νέα, 2013.

Some rare books found online

Bibliography of Historical books and documents used in my research. Some may not have previously cited. Some of the books are rare and only available online from the GOOGLE library.

Ιστορία της Ελληνικής Επαναστάσεως, Σπυρίδωνος Τρικούπη, ΤΟΜΟΣ Β, 1860-1862. HISTORY OF THE GREEK REVOLUTION by Spirdonos Trikoupis, Volume B, (PETER HESS), https://anemi.lib.uoc.gr
This is available as a PDF in Greek and available on the Internet.

An Historical Sketch of the Greek Revolution, Samuel G. Howe, M.D. 1828, 452 pages.
This is in English and may be available from Google on the Internet.

Χιακόν αρχείον Ιωάννου Βλαχογιάννη, ΤΟΜΟΣ 1, ΑΘΗΝΑΙΣ 1924, ΕΚΔ. Π. Δ. ΣΑΚΕΛΛΑΡΙΟΥ, 487 σελίδες. - Archives of Chios Ioannis Vlachogiannis, 1924, Volume 1, 452 pages. A collection of letters documenting the events from Chiotans from Nafplio in 1831 beginning with 1821. See pages 451 - 453 regarding Antonios Bournias.
This is in Greek and may be available on the Internet.

A HISTORY OF THE ISLAND OF CHIOS, A.D. 70-1822, as translated from the second part of the work entitled "**XIAKA**" (pronounced HE AKA) or "**The History of the Island of Chios from the earliest times down to its destruction by the Turks in 1822**" by Dr. Alexander M. Vlasto, London 1913, 204 pages.
This is in English and may be available from Google on the Internet.

ΙΣΤΟΡΙΑ ΤΗΣ ΧΙΟΥ, Α. Π. ΧΑΝΔΡΑ – ΡΟΔΑΚΗ, Εκδ. Ελευθερη Σκεψις, date unknown.
The History of Chios is based on another book by G. Zolota written in 1921 – 26.

Χιακά: ήτοι ιστορία της νήσου Χίου από των αρχαιοτάτων χρόνων μέχρι της έτει 1822 γενομένης καταστροφής αυτής παρά των Τούρκων / Αλεξάνδρου Μ. Βλαστού, Ερμούπολει 1840, (A History of the Island of Chios: A. D. 70-1822) (Classic Reprint), Alexandros M. Vlastos, ISBN 1528288920, 9781528288927, 200 pages.

Χιακόν αρχείον Ιωάννου Βλαχογιάννη, ΤΟΜΟΣ 1, ΑΘΗΝΑΙΣ 1924, ΕΚΔ. Π. Δ. ΣΑΚΕΛΛΑΡΙΟΥ, 487 σελίδες.
Archives of Chios Ioannis Vlachogiannis, 1924, Volume 1, 452 pages.
PDF Collection of letters documenting the events from Chiotans from Nafplio in 1831 beginning with 1821. See pages 451 - 453 for Antonios Bournias
This is available as a PDF in Greek and available on the Internet.

Γεώργιος Ι. Αναστασιάδης, Georgos I. Anastasiadis a council member of the National Revival of Asia Minor, pp.224, notes that based on the decision of the awards committee of the date, 30th of April / 12th of May 1838, under protocol number 23 Hatzi-Antonios Bournias of Chios received the Silver Medal.

Ιστορία της Νήσου Σύρου, (History of the Island of Syros), Τιμολέοντος Δ. Αμπελάς, 1874, 786 pages, 1874.
A list of those who escaped from various islands during the period of the revolution.
An incredible collection of statistics for the time towards the end of the book.
This is in Greek and may be available from Google on the Internet.

Χιώτες Πρόσφυγες στη Σύρο, (Chiot immigrants in Syros), Απόστολος Κουφοδήμος, 92 pages, 2007. This document contains numerous names of Chiots that escaped during the period of the revolution.
This is in Greek and may be available from Google on the Internet.

Αρχεία της Νεωτέρας Ελληνικής Ιστορίας, Ιωάννου Βλαχογιάννη, Τόμος Πρώτος, 1901, 576 σελίδες. (Archives of the Neo Greek History, Ioannis Vlachogiannis, Volume 1, 1901, 576 pages.). This is in Greek and may be available on the Internet.
Αθηναϊκόν αρχείον Ιωάννου Βλαχογιάννη - 1.pdf
This is available as a PDF in Greek and available on the Internet.

Οι Έλληνες του Ναπολέοντος / Υπό Κωνσταντίνου Ν. Ράδου, Νικόλαος Τσεσμελής ή Παπάζογλους (1758-1819), 1916.
(THE GREEKS OF NAPOLEON Nicholas Tsesmelis or Papazoglous (1758-1819), 1916.)
This has an account from his nephew Petros D. Bournias verifying that Demetrios was the brother of Antonios. https://anemi.lib.uoc.gr
This is available as a PDF in Greek and available on the Internet.

ΕΛΛΗΝΕΣ ΜΙΣΘΡΦΟΡΟΙ ΣΤΗΝ ΥΠΗΡΕΣΙΑ ΤΗΣ ΕΠΑΝΑΣΤΑΤΙΚΗΣ ΓΑΛΛΙΑΣ (1789 – 1815), ΦΟΙΒΟΣ ΟΙΚΟΝΟΜΟΥ, ΔΙΔΑΚΤΟΡΙΣΗ ΔΙΑΤΡΙΒΗ, ΘΕΣΣΑΛΟΝΙΚΗ 2007.
Greek Merceneries in the Service of the French Revolution, Phoivos Oikonomou, Dissertation, Thesaloniki 2007.
This is available as a PDF in Greek and available on the Internet.

Charles Fabvier: Napoleonic Soldier & Greek Hero, from the website of Shannon Selin.
English, from the website https://shannonselin.com/2016/04/charles-fabvier/

Έρση-Αλεξία Χατζημιχάλη, Περίπατος με την Αγγελική, (Walking with Angeliki), Φεβρουάριος 1999, ΕΚΣΟΣΕΙΣ ΚΑΚΤΟΣ, 328 σελίδες, ISBN: 9603525154
Greek, from the website https://www.kaktos.gr/
ΧΙΟΣ ΚΑΙ ΧΙΟΙ, ΔΙΑ ΜΕΣΟΥ ΤΩΝ ΑΙΩΝΩΝ, Φιλίππου Λ. Χρυσοβελόνη, ΑΘΗΝΑΙ, 1938, 130 σελίδες. A history from 1500 BC to 1937 AD, names of chiots with some biographical info including Antonios A. Bournias and his grandchild Georgios A. Bournias born 1870, father Apostolos, battle of Karfotou 1912. Vios, Stylianos G. born 1881, Kardamyla, Chios. Teacher of Philology and co-author of Chiaka Language 1920,
This is in Greek and may be available on the Internet.

(Massacre at Chios from the mouth of the Chiot People,)
Η σφαγή της Χίου εις το στόμα του χιακού λαού, Στυλιανός Γ. Βίος
ΔΙΗΓΗΣΙΣ Πέτρου Μπουρνιά (Εκ Πυραμάς, κατοίκου Λειβαδίων)
ΔΙΗΓΗΣΙΣ Παπά Δημητρίου Χανιώτου (Εκ Πυραμάς)
References from the book in Greek, "The Slaughter of Chios" by Stylianos G. Viou, #1, Chios 1987 from the Omiros Spiritual Center, Municipality of Chios.
Excerpts from "*The Massacre at Chios*" were translated for the "*Historical testimonials for Antonios Bournias,*" P. Bournias, 2013.

The Massacres of Chios, described in Contemporary Diplomatic Reports. Edited, with an Introduction, by Philip P. Argenti, Pp. xxxiv + 242; London: John Lane, 1932
Incorrect classification of the origin and spelling of Bournias as Bourgna.
It appears to me that Philip P. Argenti negatively influences the author John Lane.
https://www.cambridge.org/core/journals/journal-of-hellenic-studies/article/abs/massacres-of-chios-described-in-contemporary-diplomatic-reports-edited-with-an-introduction-by-philip-p-argenti-pp-xxxiv-242-3-plates-london-john-lane-1932-12s-6d/7D3180D77526CBD6B03F19EC2EA96B6B

CHIUS VINCTA or The Occupation of Chios by the Ottomans (1566) & their Administration of the Island, has some information that pirates did not like the Ottomans who controlled the island and they established their base there and attacked Ottomans ships.
English, from the website https://books.google.gr/books

CHIUS LIBERATA or The Occupation of Chios by the Greeks in 1912, John Lane, Philip P. Argenti, 1933.
The Expedition of Colonel Fabvier to Chios, described in contemporary diplomatic reports.
English, from the website https://books.google.gr/books

Extracts from the diaries of John Covel (1870-1879), In Bent, J. Theodore (ed.).
Early voyages and travels in the Levant. London: Hakluyt Society. pp. 99–287, 1893, Dallam, Thomas, ca. 1575-ca. 1630; Covel, John, 1638-1722; Bent, J. Theodore (James Theodore), 1852-1897, English, from the website
https://archive.org/details/earlyvoyagestrav00dallrich/mode/2up

Catholic Pirates and Greek Merchants, A maritime history of the Mediterranean
This is in English and may be available from Google on the Internet.
English, from the website https://books.google.gr/books

Κουρούνια Ιστορία, Αθήνα 2013, ΜΙΧΑΛΑΚΗΣ, ΓΙΑΝΝΗΣ, Kourounia History, Athens 2013, Mixalakis, Giannis, Greek, from the website https://issuu.com/christosapostolou3/docs

(Cohabitation of the Greeks and Ottomans on Chios before 1822)
ΣΥΜΒΙΩΣΗ ΕΛΛΗΝΩΝ ΚΑΙ ΟΘΩΜΑΝΩΝ ΣΤΗ ΧΙΟ ΠΡΙΝ ΑΠΟ ΤΟ 1822, ΕΙΡΗΝΗ ΚΑΡΑΒΟΛΟΥ, Η ΤΥΧΗ ΤΩΝ ΑΙΧΜΑΛΩΤΩΝ ΚΑΙ Η ΕΙΚΟΝΑ ΤΩΝ ΟΘΩΜΑΝΩΝ ΤΟΥΡΚΩΝ ΩΣ "ΑΛΛΩΝ" ΣΤΙΣ ΑΦΗΓΗΣΕΙΣ ΤΗΣ ΚΑΤΑΣΤΡΟΦΗΣ ΚΑΙ ΣΕ ΑΛΛΕΣ ΠΗΓΕΣ ΤΟΥ 19ου ΑΙΩΝΑ, ΔΙΔΑΚΤΟΡΙΚΗ ΔΙΑΤΡΙΒΗ, ΙΩΑΝΝΙΝΑ ΜΑΡΤΙΟΣ 2019, 504 σελίδες.
This is available as a PDF in Greek and available on the Internet.

(The Greek Community in Egypt and the Second World War)
Η Ελληνική παροικία στην Αίγυπτο και ο Δεύτερος Παγκόσμιος Πόλεμος, 1981, Alexander Kitroeff, 32 Pages, (The Greek Province in Egypt and the Second World War).
https://www.academia.edu

REFERENCES AND NOTES

#51 of the link below refers to Xatzi-Antonios Bournias and translates as:
The political conflicts in Chios were fierce, many of which were initiated by the **Filiki Eteria** or **Society of Friends**, and the military leader of the rebels was X. A. Bournias*, a former officer of Napoleon and fanatic democrat.

* X. A. Bournias is Xatzi-Antonios Bournias also known as Antonios Bournias as explained elsewhere.

The above mentions information from pages 336, 419, 451- 453 of the Greek book known as:
Χιακόν αρχείον Ιωάννου Βλαχογιάννη published in Greek in five volumes by Ioannis Vlachogiannis as *Archives of the Chiots*.

51. Η Επανάσταση στη Θεσσαλία-Μαγνησία, που ξεκίνησαν ο Α. Γαζής, ο βιοτέχνης Χατζή-Ρήγας κ.ά. Φιλικοί (μεταξύ τους και πολλοί αρματολοί), πνίγηκε στο αίμα από τις υπέρτερες τουρκικές δυνάμεις, με την αμέριστη συνεργία των προκρίτων και του ανώτερου κλήρου («Αρχείο Κουντουριώτη," τ.Α., 11-12, Γ. Κορδάτο: «Η Επανάσταση της Θετταλομαγνησίας στο 1821», εκδ. «Επικαιρότητα»). Ιδια κατάσταση και στην Κρήτη («Αρχεία Ελληνικής Παλιγγενεσίας," τ. Α, 1857, σελ. 505-532). «Ατυχή» κατάληξη είχαν οι αντίστοιχες προσπάθειες του Φιλικού τραπεζίτη Εμ. Παπά στη Μακεδονία (για τη «στυγερή και άτιμη» στάση των Αγιορειτών βλ. Δ. Κόκκινου: «Ελληνική Επανάστασις», τ. Β, εκδ. «Μέλισσα, σελ. 437). Σφοδρότατες ήταν επίσης οι συγκρούσεις στη Χίο, απ' όπου πολλοί έμποροι ήταν μυημένοι στη Φ.Ε., ενώ στρατιωτικός ηγέτης των επαναστατών είχε τεθεί ο Χ. **Α. Μπουρνιάς, πρώην αξιωματικός του Ναπολέοντα και φανατικός δημοκράτης** («Χιακόν Αρχείον," σελ. **336, 419, 451-453** κ.α.). Στην Κάλυμνο οι επαναστάτες κατέλυσαν τα προνόμια των προκρίτων, στήνοντας δημοκρατική διοίκηση. Οι τελευταίοι όμως κατάφεραν τελικά να επικρατήσουν, εκδιώκοντας τους ηγέτες της επανάστασης από το νησί. Εκείνοι θα επιστρέψουν συνοδεία του ελληνικού στόλου το 1824. (Γ. Κορδάτου: «Ιστορία της Ελλάδας», τ. Χ, εκδ. «20ός αιώνας», 1957, σελ. 296-298).

Ξεφυλλίζοντας τα πεπραγμένα περασμένων Βουλευτικών εκλογών στην Χίο 1915-1964, Καββάδας, Κώστας Στεφ., alithia.gr, Λονδίνο, Αύγουστος 2019, Greek, from the website https://www.alithia.gr/politiki/xefyllizontas-ta-pepragmena-perasmenon-voyleytikon-eklogon-stin-hio-1915-1964

ekloges_sti_chio_1915-2015, ΠΑΡΑΔΕΙΣΗΣ, ΣΩΤΗΡΗΣ, self-published, 2019, a reference to Leonidas Bournias page 2.

Τι ήταν τα Ταμπάκικα; (What were the Tambakika?)
Τα ταμπάκικα, η δερματεμπορία και η βυρσοδεψία, Hides and Skins factory, the leather trade and tannery. From the website of Aplotaria in Chios, 1 April 2014, https://www.aplotaria.gr/tampakika-chios/

A People's History of the Second World War, Resistance versus Empire, Donny Gluckstein, ISBN 978 1 84964 719 9 PDF, ISBN 978 0 7453 2803 4 Hardback

Art of War Papers Instilling Aggressiveness, William D. Harris, Jr., Major, US Army, ISBN 978-1782663935

White Book National Liberation Front EAM, 1945, ISBN 978-1501097997

Power, Faith, and Fantasy, Michael B. Oren, ISBN 978-0393330304

1881 and 1949 earthquakes at the Chios-Cesme Strait (Aegean Sea) and their relation to tsunamis, y. Altinok, B. Alpar, N. Özer, C. Gazioglu. 1881 and 1949 earthquakes at the Chios-Cesme Strait, (Aegean Sea) and their relation to tsunamis. Natural Hazards and Earth System Sciences, Copernicus, Publ. / European Geosciences Union, 2005, 5 (5), pp.717-725, hal-00299270.

Movies Regarding Greek History

Some movies regarding Greek history that are available in English and Greek.
I am including this to introduce the Diaspora to more Greek culture.

Psyhi vathia 2009 ***Ψυχή βαθιά*** directed by Pantelis Voulgaris with Thanasis Vengos, a famous Greek comedian.
A story about the Greek Civil War and two brothers find themselves in opposite sides.

Nyfes 2004 ***Νύφες*** directed by Pantelis Voulgaris
A story in English about mail order brides from Greece and other areas to the USA.

Ulysses' Gaze or ***To vlemma tou Odyssea***, 1995, directed by Theodoros Angelopoulos
A story about a journey through time.

SMYRNA: THE DESTRUCTION OF A COSMOPOLITAN CITY, 1900-1922, 2012
http://www.smyrnadocumentary.org/?id=77#!page/77
An examination of the destruction of cosmopolitan city Smyrna in 1922.

RESOLUTIONS OF GREEK HISTORY

History is an inter-twined timeline of facts, consequences, circumstances, and delusions.

The 20th century provided us with the Internet and some examples are shocking as to what the lack of historical knowledge or its distortion cultivates.

The following notes by the author may be regarded as his own opinion.

Is Greece inferior as a country and is it a western country?
Anyone wanting a complete answer to this MUST understand the historical relation to the Industrial Revolution that Greece did not undergo with the rest of Europe, nor did urbanization of the population occur the same way.
Greece is considered a western country but again based on its history many think that Greece falls to the left, even though the communist party is less than ten percent.
In essence, Greece prefers to be a neutral and independent country but due to numerous bankruptcies, independence is questionable when finances are controlled by third parties.
There is no short explanation for either of these questions.

The British Empire and Anti-Americanism
What does this phrase have in common? Again, the reader must delve into history books to understand that anti-Americanism by some Greeks is not simply related to any left wing association with Russia. It is due to the imposition of power by Great Britain upon the Greek people, either by royalty and/or by the attempted extermination of left wing Greek Resistance known as EAM and/or ELAS after they successfully opposed the German military in WWII.

The British government from 1943 to 1949 declared these groups as communists, Churchhill appointed Christopher Montague "Monty" Woodhouse to implement his plan for the election of the Greek Prime Minister Metaxas, a dictator, to eliminate the "communist threat" of the partisans known as "andartes" in Greek by putting them in concentration camps or political prisons such as on the island of Makronisos (a small island near Cape Sounion, or by execution.

"A riot (the Dekemvriana) erupted; and Greek government gendarmes, with British forces standing in the background, opened fire on a pro-EAM rally, killing 28 demonstrators and injuring dozens.," an excerpt from Wikipedia Greek Civil War. By these actions, Britain started the third Greek Civil War.

"Nevertheless, Churchill told General Scobie: 'Do not hesitate to fire at any armed male in Athens who assails the British authority or Greek authority ... [A]ct as if you were in a conquered city where a local rebellion is in progress.' Even the Greek PM (Prime Minister) was appalled and threatened to quit. Churchill told his ambassador in Athens:

'Force [George] Papandreou to stand on his duty ... Should he resign he should be locked up till he comes to his senses.'," an excerpt from the book "A People's History of the Second World War."

From 1947 to the 1960's, the Great Britain then passed the situation onto the Americans who, whether they realized the political consequences or not, appointed James Van Fleet US Army. During the so-called aid to the British and Greece, the United States used napalm to decimate the EAM and ELAS communist insurgency.

An excerpt from Wikipedia Napalm
"In its first known post - WWII use, U.S. - supplied napalm was used in the Greek Civil War by the Greek National Army as part of Operation Coronis against the Democratic Army of Greece (DSE) – the military branch of the Communist Party of Greece (KKE)."

The Cold War between the United States and the Soviet Union began in 1947.

So where and what was Russia doing?
Russia has been a part of Greece's history since (Russo-Turkish War 1768 – 1774) the days of Ottoman rule. Russia aided Greece during the fighting in Asia Minor, Crete, the Peloponnese, and provided aid to the Greek resistance. The Orthodox Religion is common to both countries.

All the killing and destruction that occurred during the world wars, despite the heroic and successful fighting by the Greek resistance from mainland Greece and those who came back from Egypt against the German military did nothing more than increase the distrust of the Greeks against foreign powers.

The consequences of the actions by Great Britain and the US created a separatism between the Greek Communist party (KKE), Great Britain and the US that continues to exist today. I still find it odd that the KKE does not rally in front of the British Embassy even though they started the anti-communism movement.

The following is a simple explanation of how and why communism exists in Greece.
Although Greece was a European nation, during the War of Greek Independence of 1821, Russia played an important part in providing assistance politically, economically, and militarily, which would become the basis for some Greeks supporting the Russian Communist movement in the years to come, and that still exist today.

INTERNET LINKS

Wikipedia Internet links that contain many characters are those provided in Greek. Those who wish to find the content may use the Wikipedia search using English wording and then locate the Greek link on the lower left. I include the Greek link because there may be more information that is not shown in the English version.

Some links may require knowledge of the English or the Greek language or an online translator.

The Greek government website to obtain certificates of birth, marriage, and death, as well as other services.
This site is used by Greek citizens, requires a login and password after registering with a Greek tax office.
https://www.gov.gr/

The Ministry of Affairs in Greece
https://www.mfa.gr/en/citizen-services/

The Special Registrar of Athens for Diaspora regarding family declarations.
https://www.ypes.gr/en/home-special-registry/home-special-registry

The American Hellenic Educational Progressive Association (Order of AHEPA).
https://ahepa.org/

Family Search is my preference to other websites that provide vital records.
https://www.familysearch.org/en/

A Website to locate information about the deceased in the USA, and worldwide.
https://www.findagrave.com

A Website to locate information about the deceased in various countries.
https://www.tributearchive.com

This website is linked to Ancestry.
https://billiongraves.com/

The General Archives of Greece new website.
http://www.gak.gr/index.php/el/

The General Archives of Greece online archives.
http://arxeiomnimon.gak.gr/index.html

The following links contain information of the General Archives of Greece regarding election material, voter records, and some records from the registry of males for Greek genealogy research. The majority of this information is in the Greek language.

The Greek Parliament Archive at the GAK that contains voter records from 1918.
Election material from the Greek Parliament Archive for 1844 to 1893, 1915
http://arxeiomnimon.gak.gr/browse/resource.html?tab=01&id=13721

The Vlachogiannis Collection is an archive of the catalogs at the GAK that contains voter records and some records from the registry of males.
Election material from Vlachogiannis Collection for 1864 to 1925
http://arxeiomnimon.gak.gr/browse/index.html?cid=13808

The Vlachogiannis Collection is an archive of the Georgios Ladas
Election material from Georgios Ladas for 1842, 1843 εως 1873
http://arxeiomnimon.gak.gr/browse/resource.html?tab=01&id=13477

The National Archives of the UK
https://discovery.nationalarchives.gov.uk

BNF Gallica France Archive
https://gallica.bnf.fr/

Daughters of Penelope
https://www.daughtersofpenelope.org/

The Sons of Pericles
The corresponding website for Greek males abroad was "*The Sons of Pericles*" but no longer exists.

Researcher note:
Some links may require the use of a VPN.
Internet links are known additionally as Digital Object Identifier (DOI).

BOURNIAS FAMILY WEBSITES

My web site has a program to record genealogy information about the family but is only available to family members because of privacy restrictions.

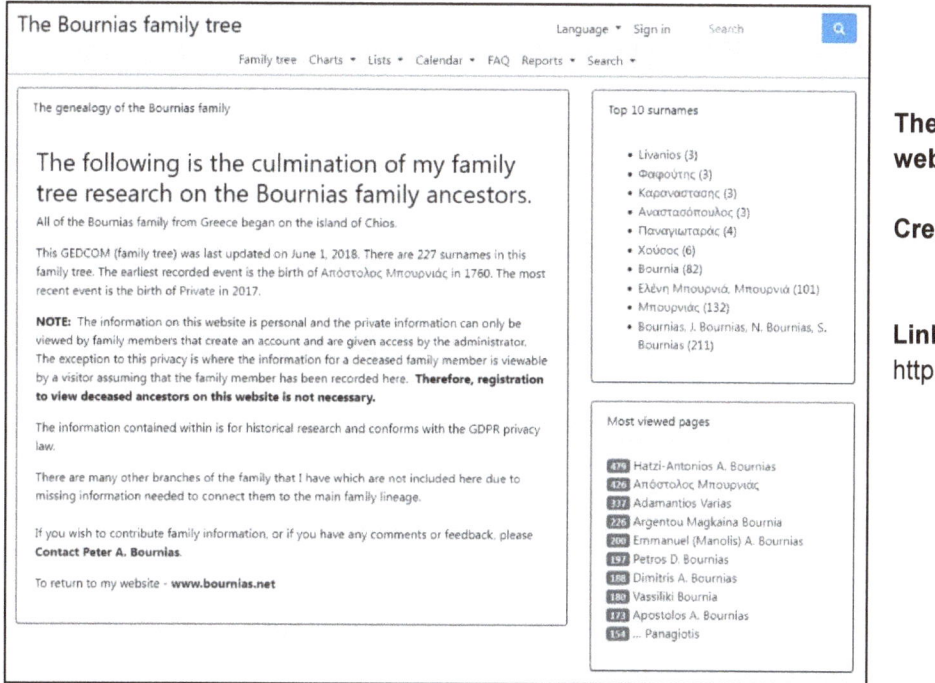

The Bournias family tree website

Creator Peter A. Bournias

Link:

http://webtrees.bournias.net

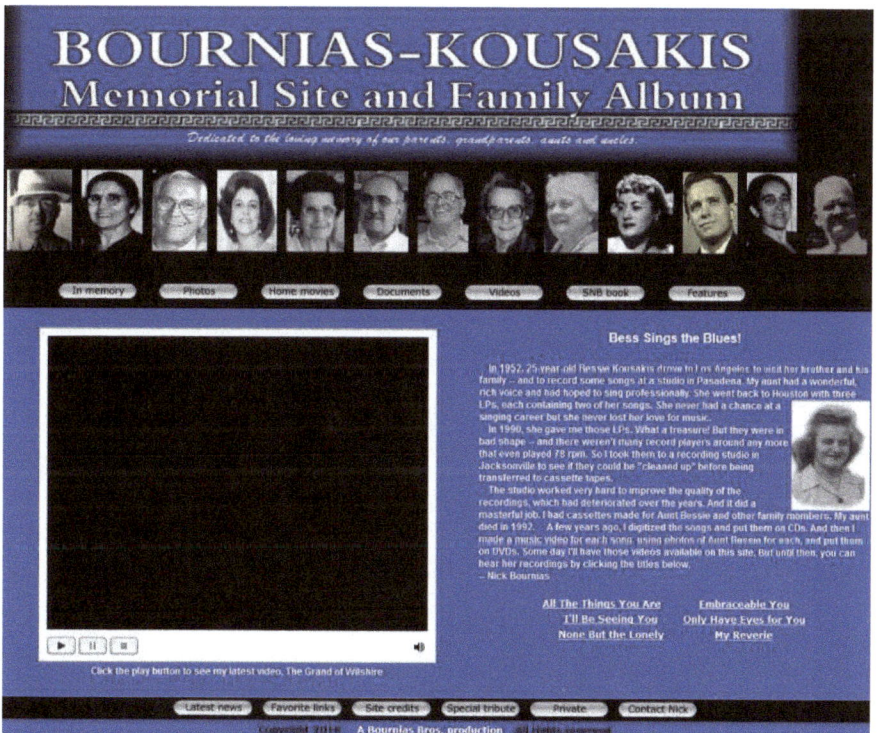

The Bournias-Kousakis website

Creator Nicholas Stanley Bournias

Sadly, this website no longer exists.

GLOSSARY / ABBREVIATIONS / ACRONYMS

A.K.A., also known as.

Chian, Chiotist or Chiotan, a person from the island of Chios Greece.

Chiotissa, a female from the island of Chios Greece.

Dates, All dates of Greek documentation use day / month / year format unless shown otherwise.

GAK, the General Archives of Greece, with offices in various areas of Greece.

IMS, the Institute of Mediterranean Studies – Forth.
This IMS organization has digitized many of the records from the registries of Syros.

KMS, the Center for Asia Minor Studies (ΚΕΝΤΡΟ ΜΙΚΡΑΣΙΑΤΙΚΩΝ ΣΠΟΥΔΩΝ).
The KMS organization gathers records and information from the survivors of the catastrophe of Asia Minor.

FB, Facebook. Useful if you wish to connect other members of the Bournias family assuming that you may need to speak or read and / or write Greek for those from Greece.

File names shown with the extension "JPG" or "PNG" are images.
File names shown with the extension "PDF" or "DOCX" are documents.

ANNOTATIONS

Hatzi or Hadji - Greek: from the vocabulary word *khatzis* 'pilgrim (to Jerusalem)'.
Completing a pilgrimage to the Holy Land was a mark of high social distinction.
Often, this surname is a reduced form of a surname with *Hatzi-* as a prefix to a patronymic, naming the ancestor who made the pilgrimage; e.g. Hatzimarkou 'Mark the Pilgrim', *Hatzioannou* 'John the Pilgrim'.

Researcher note:
Hatzi or Hadji, http://en.wikipedia.org/wiki/Chatzi

A Legacy of Islam in Greece: 'Ali Pasha and Ioannina
http://www.jstor.org/discover/10.2307/194383?uid=3738128&uid=2129&uid=2&uid=70&uid=4&sid=21102512488267

Common prefixes of Greek names, http://en.wikipedia.org/wiki/Greek_name

Apparently, historians have not clarified the use of the prefix Hatzi or Hadji very well.
The correct meaning of the use of this prefix in this document is for Christians.
A similar prefix exists for Muslims.

ACKNOWLEDGEMENTS

Thanks to Nicholas "Nick" S. Bournias for meeting with me in Florida, for sharing family information, and for creating the Bournias-Kousakis website, which unfortunately no longer exists.

Thanks to Billy Bournias, spouse of Sam Bill Bournias Jr. and a DAR - Daughter of the American Revolution, who also became the family genealogist for the Bournias family that settled in the state of Texas.

Thanks to Panagiotis G. "Pete" Bournias and his niece Irene F. Frangou, relatives of the Bournias family from Messinia and a branch of the same family that settled in Texas.

Thanks to Ioannis P. Bournias and his son Pantelis I. Bournias from Spartounta Chios for meeting with me, sharing family information, and answering questions about the families.

Thanks to Dr. Martha Bournia and Dr. Michalis Bournias for sharing family information.

Thanks to Maria Spyrakis-Karnieris nee Bournia for sharing family information.

Thanks to Anna Katos for sharing family information regarding her family of Spartounta.

Thanks to Gregory and Staci Bournias for sharing family information.

Many thanks to the related individuals that answered emails or messaging through Facebook who provided some answers to questions about their family lineage.

Many thanks to Mr. Leonis Stylianos. While in Chios, I visited the villages of Pirama and Parparia again and had the wonderful pleasure of meeting one of its most senior members, Mr. Leonis Stylianos. After speaking with the 88 year old, he conveyed to me the gratitude and respect that he had for the man known as Antonios Bournias, and allowed me to read and photograph some of the notes that he had produced over his lifetime from the stories that had been passed down by his family. Additionally, Mr. Stylianos' brother was the artist created the detailed bust of Antonios Bournias that decorates the town square next to the church.

Thanks to Tasos Spiliotopoulos for sharing family information about his grandfather Ioannis Bournias.

Thanks to Sophia D. Axioti for sharing family information.

Thanks to Cindy Petridis for sharing family information.

Many thanks to the General Archives of Greece, especially the offices of Chios, Aegina, Messinia, and Syros for the work they do to preserve the history of Greece and its people.

Many thanks to the Greek Orthodox Mitropoli (Diocese) of Chios and Messinia for providing access to the record books of births, baptisms, and marriages.

Many thanks to the KEP of Greece for their assistance in providing vital records when and where available.

Many thanks to the Military Archive services for their assistance in answering questions and providing me with my grandfather's file.

Many thanks to the IMS, the Institute of Mediterranean Studies for providing access to the records of births, baptisms, and marriages from Syros, Mykonos, and Chios.

Many thanks to the KMS, the Center for Asia Minor Studies (ΚΕΝΤΡΟ ΜΙΚΡΑΣΙΑΤΙΚΩΝ ΣΠΟΥΔΩΝ) for their assistance.

Many thanks to the Family Search website for providing access to the record books of births, baptisms, and marriages.

Many thanks to the Bibliothèque Nationale de France for their excellent archiving and the extraction technology of their website, and in making their archived materials available.

Many thanks to the National Library of Greece for their reference materials.

Many thanks to The National Archives U.K. for making their archived materials available.

Many thanks to Prof. Stephanos Kaklamanis for sharing his insight on literature and history.

Google and all Google provider data provider(s), such as "Map data: Google Search data, are trademarks of Google LLC and this book is not endorsed by or affiliated with Google in any way with the author, publisher, distributor, or printer of this book.

Many thanks to the Tazedakis Law Firm for their legal support and advice pertaining to the privacy laws, dealing with Greek government services, and other legalese.

CLOSING REMARKS

I hope that you find this non-fiction work interesting and that it becomes a part of the personal library in every Bournias family. I have tried to answer as many questions as possible about family members with the limitations of the government registries and the perplexing bureaucracy regarding privacy, and hope that whatever I have not answered can provide you with a solution for your own family research by cross referencing information from my texts.

In the end, this is about the Bournias family history and ancestry whether you live in Greece or abroad. The Greeks have a saying "*If you don't know where you came from then you can never really know where you are going!*" This may have originated from Greek sailors but it does merit wisdom. Based on the success of many Bournias family members, you can exceed if you put your mind to it.

Some readers may be surprised about some of my comments, but as I have been a resident of Greece for over thirty years, I have experienced much more than I reveal here about life in Greece today.

I hope that I have not deviated too much in my writing as I added some information and images that may not be considered objective by some or be based on verifiable records but this a collection of information about the Bournias families and the homeland island and villages (*patrida - πατρίδα*) of Chios.

Although there is a multitude of information that I discovered over the years, the fact that Greece did not progress in documentation and technology due to wasted years by politicians and civil employees means that there should and probably will be more information to be discovered in the future for anyone interested in furthering the family history. I have seen new information being produced regarding the historical aspects by university students through their dissertations.

Finally, this is probably the most valuable resource of the Bournias family lineage, which I hope that family members and their children will keep as a reference and can be proud of, as the Bournias family is a powerful and dynamic family.

Peter Anthony Bournias a.k.a. Petros Antonios I. Bournias
March 2023

BIOGRAPHY OF THE AUTHOR

Peter Anthony Bournias was born on the island of Manhattan in New York State in August of 1954. His father and mother were Ioannis P. Bournias from Chios Greece and Maria Christina Rivera Martinez from Mayaguez Puerto Rico.

He is a first generation American, born and raised in the Chelsea area of New York City. He attended the Catholic schools of St. Columba and Bishop Dubois High School; he then attended Suffolk County Community College on Long Island, and graduated from Pace University in June 1981.

His spouse is an Athenian with ancestry from Smyrna and Cappadocia in Asia Minor.

After a "working" life in New York, he moved to Athens Greece in 1983, attained dual citizenship, and successfully adjusted to the mentality, culture, and language of his the Greek environment where he "lives" the second half of his life as Petros-Antonios Bournias.

The researcher and author of this genealogy research.

Thank you for reading the Bournias Family Ancestry, Heritage, and Personal Legacies.

It is challenging researching, discovering, extracting, and organizing the information in this book but it brought me closer to the history of Greece and learning about my Greek relatives, as I hope that it will bring you closer to yours.

Please contact me if you have any information to share, questions, comments, or to introduce yourself:

bourniasfamily@bournias.net

or through my web site at www.bournias.net

Thank you!

INDEX

15th catalog of immigrant farmers
    Emmanouil A. Bournias 82
a historical clarification
    THE REVOLUTION ON CHIOS ABRIDGED 72
A RARE MAP OF CHIOS 59
About Freedom
    OUR family relationship with Antonios A. Bournias ... 76
ACKNOWLEDGEMENTS 203
Adamantios P. Bournias 101
Akropolis Newspaper
    Gregorios A. Bournias 85
Alexandros Ypsilantis
    THE REVOLUTION ON CHIOS ABRIDGED 69
Anastasia "Tacia" W. Bournias
    William P. Bournias 118
Anastasios G. Bournias 126
Anastasios P. "Ernest" Bournias 115
Anastasios P. Bournias 121
Angeliki Bournia Chatzimihali
    home of Gregorios A. Bournias 141
Angeline Bournias
    Census Records for the USA 184
Anna Kattou
    Pantelis G. Bournias 106
ANNOTATIONS 202
anti-royalists
    Ioannis G. Bournias 124
Antonios A. Bournias 67
    APOSTOLOS BOURNIAS 66
Antonios Bournias Street
    OUR family relationship with Antonios A. Bournias ... 76
Antonios Bournias was found not guilty
    OUR family relationship with Antonios A. Bournias ... 76
Apostolis A. Bournias 86
Apostolis I. Bournias 96
Apostolos A. Bournias
    Antonios A. Bournias 68
APOSTOLOS BOURNIAS 66
Apostolos Bournias a Soldier 134
Ariadni Bournia 133
Aris Portosalte
    OUR family relationship with Antonios A. Bournias ... 76
Asia Minor Campaign 50
Asia Minor Catastrophe 21
Asimine "Minnie" S. Bournia 110
Athena "Edna" P. Bournias
    Frank P. Bournias 120
Balkan wars 48
BAPTISM
    FAMILY RECORDS 148
Battle of Karfotou
    Georgios A. Bournias 91
Bessie W. Bournias
    William P. Bournias 118
Bibliography 190

BIOGRAPHY OF THE AUTHOR 206
Birth Certificate of Ioannis P. Bournias
    FAMILY RECORDS 147
BNF Gallica Archive of France 182
Bounias (Léon)
    BNF Gallica Archive of France 182
BOURNIAS Apostolos
    BNF Gallica Archive of France 182
Bournias Basil – Vasilios, K.
    BOURNIAS FALLEN IN ACTION 170
Bournias Charalambos
    BOURNIAS FALLEN IN ACTION 170
BOURNIAS FALLEN IN ACTION 170
Bournias family members not linked on my Genealogy
    Charts 131
BOURNIAS FAMILY WEBSITES 201
Bournias from Spartounta 102
Bournias Ioannis, V.
    BOURNIAS FALLEN IN ACTION 170
Bournias Leonidas, A.
    BOURNIAS FALLEN IN ACTION 170
BOURNIAS SURNAME 22
BOURNIAS SURNAME IN THE UNITED KINGDOM 136
Bournias-Kousakis Memorial web site
    Stylianos S. Bournias 104
Bouzouki
    Pantelis P. Bournias 93
British Ambassador in Constantinople
    THE REVOLUTION ON CHIOS ABRIDGED 72
British, Austrian and French vice-consuls
    THE REVOLUTION ON CHIOS ABRIDGED 71
brothers and sisters
    Panagiotis G. Bournias 130
bust representing the figure of Antonios A. Bournias 74
candidate for the position of Deputy Mayor of Athens
    Othonos I. Bournias 87
Candy Kitchen 111
Captain Adamantios P. Bournias
    Adamantios P. Bournias 101
CATHOLIC CHURCH IN GREECE 44
Cemeteries 169
Census Records for the USA 184
CENSUS RECORDS OF GREECE 173
Charilaos I. Bournias
    Ioannis Bournias 131
CHIAN SURNAMES 28
CLOSING REMARKS 205
Conclusion of Research 146
DEDICATION 8
Demetra P. Bournia 115
Demetrios A. Bournias
    APOSTOLOS BOURNIAS 66
Demetrios Chaniotis
    APOSTOLOS BOURNIAS 66
Demetrios L. Bournias 88

Demetrios Mihail Bournias
   PESONTES OF THE GREEK ITALIAN WAR OF 1940 AND 1941 171
Demtrios Ypsilantis
   THE REVOLUTION ON CHIOS ABRIDGED 69
Descriptive characteristics of Antonios A. Bournias
   bust representing the figure of Antonios A. Bournias .. 74
Efthymia P. Bournia 115
Election List Chios Spartounta 1930 153
   Municipality of Kardamyla, Chios 154
Electoral List Municipality Chios 1930 103
Electoral List Municipality Chios by local churches
   GAK OF CHIOS 151
Electoral List Municipality Syros 1871 159
Eleftherios A. Bournias
   Antonios A. Bournias 68
Eleni Maria Dareiotaki
   Panagiotis Bournias 114
Emmanouil A. Bournias 82
Emmanouil Bourniadakis
   Emmanouil A. Bournias 82
Emmanuil A. Bournias
   Antonios A. Bournias 68
Ersi-Alexia Hatzimihali
   Antonios A. Bournias 68
Evgenia "Virginia" Pontiki
   William P. Bournias 118
Evgenia P. Bournia 115
EVZONS 47
executed by the Nazis
   Loukas D. Demetrios 97
executed in Alexandroupolis
   Ioannis G. Bournias 122
Faculty of Law
   Ioannis A. Bournias 92
FALLEN IN ACTION 45
FAMILY RECORDS 147
Fannie W. Bournias
   William P. Bournias 118
Figelia S. Bournia 110
fighters from Samos
   Testimonial evidence of Antonios A. Bournias 78
First Cemetery of Athens
   Apostolls I. Bournias 96
   Ioannis A. Bournias 92
First Gymnasio 42
First Names of Greeks Abroad 35
First photography on Chios
   Census Records for the USA 187
First Women Photographers in Greece
   Census Records for the USA 188
Folklore and Artifacts 16
Foreign first names 35
FOREIGN INFLUENCE AND POLITICS 56
Fort Roupel
   Apostolos Bournias a Soldier 134
FORWARD 7
Frank P. "Fotis" Bournias 115
Frank P. Bournias 120
GAK Athens
   Othonos I. Bournias 87
GAK ATHENS 163
GAK ERMOUPOLI SYROS AND MYKONOS 161
GAK KALAMATA 164
GAK OF CHIOS 151
GAK OF ERMOUPOLI SYROS AND MYKONOS 155
GAK Syros for Ioannis Bournias 1844 156
Genealogical Charts 186
GENEALOGY CHARTS 186
GENEALOGY OF THE BOURNIAS FAMILIES 58
GENEALOGY SHORTHAND 61
General Archives of Chios 42
GEOGRAPHICAL MAPPING OF THE SURNAME 24
Georg. Bournias
   POLITICS 55
George S. Bournias 108
Georgios A. Bournias 90
Georgios Bournias
   Sweets From Chios 17
Georgios E. Bournias
   Emmanouil A. Bournias 82
Georgios Konstantinos Bournias
   PESONTES OF THE GREEK ITALIAN WAR OF 1940 AND 1941 171
Georgios P. Bournias 115
German Luftwaffe
   Anastasios G. Bournias 126
Germany began their invasion
   Anastasios G. Bournias 128
GLOSSARY / ABBREVIATIONS 202
Gosteis Bournias
   Census Records for the USA 184
Greco-Turkish War 21
GREECE SURVIVED FORTY-EIGHT (48) YEARS OF WAR 52
Greek Army in Epirus
   Anastasios G. Bournias 128
GREEK MILITARY 45
Greek Naming Conventions 34
Greek Orthodox Church baptism and Marriage Records of Chios 167
Greek Orthodox religion 43
GREEKS WITH THE SURNAME BOURNIAS IN GREECE 25
Gregorios A. Bournias
   Gregorios A. Bournias 85
Gregoris A. Bournias
   Antonios A. Bournias 68
Harlem Riots in 1964
   Ioannis P. Bournias 99
Helen Elaine W. Bournias
   William P. Bournias 118
Helen Kandis (Capogiannis)
   Nicholas S. Bournias 109
Helen P. Bournias
   Frank P. Bournias 120
Hippocrates of Chios 15
historical Plaka area of Athens
   home of Gregorios A. Bournias 141
home of Antonios A. Bournias in Parparia Chios 139
home of Gregorios A. Bournias 141
Homer 15

Hora the central city of Chios
    TRAVELING ON A STEAMSHIP 144
How to interpret middle initials 36
INCEPTION OF THE BOURNIAS SURNAME 23
INDEX 208
Individuals of the Bournias family 62
INTERNET LINKS 199
INTRODUCTION 6
Ioannis "Yangos" A. Bournias
    Apostolis I. Bournias 96
Ioannis A. Bournias
    Ioannis A. Bournias 92
Ioannis Bournias 80
Ioannis Demetrios Haniotis
    home of Antonios A. Bournias in Parparia Chios 140
Ioannis G. Bournias 122
Ioannis P. Bournias 98
Ioannis Vagias
    Maritsa P. Bournia 100
Irish Dragoon Guards
    BOURNIAS SURNAME IN THE UNITED KINGDOM 137
island of Makronissos
    Ioannis G. Bournias 123
Italian invasion
    Anastasios G. Bournias 128
James "Jim" S. Bournias 108
James Gus "Jim" Bournias
    Konstantinos P. "Gus" Bournias 120
James N. Bournias 108
Jane N. Bournias 109
Karavasileiou
    Emmanouil A. Bournias 83
Karystos Evia
    Ioannis A. Bournias 92
Katerini "Katina" Pala
    Anastasios P. Bournias 121
Katina D. Bournia
    Loukas D. Demetrios 97
Kelebesion Anneon region
    Emmanouil A. Bournias 82
Konstantinos A. Bournias
    Leonidas A. Bournias 95
Konstantinos P. "Gus" Bournias 115, 119, 120
Koroni Messinia
    Panagiotis Bournias 114
Koroni, Kalamata, and Texas
    Bournias from Spartounta 102
Kybelis G. Bournias
    Ioannis A. Bournias 92
Land Registry
    Individuals of the Bournias family 62
Language and the Dialect of Chios 19
Larry P. Bournias
    Frank P. Bournias 120
Leonidas A. Bournias 95
Leonidas Bournias
    POLITICS 55
Lineage of the Bournias Ancestry chart of Texas and Messinia 107
Lineage of the Bournias Ancestry Main Chart 63

list of Bournias family members
    SHIP MANIFESTS 174
Loukas D. Demetrios 97
Lycurgus Logothetis
    THE REVOLUTION ON CHIOS ABRIDGED 69
Macedonia Greece
    Apostolos Bournias a Soldier 134
Major Anastasios Stymfaliadis
    Georgios A. Bournias 91
Margaret Kandis
    Konstantinos P. "Gus" Bournias 120
Maria C. Martinez
    Ioannis P. Bournias 98
Maria Charuhaus
    Nicholas F. Bournias 125
Maritsa P. Bournia 100
Marriage Certificate of Pantelis Petros Bournias
    FAMILY RECORDS 149
Mary G. Bournias
    Konstantinos P. "Gus" Bournias 120
Mary S. Bournia 110
Massacre at Chios by Eugene Delacroix 73
Massacre at Chios from the mouth of the Chiot People
    OUR family relationship with Antonios A. Bournias 75
Mayor of Athens
    home of Gregorios A. Bournias 141
meaning of the surname Bournias 37
Messinia
    Ioannis G. Bournias 122
Michael S. Bournias 110
Michail A. Bournias 89
military base of Katechaki
    Georgios A. Bournias 91
Military Preparatory School of Corfu
    Georgios A. Bournias 90
military record
    Pantelis P. Bournias 94
modern day map of Chios 18
Monastiraki
    Michail A. Bournias 89
Movies Regarding Greek History 196
Municipality of Chios
    Demetrios L. Bournias 88
Municipality of Ermoupoli
    Ioannis Bournias 80
Municipality of Kalamata
    Ioannis Bournias 131
Municipality of Kardamyla, Chios 154
Municipality Records Koroni
    GAK KALAMATA 164
MUNICIPALITY RECORDS OF KARYSTOS EVIA 166
Myths 37
Name Days and Birthdays 36
Naming Conventions and Traditions 32
Napoleon
    THE REVOLUTION ON CHIOS ABRIDGED 69
Nathaniel Hurst born BOURNIAS
    BOURNIAS SURNAME IN THE UNITED KINGDOM 136
Nature and the Destruction of Greek Vital Records
    OBSTRUCTIONS IN GREEK GENEALOGY 53

Navy Archives
    Anastasios G. Bournias 128
newspaper Eleftheria
    Georgios A. Bournias 90
Nicholas F. Bournias 125
Nicholas P. Bournias
    Frank P. Bournias 120
Nicholas S. Bournias 109
Nick G. Bournias
    Konstantinos P. "Gus" Bournias 120
Nicknames or Paratsoukli 35
Nicoletta "Edith" P. Bournias
    Frank P. Bournias 120
Nola "Nellie" (Annoula) N. Bournias 108
OBSTRUCTIONS IN GREEK GENEALOGY 53
OLD & NEW PROFESSIONS 39
Origins of Greek Surnames 33
Othonos I. Bournias 87
OUR family relationship with Antonios A. Bournias 75
Panagiotis Bournias 114
Panagiotis Bournias of 1842
    Stylianos S. Bournias 104
Panagiotis G. Bournias 130
    Panagiotis Bournias 114
Panayiota "Teetsa" Bournias
    William P. Bournias 118, 119
Pantelis G. Bournias 106
Pantelis P. Bournias 93
Parliament Library Collection for Bournias 172
Parparia or Pirama to Kastron
    A RARE MAP OF CHIOS 59
PESONTES OF THE GREEK ITALIAN WAR OF 1940 AND 1941
.... 171
Peter G. Bournias
    Konstantinos P. "Gus" Bournias 120
Peter N. Bournias 109
Peter P. Bournias
    Frank P. Bournias 120
Peter S. "Gus" Bournias 108
Petros D. Bournias 81
PHOTOGRAPHY AND HISTORY 187
Pirama, Parparia, Spartounda
    Stylianos S. Bournias 105
PIRATES 57
PLAQUE ON THE HOME OF ANTONIOS A. BOURNIAS
    home of Antonios A. Bournias in Parparia Chios 140
Political Minister (MP) of Evia
    Apostolis I. Bournias 96
POLITICS 54
Port of Piraeus
    Anastasios G. Bournias 126
Port of Piraeus to Chios
    TRAVELING ON A STEAMSHIP 143
PREFACE 13
Queen Elizabeth
    Nicholas F. Bournias 125
Records of the Registry of (Boys) Males
    GAK KALAMATA 165
REFERENCES AND NOTES 194
Registry of Birth

FAMILY RECORDS 147
Registry of Boys
    Emmanouil A. Bournias 84
Registry of Citizens of the Municipality of Ermoupoli
    GAK Syros for Ioannis Bournias 1844 158
Registry of Marriages
    FAMILY RECORDS 149
RESOLUTIONS OF GREEK HISTORY 197
Ruby or Roubini or Roubinia S. Bournia 110
sacrificial Muslim ritual
    Testimonial evidence of Antonios A. Bournias 70
Sam Bill W. Bournias
    William P. Bournias 118
Sam Gus Bournias
    Konstantinos P. "Gus" Bournias 120
School Record of Student Grades
    GAK KALAMATA 164
Second Boys High School of Athens
    Ariadni Bournia 133
SETTLEMENTS NAMED BOURNIAS 138
Ship Crew Lists 181
SHIP MANIFESTS 174
Sifnos
    Ioannis Bournias 132
SKAI Channel
    OUR family relationship with Antonios A. Bournias 76
Smaragda A. Bournia
    Antonios A. Bournias 68
Smidgen of History about Chios 20
Smyrna Turkey
    Georgios A. Bournias 91
Sofia G. Fragou nee Bournia 129
Some rare books found online 190
Sophia G. Bournia
    home of Gregorios A. Bournias 141
SOURCES OF NAMES AND VITAL RECORDS 41
SS Patris 145
Stamatios Bournias 103
Stanley N. Bournias 109
Stylianos A. Bournias
    Stylianos S. Bournias 104
Stylianos S. Bournias 104
Sweets From Chios 17
TABLE OF CONTENTS 9
tannery factory
    Pantelis P. Bournias 93
Tasos Spiliotopoulos
    Ioannis Bournias 132
Testimonial evidence of Antonios A. Bournias 77
Testimonial references
    Testimonial evidence of Antonios A. Bournias 79
The Greek Merchant Marine
    Leonidas A. Bournias 95
The Massacre at Chios
    THE REVOLUTION ON CHIOS ABRIDGED 71
THE REVOLUTION ON CHIOS ABRIDGED 69
The Voice
    Ioannis P. Bournias 99
travelers from Greece to the USA
    SHIP MANIFESTS 175

TRAVELING ON A STEAMSHIP 143	war of 1897
Turkification 21	Georgios A. Bournias 91
U.K. National Archives	WARS IN GREECE AND CHIOS 46
BOURNIAS SURNAME IN THE UNITED KINGDOM 136	William Donahoe born BOURNIAS
Voting Records of the United St 185	BOURNIAS SURNAME IN THE UNITED KINGDOM 136
Vournias 27	William N. "Billy" Bournias 109
Vournias Family	William P. Bournias 117
Emmanouil A. Bournias 82	William Pete "Bill" Bournias 115
Vournias or Bournias	WORLD WAR I 49
Emmanouil A. Bournias 83	WORLD WAR II 51
Vrontados Chios	Zabella A. Varia
Ioannis P. Bournias 98	Pantelis P. Bournias 93
Vrontados Chios from about 1930 189	

Page intentionally left blank for notes

ISBN (International Standard Book Number): 979-8-218-16241-2
(PRINTED BOOK ONLY hard or soft cover)

LCCN (Library of Congress Control Number): 2023903752

www.ingramcontent.com/pod-product-compliance
Lightning Source LLC
Chambersburg PA
CBHW040356010526
44108CB00049B/2920